MILADY STANDARD COSMETOLOGY

Situational Problems

MILADY STANDARD COSMETOLOGY

Situational Problems

Australia • Brazil • Japan • Korea • Mexico • Singapore • Spain • United Kingdom • United States

Milady Standard Cosmetology Situational Problems
Catherine M. Frangie

President, Milady: Dawn Gerrain

Senior Product Manager: Philip Mandl

Editorial Assistant: Maria K. Hebert

Director of Beauty Industry Relations: Sandra Bruce

Executive Marketing Manager: Gerard McAvey

Associate Marketing Manager: Matthew McGuire

Production Director: Wendy Troeger

Senior Content Project Manager: Nina Tucciarelli

Art Director: Benj Gleeksman

For product information and technology assistance, contact us at **Professional & Career Group Customer Support, 1-800-648-7450**

For permission to use material from this text or product, submit all requests online at **cengage.com/permissions**. Further permissions questions can be e-mailed to **permissionrequest@cengage.com**.

Library of Congress Control Number: 2010903896

ISBN-13: 978-1-4390-5920-3
ISBN-10: 1-4390-5920-9

Milady
5 Maxwell Drive
Clifton Park, NY 12065-2919
USA

Cengage Learning products are represented in Canada by Nelson Education, Ltd.

For your lifelong learning solutions, visit **milady.cengage.com**
Visit our corporate website at **cengage.com**.

Printed in United States
1 2 3 4 5 XX 15 14 13 12 11

Dedication

To my mother, Wadad Frangie, who taught me
everything she knows about love, life, and,
of course, the beauty business!

Contents

INTRODUCTION

Welcome to the professional beauty industry! You have chosen a wonderful and exciting career opportunity. To be successful, you will have to sharpen your ability to think through the situation at hand and choose the best solution for all the parties involved. Remember, you will be working with lots of people—clients, coworkers, managers, vendors—and each could have a different perspective on every encounter or situation. While there may be many possible outcomes to those encounters or situations, to be successful as a professional cosmetologist you will have to find a way to make sure that every outcome is positive.

Milady Standard Cosmetology Situational Problems was created to acquaint you with the types of dilemmas you may encounter in your daily life as a professional cosmetologist. As you read the stories and answer the questions, keep in mind that this workbook gives you the opportunity to sharpen your decision-making and relationship skills and to determine how you will handle similar situations in your career. So take your time, think through each situation, and make the best decision you can based on the information you are given.

Once again, I want to congratulate you on your professional career choice and wish you much success in your career!

—Catherine M. Frangie

PREFACE

How to Use This Book

Milady Standard Cosmetology Situational Problems was created to be used with the *Milady Standard Cosmetology*. As you will see, the chapters in this *Situational Problems* book correspond to the chapters in the *Milady Standard Cosmetology* and provide you with real-life scenarios that illustrate core concepts and points in the textbook.

Each scenario is categorized by topic, making it easy for you to look up information in the textbook. As you work your way through the scenarios, you will have the opportunity to build upon your knowledge of the principles and theories taught in the *Milady Standard Cosmetology* and to see how they apply to salon life.

There are many ways you can use *Milady Standard Cosmetology Situational Problems* with the *Milady Standard Cosmetology*: after completing your reading assignments, during theory class, to review for tests, or to prepare for clinic work. Whatever way you decide to use the book, it is recommended that you talk about these scenarios with your instructors during class and make them the basis for discussions and debates.

CHAPTER 1 History and Career Opportunities

Marsha is about to graduate from cosmetology school and in her last three weeks of class, her instructor, Ms. Smith, asks her to research various career opportunities available to a licensed cosmetologist and to create a career plan for herself. Marsha takes advantage of the career fair her school is sponsoring to gather information about various career options available to her. At the career fair, Marsha speaks to April, a haircolor specialist; Anderson, a texture specialist; Morris, a cutting specialist; Alfredo, a salon trainer; and Barry, a distributor sales consultant.

1. April is a haircolor specialist, which means she:
- **a.** selects haircolors the staff should wear
- **b.** creates new chemical formulas for haircolor
- **c.** designs haircolor containers and implements for use in the salon
- **d.** trains herself and others to perform haircolor services in the salon

2. A texture specialist like Anderson, would most likely spend his days:
- **a.** painting textured patterns on salon walls
- **b.** creating new formulas for permanent waves
- **c.** performing texture services for salon clients
- **d.** writing manufacturer guidelines and product instructions

3. Morris would have to __________ to be an effective cutting specialist.
- **a.** have a dedicated interest in learning various cutting styles and techniques
- **b.** travel to the most elaborate trade shows for cosmetology
- **c.** purchase expensive equipment that he would have to carry with him at all times
- **d.** wear outrageous haircuts and haircolor

4. As a salon trainer, Alfredo is primarily responsible for:
- **a.** managing the exercise routine of the salon staff
- **b.** developing the skills of salon staff and personnel
- **c.** determining the product lines a salon will carry and maintaining their inventory
- **d.** issuing credits to dissatisfied clients

5. As a distributor sales consultant (DSC), the most important thing that Barry takes care of is:
   a. the relationship between the salon and its employees
   b. the relationship between the salon and the distributor
   c. the relationship between the salon and its landlord
   d. the relationship between the distributor and the manufacturing company

6. While discussing his job, Barry mentions that a manufacturer educator will be in town in the coming months and that Marsha may want to speak with her. A manufacturer educator's primary function is to:
   a. train stylists and salon staff to understand and use a company's hair care, haircolor, and chemical-service products
   b. train stylists and salon staff to understand and use all of the retail products in their salon
   c. train stylists and staff on the newest rulings regarding infection control, as mandated by OSHA
   d. develop and create products for the company by working closely with the research and development department

7. Marsha has had an example of a very viable cosmetology career option all the time she was in beauty school. Who might that have been?
   a. a platform artist
   b. her cosmetology instructor
   c. the school's business manager
   d. a salon manager

8. Marsha, who feels she has a sharp business mind, also considers becoming a:
   a. a platform artist
   b. a cosmetology instructor
   c. the school's curriculum director
   d. a salon manager

CHAPTER 2 Life Skills

John has always dreamt of becoming a very successful professional. He has carefully thought through and imagined who he wants to be. John has taken a position with a very prestigious salon, where he has been working for five years. John drives an expensive automobile and rents a pricey apartment in a chic neighborhood. His wardrobe consists of designer and name-brand clothing and fashionable shoes and accessories, and he is always impeccably dressed. John spends a lot of time and money on his appearance and he wishes he were better compensated for his work because he has difficulty paying his other expenses—his car and rent—each month. However, he is reluctant to reduce his expenses because he is concerned that the salon's well-to-do clients won't patronize him if he doesn't live up to their standards of living. Because John works about 70 hours per week, he doesn't have a lot of time to devote to activities other than his work. John hardly ever sees his friends and family and rarely takes any time to enjoy sports or music, his favorite pastimes.

1. John's self-esteem appears to be based on:
- **a.** his inner strengths
- **b.** his ability to possess things
- **c.** his ability to care for his things
- **d.** his physical strengths

2. John has used the technique of visualization to:
- **a.** picture himself as a complete success
- **b.** improve his sleep
- **c.** picture himself as a complete hairstylist
- **d.** improve his ability to concentrate

3. Truly successful people do not:
- **a.** get enough rest
- **b.** pace themselves to prevent fatigue
- **c.** allow business to be the only focus of their life
- **d.** socialize with people outside of their business

4. John's lifestyle requires him to spend all of his time:
- **a.** visiting with family
- **b.** exercising
- **c.** visiting with friends
- **d.** working

5. John's definition of success includes:
   a. dividing his time between work and pleasure
   b. increasing his education
   c. having a daily exercise routine
   d. keeping up appearances

6. Whose definition of success is John attempting to achieve?
   a. his family's.
   b. his coworkers'.
   c. his clients'.
   d. his friends'.

Ramona is a busy person. She has a part-time job and a small child; she attends cosmetology school and has many other tasks and responsibilities to take care of each day. Now that she is about to graduate and begin looking for a job in a salon, Ramona knows that she has to get better organized but she is always feeling frustrated by how much she has to do and how little time she has to do it. Ramona has good intentions but often gets so caught up in the day's activities and events that she forgets important errands she needs to run or appointments she has made. Ramona has resolved to use her time more efficiently.

7. The first thing Ramona must do is:
   a. reorganize her living room to make the flow of furniture work better
   b. prioritize the list of tasks that need to be done
   c. take on an additional project for her current employer
   d. drop every other task she has until she finds a salon job

8. Ramona needs to have some specific time with her young child each day. She can accomplish this by:
   a. taking the child to school an hour later each day
   b. designing a schedule for herself that includes blocks of unstructured time
   c. taking her child to work with her each evening
   d. designing a play space in the salon

9. Which of the following will NOT save Ramona time in her busy schedule?
   a. Reducing as much stress as possible.
   b. Saying no when being asked to take on more than she can handle.
   c. Relying on others to problem-solve and uncover solutions she can use.
   d. Taking a time-out whenever she is frustrated, overwhelmed, irritated, worried, or feeling guilty.

10. When Ramona is feeling overwhelmed by the circumstances of her hectic life she could try a technique called:
- **a.** shallow breathing
- **b.** deep breathing
- **c.** shallow sighing
- **d.** deep sighing

11. To aid Ramona in remembering important notes and reminders she should carry:
- **a.** a memo pad or day planner
- **b.** her favorite music CD
- **c.** a computer
- **d.** her address book

12. Ramona might consider scheduling her time in _________ intervals to study for a major exam.
- **a.** 10-minute
- **b.** 15-minute
- **c.** 30-minute
- **d.** 60-minute

13. To make the most of her time, Ramona should schedule activities that require alert, clear thinking during times when she is:
- **a.** wearing comfortable clothing
- **b.** distracted and can't concentrate
- **c.** highly energetic and able to focus
- **d.** not feeling well and needing medication

14. Which of the following is NOT a healthy way for Ramona to reward herself for a job well done?
- **a.** taking a bubble bath
- **b.** going to a movie
- **c.** taking a nap
- **d.** smoking a cigarette

15. Another activity Ramona must consider scheduling to promote clear thinking and planning is:
- **a.** exercising
- **b.** eating dessert
- **c.** reading magazines
- **d.** oversleeping

16. Which of the following tools would best help Ramona keep focused on the tasks she needs to complete each day?
   a. a mission statement.
   b. a goal statement
   c. a to-do list
   d. a long-range plan

Hector is a dedicated student who wants very badly to progress through school and become a licensed professional. While he is happy to be in school, he has difficulty staying focused during lectures and studying for and taking exams. He usually ends up cramming the night before an exam, even for important tests that cover many topics. Hector is frustrated and wants to have an easier time with this part of his schooling. He knows that he is a capable and serious student and he is willing to try some new techniques to lessen his fears and anxieties about test-taking.

17. What is missing from Hector's educational background?
   a. a desire to work hard
   b. good study skills
   c. a desire to succeed
   d. good people skills

18. When Hector feels overwhelmed by his courses and upcoming tests, he can focus on __________ to feel better about himself and his progress.
   a. rereading the entire chapter in his textbook
   b. checking out more reference books from the school library
   c. accomplishing small tasks, one at a time
   d. fun activities that make him feel less nervous

19. Instead of cramming the night before an exam, Hector should:
   a. study for up to three hours at a stretch for the two days before the exam
   b. study for one hour just before taking the exam
   c. study in small intervals when the lesson is presented so that it won't be necessary to review before the test
   d. study the day's lessons each day and then review all the material before the exam

20. Which of the following techniques will help Hector to stay focused when his mind begins to wander in class?
   a. Write notes to fellow students.
   b. Think about becoming a successful professional.
   c. Write down key words and discuss them with the instructor.
   d. Look up definitions of terms in his textbook.

21. If Hector decides to form or join a study group, what should he look for in the group?
    a. Students who will give him the information he needs.
    b. Students who are willing to be helpful and supportive.
    c. Students who have the same interests as he does.
    d. Students who have a good sense of humor and are fun to be with.

22. If Hector were to find a "study buddy," what would this person's job be?
    a. to introduce him to other students
    b. to eat lunch with him everyday
    c. to help him stay focused on studying
    d. to practice finger waving with him

Hakim and Jackie are senior stylists and assistant managers at La Bella Luna Salon and Spa. Both have excellent technical skills and are attractive-looking professionals who are intelligent and capable. Hakim's behavior is hallmarked by a sense of calm; he manages his fellow coworkers with honest and open communications, he is respectful of clients, and he never gossips. However, when he has problems at home, he often calls in sick for the day with little notice to the salon. Jackie, the other senior stylist, is quick to complain about other people, is sometimes bossy and uncaring about the feelings of others, and acts as if the salon's rules and policies do not pertain to her, yet Jackie is always at work on time and she rarely ever takes unscheduled time off. Adam, the salon's owner, has a salon manager opening to fill and Hakim and Jackie are the two candidates he has to choose from.

23. In making his decision, Adam must choose the person who is best at:
    a. fixing haircolor mistakes
    b. socializing with other stylists
    c. speaking honestly to stylists
    d. scheduling appointments

24. In assessing Hakim and Jackie, which of the following does NOT indicate a high standard of professionalism?
    a. identifying one's values
    b. avoiding all conflict
    c. maintaining one's principles
    d. developing a sense of genuine concern for others

25. As a service provider, Hakim must be able to practice:
   a. self-sufficiency
   b. self-care
   c. self-indulgence
   d. self-deprivation

26. When determining Jackie's and Hakim's sense of integrity, Adam will need to assess:
   a. if their communications and actions match their personalities
   b. if their behavior and actions match their values
   c. if their values and sense of humor match their behavior
   d. if their behavior and actions match their personalities

27. For Jackie to display a genuine sense of integrity she would have to behave in the following manner:
   a. use high-end products only
   b. provide the best scalp massage in the salon
   c. market to clients from previous employers
   d. recommend products and services that will benefit the client

28. When Jackie gossips with other stylists about a client's personal situation she is lacking:
   a. deception
   b. personality
   c. discretion
   d. politeness

29. Which of the following indicates that Hakim is using ethical behavior in his communication with customers and the other people he works with?
   a. buying lunch
   b. being indirect
   c. being direct
   d. wearing trendy clothing

Tishla is the receptionist at the Salon Omega. One of her most important duties is to schedule clients effectively and efficiently so that neither the stylists nor the clients are waiting for long periods of time. Tishla has scheduled Mr. Everett for a haircut and scalp massage with Jane for 6 p.m. At 6:20 Mr. Everett calls from his cell phone to say that he is stuck in traffic and would like to change his appointment to 7 p.m. Tishla looks at Jane's schedule and sees that she has 7 p.m. and 7:30 p.m. appointments, so there is no way that she can reschedule Mr. Everett for this evening. Annoyed, Tishla says to him, "Well, if you had called immediately, I may have been able to move a later appointment up. You should have called sooner to reschedule, like when you first got stuck in the traffic jam! There's nothing I can do now, Jane has no openings until next week."

Mr. Everett explains, "I thought the traffic would clear up sooner and that I'd make it in time. I'm sorry if I caused any problems. I'd like to make another appointment."

Tishla says, "Okay but Jane is sitting here waiting for you while two other clients have walked in and she could have been servicing them!" Tishla looks at the appointment calendar and says that she can make an appointment for Mr. Everett for the following week but, she warns, "You have to be sure you're going to make it on time and if you can't be on time, you have to call me right away and let us know." Mr. Everett says he would like to take the appointment; Tishla marks his name in the calendar and then completes the call.

30. From her response, what kind of attitude does Tishla have about people who are late?

- **a.** She is understanding and helpful.
- **b.** She is sad but accommodating.
- **c.** She is impatient and distrusting.
- **d.** She is angry but cooperative.

31. How would you rate Tishla's ability to handle the situation with Mr. Everett tactfully?

- **a.** Excellent—she was able to reschedule Mr. Everett's appointment without incident.
- **b.** Good—she clearly stated that his tardiness could not happen again.
- **c.** Fair—she wasn't very sympathetic but managed to reschedule the client.
- **d.** Poor—she argued with the client and he promised to never return to the salon.

32. How should Tishla have handled the conversation with Mr. Everett?

- **a.** She should have become annoyed and repeated that his tardiness was a problem.
- **b.** She should have flown into a rage at his inconsiderate behavior.
- **c.** She should have calmly informed him that Jane lost money waiting for him and that she didn't want to service clients like him.
- **d.** She should have let him know that missing his appointment was a problem and asked him if he'd prefer to be the last client of the day to give him ample time to get to the salon.

33. How sensitive was Tishla to Mr. Everett?

- **a.** extremely
- **b.** moderately
- **c.** somewhat
- **d.** not sensitive at all

34. Based on Tishla's response to this situation, what do you think her values and goals are?

- **a.** empathy and harmony
- **b.** sensitivity and caring
- **c.** precision and efficiency
- **d.** accusation and blame

35. What will likely be the effect of Tishla's communication on Mr. Everett?

- **a.** He will feel understood.
- **b.** He will feel reprimanded.
- **c.** He will feel insignificant.
- **d.** He will feel guilty.

CHAPTER 3 Your Professional Image

Maggie is always rushed and is frequently late for work. To save time in the morning, she sometimes showers in the evening before going to bed so that the time she spends getting ready for work in the morning is lessened. Maggie awakens a half an hour before she needs to leave her house, quickly washes her face, brushes her teeth, puts on her makeup, dresses, and runs out the door to get to the salon. Several days a week after working at the salon, she goes to her evening job as a waitress, often without freshening her clothes, herself, or her makeup. Maggie's clients and colleagues noticeably pull away from her when she is speaking to them and coming in close contact with them. Behind her back, some of Maggie's colleagues make fun of her and call her names like "sloppy" and "disheveled" because she is always late, seemingly forgetful, and never looks well put together or freshly bathed. Maggie is always tired and she is becoming increasingly unhappy.

1. Based on the reaction from Maggie's colleagues, how would you rate her personal hygiene?
   a. excellent
   b. very good
   c. good
   d. fair

2. Which of the following should Maggie NOT do to improve her personal hygiene between jobs?
   a. brush her teeth
   b. use underarm deodorant
   c. freshen her makeup
   d. douse herself with perfume

3. What is most likely the cause of coworkers and clients pulling away from Maggie when she is speaking to them?
   a. fresh breath
   b. foul language
   c. bad breath
   d. complicated language

4. What does Maggie's disheveled appearance say about her professionalism?
   a. That she is a meticulous professional.
   b. That she is proud to be in her profession.
   c. That she is happy with her job and lifestyle.
   d. That she is feeling stress and cannot manage her time.

Paige is in her early twenties and loves to wear her short, cropped hair messy with styling glue; she describes her style as the "bad-girl-meets-the-beauty-biz." She also often wears sleeveless or short-sleeved shirts to show off her numerous tattoos. Paige loves to wear dark, colorful makeup applied in a "gothic" fashion. Since she really needs a job, Paige has decided to apply at the luxury spa that has just opened a few blocks from her home. A couple of days before her interview, Paige goes into the spa and observes that the spa employees are all wearing simple black clothing with white smocks over them. She notices that their hair is styled into simple and classic looks and their makeup is very simple, employing natural colors and techniques. Paige decides that in order to have a shot at the job she wants so desperately she will dress in accordance with the other spa staffers during her interview and then slip into her own style once she has gotten the job.

5. How should Paige go about finding the best place for her to work?
- **a.** Visit several salons and determine which one is most in line with her own sense of style.
- **b.** Apply for a position at a mall salon and take the job when it is offered.
- **c.** Agree to be a salon assistant for at least one year before making a decision.
- **d.** Ask her friends what type of salon they are looking for and follow their lead.

6. From the description, what seems to be the energy and image of the spa Paige is interviewing at?
- **a.** a chic spa with celebrity clients
- **b.** a low-cost salon specializing in short, layered cuts
- **c.** a high-end spa with an exclusive clientele
- **d.** a high-end color-only salon

7. What type of salon seems most appropriate for someone with Paige's sense of style to work in?
- **a.** A color-only salon catering to clients who want to cover gray hair.
- **b.** A moderately priced salon that caters to young clients who have a sense of adventure.
- **c.** A moderately priced salon that caters to businesspeople.
- **d.** A mall salon that caters to families and children.

8. Is Paige's approach to getting this job ethical?
   a. Yes, because she really needs the job and she will be a good employee.
   b. Yes, because the salon should be hiring her for her skill and not her appearance.
   c. No, because she isn't being honest about who she really is.
   d. No, because she can help the salon change its culture.

Peter loves to have a good time. Almost every day after working at the salon, he meets up with his buddies to hang out. They go to one another's apartments and order pizza and drink and watch television until late into the night. Often, because Peter is so tired, he sleeps on his friend's couch and then gets up the next day and goes directly to work. His salon coworkers always know when Peter has been out with his friends the night before because he is barely awake, is unshaven, and is wearing the same clothes he wore the day before. Peter gets teased by some of the other salon employees for being a "free spirit," but Allie, the salon manager, isn't as able to dismiss his messy appearance because he is often so disheveled that he is off-putting to salon clients. Allie decides to have a conversation with Peter about his appearance and general hygiene.

9. The best time for Allie to approach Peter would be:
   a. When they are in a staff meeting.
   b. When Peter's with a client.
   c. When they are alone in the salon.
   d. When Allie is in a managers' meeting.

10. What should Allie discuss with Peter?
   a. his personal appearance and its effect on the salon's clients
   b. his attitude about partying too much
   c. his irresponsible behavior toward his family
   d. his favorite television shows

11. What could Peter do to make sure he is fresh for work even on nights when he doesn't sleep at home?
   a. take a shower the evening before so he doesn't have to worry about it in the morning
   b. spray himself with some cologne on the way in to work
   c. keep clean clothing in his car and freshen up before arriving at the salon
   d. spray his worn clothing with something that eliminates odors

12. The image that Peter is projecting to clients suggests that he is:
   a. a serious professional concerned with learning more on the job
   b. between apartments and sleeping wherever he can
   c. concerned with doing an excellent job at the salon
   d. sad and unhappy in his work

Marilyn is both a hairstylist and nail tech who works about eight hours a day servicing clients. When she is standing, she very often leans on one hip or the other, shifting her weight from one side to the other, and when she is seated she's usually leaning forward with her legs either crossed or tucked underneath her body. At the end of the day Marilyn is often in pain–her legs and back are cramping and her arms, shoulders, and neck feel tired and strained. By the time she arrives home at night she hardly has enough energy to do routine chores before plopping in front of the television set for the evening.

13. What does Marilyn's physical presentation indicate?
   a. excellent personal style
   b. poor posture
   c. decreased ability to retain clients
   d. incredible physical strength

14. To achieve and maintain a good work posture, what position should Marilyn's neck be in?
   a. level with her elbow
   b. tilted forward at a 45-degree angle
   c. elongated and balanced directly above shoulders
   d. tilted backward at a 45-degree angle

15. To relieve the tension in her shoulders, Marilyn should:
   a. scrunch them together
   b. level and relax them
   c. lift one higher than the other
   d. bring them in close to the body

16. When standing, what position should Marilyn's back be in?
   a. curved laterally
   b. swayed to the left
   c. swayed to the right
   d. straight

17. A sitting posture that would alleviate Marilyn's back and neck pain would include:

- **a.** curving her back forward
- **b.** stretching her back from left to right
- **c.** keeping her back straight
- **d.** crossing her feet at the ankles

18. How can Marilyn make her work environment more ergonomically correct for herself?

- **a.** She can bend forward to reach her clients better.
- **b.** She can adjust the client's chair.
- **c.** She can ask the client to lean forward.
- **d.** She can stand during all of the services.

CHAPTER 4 Communicating for Success

Tyrone is a distributor sales consultant who is calling on Eva, a salon owner. Eva placed an order two weeks ago but it still has not been delivered. Eva is angry because she has missed several opportunities to make retail sales and to service clients because she can't get the products she needs. When Tyrone walks in to the salon for his monthly sales call, Eva quickly and loudly complains about her order situation to Tyrone. Frustrated because Eva is the fourth salon owner he has called on this week with the same complaint, Tyrone slams his sales book shut and tells Eva, "I've told you already that the products are back-ordered from the manufacturer and there's nothing I can do about it. If you aren't interested in seeing this new brush line, then I guess there's nothing else I can do for you!"

1. Tyrone's reaction to Eva indicates that he was:
   - **a.** aware of the problems with the delivery and had an alternative plan
   - **b.** not rattled by her complaints and able to offer another solution
   - **c.** unprepared for her complaints and took them personally
   - **d.** aware that she was overreacting out of frustration and a lack of communication

2. If Tyrone had a strong sense of his abilities, how would he have behaved with Eva?
   - **a.** Just as he did.
   - **b.** He would have patted her hand and told her whatever he could to calm her down.
   - **c.** He would have blamed his manager and had Eva call him right then.
   - **d.** He would have called her with a delivery date and proposed some alternative options.

3. Had Tyrone really been listening to Eva's complaint, what opportunity might he have been presented with?
   - **a.** the chance to sell her a new product line to try
   - **b.** the chance to take an additional order
   - **c.** the chance to transfer her account to another rep
   - **d.** the chance to tell off his manager and feel justified in doing so

4. What would have been the best way for Tyrone to attend to Eva's needs?
   a. ignoring her complaints and moving on with his sales call
   b. joining her in complaining about the company
   c. agreeing with her complaint and asking what he could do to help her in the short term
   d. simply listening to her and offering no reaction at all

5. From Tyrone's reaction to Eva, what can you infer about his job satisfaction?
   a. He is very happy at work and is looking forward to being promoted.
   b. He is frustrated by his working conditions and is able to discuss this with his manager.
   c. He is happy at work and looks forward to his next paycheck.
   d. He is unhappy at work and is not handling his frustrations in a positive manner.

Victoria is out shopping when she sees a salon and decides to go in for some advice. Abe, the stylist who happens to be sitting behind the reception desk, asks if he can help her. "Yes," says Victoria, "I need some help with my hair."

Abe smiles and says, "Sure, what kind of help do you need?"

Victoria thinks for a moment and then points to her wilted style and replies, "Well, I don't know, I'm not really happy with it right now." Abe asks her if she is unhappy with the length or the style. She shakes her head no and then replies "I guess I need something that will help me get and keep body in my hair."

"You want something that will help you get and keep body in your hair?" asks Abe.

Victoria nods her head and says, "Yes, an hour after drying and curling my hair, it's flat again."

Abe grabs a couple of hair magazines from the counter and asks Victoria to find a photo that is closest to the finished look she desires. Once he sees her selection he says, "I see, you want a bit of height on top but not too much width at the temple area?" Victoria nods her head in agreement and Abe hands her a bottle of styling gel, which he explains is useful when styling her wet hair, and a can of super-hold hairspray, to use once her hair is dry to keep the look she desires perfect all day.

Victoria thanks him for listening to her and taking the time to recommend products for her specific needs. Victoria pays for the products and takes one of Abe's business cards before leaving the salon.

6. When Victoria first walked into the salon, what had she neglected to do?
   a. decide on a new hair style
   b. check on the name of the salon
   c. collect her thoughts
   d. make an appointment

7. When Victoria told Abe that she needed help with her hair, how did Abe help her to articulate her thoughts more clearly to him?
   a. by booking her for a perm
   b. by suggesting a new haircolor
   c. by recommending another stylist
   d. by asking her questions

8. How did Victoria clarify her desires to Abe?
   a. by referring to another client in the salon
   b. by showing him a photo in a magazine
   c. by pushing her hair into place and recreating her look
   d. by describing the style in minute detail

9. When Abe describes the attributes of the style she has selected back to Victoria, he is using a technique called:
   a. passive listening
   b. articulating
   c. reflective listening
   d. communicating

10. Based on the exchange between Abe and Victoria, what is the outcome likely to be?
   a. Victoria will probably never return to the salon.
   b. Victoria may return to the salon, but will not request Abe's services.
   c. Victoria will probably try a brand new salon and stylist for her next service.
   d. Victoria will return to the salon and request Abe's services.

11. By going the extra mile to fully understand Victoria's needs, Abe was attempting to build a strong ____________.
   a. relationship
   b. client base
   c. pay base
   d. commission

Dennis is in the planning stages of opening a new, full-service salon that will offer hair, nail, and skin care services. As he works with his contractor to make the space usable for his needs, Dennis plans a consultation area that is separate and private from the styling and service areas of the salon. Once Dennis leaves his meeting with the contractor he begins to make a list of the things he will need to provide for the consultation space so he can prepare for the salon's opening.

Dennis has opted to use the intake form on the following page for all of his salon's client consultations. Use the form as a basis for answering the following questions.

12. Having clients fill in all of the questions pertaining to their address and other personal information allows Dennis's salon to:
- **a.** sell a list of client information to other businesses
- **b.** correctly identify each client
- **c.** determine the number of dollars in sales they will potentially create each year
- **d.** retain clients even after a stylist leaves the salon

13. Knowing when the client last visited a salon will help the stylists in Dennis's salon to:
- **a.** determine how much return business can be expected from this client
- **b.** assess the client's commitment to his or her style upkeep
- **c.** determine how much to charge for a service
- **d.** assess how much retail product to sell the client

14. Asking clients which services they have had in the previous year allows the salon to:
- **a.** assess the number of times clients cut their own hair
- **b.** determine if the client can afford more services this year than last
- **c.** identify the chemical treatments that clients have been happy with
- **d.** determine clients' history and hair condition

15. Why is it useful for Dennis to ask clients about the medications that they take?
- **a.** So he can notify the closest pharmacy.
- **b.** So he can prescribe additional medications.
- **c.** So he can assess the effect of the medication on their beauty regimen.
- **d.** So he can notify clients' physicians of the services he will perform.

16. Dennis requires clients to answer questions about their skin and nail care because:
    a. he is opening a full-service salon
    b. he is opening a nail salon
    c. he is opening a haircolor salon
    d. he is opening a luxury spa

17. Why is it important for Dennis to know how often clients wash and condition their hair?
    a. So he can recommend a pricey shampoo for them to purchase.
    b. So he can determine their hair care routine and suggest services that will work for them.
    c. So he can recommend a pricey conditioner for them to purchase.
    d. So he can determine whether or not to shampoo their hair before beginning their service.

18. Asking clients about their allergies allows Dennis to:
    a. protect staffers from allergic reactions
    b. prescribe appropriate treatments
    c. protect clients from products or services that may harm them
    d. find holistic treatments to cure clients' allergies

19. Which of the following is exactly the type of information Dennis's stylists should include in the Service Notes section of the intake form?
    a. any notes pertaining to the client's personality during the service
    b. any notes pertaining to the client's sense of humor during the service
    c. any notes pertaining to the client's clothing during the service
    d. any notes pertaining to the client's hair or its reaction during the service

Angie has been referred to Marshall by a friend who is one of Marshall's long-time clients. Angie loves the way he cuts and styles her friend's hair and she is eager to meet Marshall and have him cut and style her hair. Angie shows up on time for her appointment. When she arrives at the salon, she finds a lot of people and confusion in the reception area and, since she has never visited this salon before, she is unsure of what to do. Angie approaches the reception desk and tells the person seated behind the desk her name and the name of the stylist she has an appointment with. The receptionist nods her head and turns her back to Angie to answer the telephone. Angie sits down and waits for Marshall. A few minutes go by and a young woman comes down to the waiting area, picks up a slip of paper and calls Angie's name, then turns and

Client Intake Form

Dear Client,

Our sincerest hope is to provide you with the best hair care services you've ever received! We not only want you to be happy with today's visit, we also want to build a long-lasting relationship with you.
In order for us to do so, we would like to learn more about you, your hair care needs, and your preferences. Please take a moment now to answer the questions below as completely and as accurately as possible.

Thank you, and we look forward to building a relationship!

Name:____________________

Address:____________________

Phone Number: (day)________ (evening)________ (cell)________

E-mail address:________

Sex: ____ Male ____ Female Age:____

How did you hear about our salon?____________________

If you were referred, who referred you?____________________

Please answer the following questions in the space provided. Thanks!

1. Approximately when was your last salon visit?________________
2. In the past year have you had any of the following services either in or out of a salon?
   - ____ Haircut
   - ____ Haircolor
   - ____ Permanent Wave or Texturizing Treatment
   - ____ Chemical Relaxing or Straightening Treatment
   - ____ Highlighting or Lowlighting
   - ____ Full head lightening
   - ____ Manicure
   - ____ Artificial nail services (please describe)
   - ____ Pedicure
   - ____ Facial/Skin Treatment
   - ____ Other (please list any other services you've enjoyed at a salon that may not be listed here).
3. What are your expectations for your hair service(s) today?
4. Are you now, or have you ever been, allergic to any of the products, treatments, or chemicals you've received during any salon serviceÑhair, nails, or skin? (Please explain)

   ____
5. Are you currently taking any medications? (Please list)

   ____
6. Please list all of the products that you use on your hair on a regular basis.

   ____

   ____
7. What tools do you use at home to style your hair?
8. What is the one thing that you want your stylist to know about you/your hair?
9. Are you interested in receiving a skin care, nail care or makeup consultation?
10. Would you like to be contacted via e-mail aboout upcoming promotions and special events?
    Yes ____ No ____

Statement of Release: I hereby understand that supervised cosmetology students render these services for the sole purpose of practice and learning, and that by signing this form, I recognize and agree not to hold the school, its employees, or the student liable for my satisfaction or the service outcome.

Client signature____________________ Date__________

Service Notes

Today's Date:
Today's Services:
Notes:

Today's Date:
Today's Services:
Notes:

Today's Date:
Today's Services:
Notes:

Today's Date:
Today's Services:
Notes:

Today's Date:
Today's Services:
Notes:

NOTE: If this card were used in a cosmetology school setting, it would include a release form at the bottom such as the one following question 10.

The client intake form gives you an opportunity to built an excellent relationship with your clients.

goes toward the shampoo area. Angie stands up but the young woman is already gone. Angie again approaches the reception desk and asks what she should do. The receptionist tells her to follow the woman, who is Marshall's assistant, to the shampoo station so she can be shampooed and prepared for Marshall. Angie rushes across the styling floor and finally sits down in a shampoo chair. After her hair is shampooed, Angie is led to a styling station and told to sit down. Another couple of minutes pass when finally a young man walks over to Angie. He begins to towel-dry her hair and says "What can I do for you today?" Angie, confused, asks if he is Marshall. He smiles and sarcastically replies, "Well, I was when I got in here this morning!"

20. Based on this scenario, Angie's first impression of the salon staff is likely to be that they are:
- **a.** extremely professional and concerned with making new clients feel welcomed
- **b.** disorganized and too confused to make a new client feel comfortable
- **c.** extremely professional but too confused to make a new client feel comfortable
- **d.** disorganized but concerned with making new clients feel welcomed

21. How should Marshall's assistant have greeted Angie?
- **a.** exactly as she did
- **b.** with a smile and a handshake
- **c.** with a solemn look on her face
- **d.** with a joke about the weather

22. When Angie arrived at the salon and checked in, what should the receptionist have offered to do?
- **a.** park her car for her
- **b.** change the music station on the radio
- **c.** give her a tour of the salon
- **d.** introduce her to the owners

23. Although the salon was obviously busy, what could Marshall's assistant have done to help direct Angie?
- **a.** get her shampooed and into the styling chair as soon as possible
- **b.** waited for Angie to get up and accompany her to the shampoo area
- **c.** called to her from the shampoo area
- **d.** skipped the shampoo and taken her directly to the styling chair

24. What should have been the first thing that Marshall said to Angie when he approached her?

a. "Hi, my name is Marshall. Welcome to the salon."
b. "How much would you like me to trim off your hair?"
c. "I'm running a bit behind, do you need to have your hair shampooed?"
d. "Did anyone explain how we charge for our services?"

It's a particularly busy day at the Newmark Salon where Susan works as a nail tech. Today a loyal salon client, Kim, has several appointments scheduled beginning with a manicure appointment at 1 p.m. After the manicure she is scheduled for an eyebrow waxing at 1:45 p.m. and a haircut at 2 p.m. Susan is booked with appointments all day long, and at 1:20 Kim still hadn't arrived. Susan decides to start her next client, Mrs. Trevino. At 1:30 Kim came into the salon. When she was told by the receptionist, Patti, that she was late for her nail appointment, Kim argued that she had made the appointment for 1:30 and was on time.

25. Patti should handle the scheduling mix up by:

a. proving that she was right by showing Kim the appointment book
b. interrupting Mrs. Trevino's service and having Susan begin kim's service
c. asking Kim to visit another salon in the future
d. apologizing for the mix up and offering to reschedule the appointment

26. If Kim insists that she needs her nail appointment today, what can Patti do to accommodate her request?

a. tell Kim that since she was late there is nothing that can be done
b. check with Susan and reschedule Kim for an appointment at the end of the day
c. make a nail appointment for her at another salon
d. cancel all of Kim's appointments for today

27. In regard to Kim's remaining appointments, the salon should:

a. be able to accommodate Kim's eyebrow waxing and haircut appointments as scheduled
b. reschedule Kim's haircut appointment
c. demand that she reschedule all of the day's appointments
d. reschedule Kim's eyebrow waxing appointment

28. If Kim is upset about not being able to have her nail service immediately, Patti should refer her to:
  a. another salon
  b. the salon's employee policy
  c. another receptionist
  d. the salon's late policy

29. What could the salon do to confirm appointments for clients on the evening before?
  a. mail reminder notices
  b. call clients and confirm appointments
  c. fax special stylist announcements
  d. e-mail clients additional services descriptions

Teneka has just cut Mrs. Mendez's hair for the first time. She felt that she really understood Mrs. Mendez's directions and requests but, now that she has completed the cut and blowdry service, her client is very unhappy about the service and has begun to cry. Teneka is understandably nervous and upset but she knows that she must address Mrs. Mendez's concerns quickly so as not to upset other salon clients.

30. Where is the best place for Teneka to have the conversation with Mrs. Mendez about what is wrong?
  a. at her styling station
  b. in the reception area
  c. at the shampoo bowl
  d. in the consultation area

31. Which of the following questions most closely resembles a question that Teneka should be asking Mrs. Mendez?
  a. "Would you like to have a free conditioning treatment?"
  b. "Would you like a cup of coffee?"
  c. "What specifically don't you like about the style?"
  d. "Would you like to book now for a perm next month?"

32. If Teneka is able to determine from Mrs. Mendez that she would prefer more layers cut into the style, what should Teneka do?
  a. cancel her next appointment and re-cut Mrs. Mendez's hair
  b. tell Mrs. Mendez to remember what she wants for the next time she gets her hair cut
  c. note Mrs. Mendez's complaints on her client consultation card and file it promptly
  d. schedule Mrs. Mendez for the next available appointment and re-cut her hair

33. In the areas around the head where the hair is already too short and more layers can't be cut into the style, Teneka must:
- **a.** pretend to cut those areas to match the others
- **b.** act as if they are not a part of the finished style
- **c.** honestly tell the client that they cannot be reshaped
- **d.** cut them shorter and hope that they blend in with the new cut

34. If Teneka is not able to determine the source of Mrs. Mendez's dissatisfaction and they are not able to come to an amiable resolution, Teneka should:
- **a.** call upon her manager or a senior stylist for help and advice
- **b.** make an appointment for her at another salon
- **c.** give her a gift certificate for a year of free services
- **d.** ask her to leave and never return to the salon

35. How can Teneka use this experience to grow as a professional stylist?
- **a.** She can use the feedback to improve her service for the next client.
- **b.** She can use the experience as confirmation that she is in the wrong industry.
- **c.** She can use the feedback to blame the miscommunication entirely on the client.
- **d.** She can chalk up the experience to having had a bad day.

Sandy has just joined the Master Hair Salon, where Bonnie and Stacy have been working for more than a year. Recently while Stacy was on vacation, Bonnie serviced one of her long-time clients and gave her some advice about her haircolor that differed from the advice Stacy had given her and that satisfied the client more with her color service than she had been previously. Now the client has become a regular client of Bonnie's, and Stacy has accused Bonnie of deliberately trying to steal her clients away. The argument has turned ugly in that each is gossiping about the other to their salon coworkers and clients, and the stress of this ongoing feud has caused a lot of tension in the salon. As the new person, Sandy has been approached by each stylist and now must decide how to proceed in this environment.

36. Sandy's best course of action is to:
- **a.** keep her clients away from Bonnie
- **b.** treat both stylists respectfully and fairly
- **c.** keep her clients away from Stacy
- **d.** treat both stylists with contempt and distrust

37. When asked whose side Sandy believes, she should:
- **a.** decide that she believes Stacy and ignore Bonnie
- **b.** remain partial to Bonnie
- **c.** decide that she believes Bonnie and ignore Stacy
- **d.** remain neutral

38. If pushed into the conflict, what should Sandy say to Bonnie and Stacy?

a. "I don't like or believe either one of you."
b. "I am really ashamed at how childish you two are acting."
c. "I think you are both terrible stylists and I would have advised the client totally differently."
d. "I like you both and don't want to be involved in your argument."

39. If Sandy continues to feel pressured about taking a side, her best course of action is to ask ____________ for help in resolving the matter.

a. her parents
b. her salon manager
c. her best friend
d. her boyfriend

40. If Sandy is feeling victimized about the pressure to get involved in the salon conflict, she may feel tempted to discuss it with other salon staff which would be:

a. an excellent way to get to know others in the salon
b. detrimental to maintaining a professional relationship at work
c. a good way to hear what the other stylists think of the conflict
d. an easy way to get around talking to Bonnie and Stacy

It's October and Bruce realizes that he will be having a meeting with his manager, Jackie, for his annual employee performance evaluation. He hopes to hear that he is doing well at the salon and to discuss some thoughts and ideas he has with Jackie as well. One thing on Bruce's mind is the construction that is occurring in front of the salon and how he feels that it is discouraging the salon's walk-in business. Another issue he hopes to discuss is the flex-time policy the salon has adopted, because he isn't sure how it should be affecting the late-evening shift that he usually ends up working alone. And finally, he wants to talk with Jackie about the possibility of working toward a promotion to assistant manager of the salon.

41. In preparation for the evaluation meeting, Bruce should think about and make a list including:

a. why he should get a larger raise than the other stylists
b. all of the problems in the salon
c. problems and possible solutions
d. the ways in which he is a better stylist than his coworkers

42. When discussing the issue of the construction outside of the salon and its effect on the salon's walk-in business, Bruce should:
- **a.** show Jackie how much money the salon is losing because of it
- **b.** calculate how many clients are leaving the salon because of the noise
- **c.** stand at the door and count how many potential new clients walk by the salon in a day
- **d.** suggest some ideas for how to work around the inconvenience of the construction

43. When discussing the flex-time policy and the fact that he is often left at the salon alone in the evening, Bruce needs to:
- **a.** complain that it isn't fair
- **b.** list all of the names of stylists who have left early when they shouldn't have
- **c.** make the case for his appointment to night manager
- **d.** ask for an explanation of the policy and how it affects the evening shift

44. When discussing any opportunities there may be for promotion, Bruce will need to be prepared to hear:
- **a.** that he can have the job
- **b.** the areas that he will need to improve on in order to be considered for a promotion
- **c.** that someone else has already asked for the promotion
- **d.** the budget restrictions that disallow for another assistant manager position

45. If Bruce is serious about working toward a promotion, he will want to ask Jackie:
- **a.** when they can come together again to discuss his progress
- **b.** if he can begin to work part-time
- **c.** why she hasn't considered him for a promotion before now
- **d.** when he can expect to be made a salon partner

46. Once the evaluation is completed, Bruce should __________ Jackie.
- **a.** thank
- **b.** flatter
- **c.** praise
- **d.** ignore

CHAPTER 5 Infection Control: Principles and Practices

Adam is a new employee at the Spiral Curl Salon. Adam will begin as an assistant and, once he is licensed, he will graduate to a junior stylist. On his first day of work his salon mentor, Mary, takes him on a tour of the salon, pointing out the various areas that will be his responsibility as they walk through the salon. Adam will have many duties; the most important of these will be to help keep the salon cleaned, disinfected, and safe for both the clients and the stylists.

1. Mary explains to Adam that __________, a federal agency, regulates and enforces safety and health standards to protect employees in the workplace.
- **a.** EPA
- **b.** MSDS
- **c.** OSHA
- **d.** HCS

2. Adams asks what is specifically addressed in these standards.
- **a.** issues relating to the manufacturing of products used in cosmetology services
- **b.** issues relating to the handling, mixing, storing, and disposing of products used in cosmetology services
- **c.** issues relating to the lack of cleanliness in a salon workplace
- **d.** general information on the ingredients contained in the products used in cosmetology services

3. Adam sees a binder on the counter in the salon dispensary labeled MSDSs and asks Mary what that is for. Mary explains that MSDSs are:
- **a.** Monthly Sales Data Sheets
- **b.** Monthly Salon Data Sheets
- **c.** Material Safety Data Sheets
- **d.** Materials Salons Discard Sheets

4. Mary further explains that MSDS contain information on:
- **a.** product safety
- **b.** medical treatment
- **c.** both of the above
- **d.** neither of the above

5. Adam asks Mary where MSDS come from. She responds that they come from:
   a. workbooks that can be purchased on the Internet
   b. product manufacturers who provide them for free
   c. distributor sales consultants who pass them out when a certain dollar amount is purchased
   d. cosmetology textbooks

6. Mary tells Adam that if a state inspector comes into the salon he or she will look for a ______, which verifies that all of the salon employees have read the information on the MSDS.
   a. certificate of completion with a completion date
   b. license from the city with an expiration date
   c. certificate of acknowledgement from the product's manufacturer
   d. sign-off sheet with employee signatures

7. Adam is reminded that there are two types of disinfectant products and that they:
   a. destroy all bacteria, fungi, and viruses (but not spores) on surfaces
   b. create a sweet smell in the salon, masking unpleasant service odors
   c. destroy all bacteria, fungi, and viruses (including spores) on surfaces
   d. create a cleanliness barrier so that no new germs can grow

8. Adam reads the label on the two types of disinfectants in the salon dispensary and is reminded that, in case someone is accidentally cut and blood is present, a _____ must be used to clean the styling station and tools.
   a. tuberculocidal disinfectant
   b. medical disinfectant
   c. hospital disinfectant
   d. disease-killing disinfectant

9. Mary explains to Adam the daily cleaning and disinfecting procedure the salon uses. Mary tells him that each time he cleans and disinfects an area of the salon, he needs to enter it into the salon:
   a. scheduling program
   b. logbook
   c. diary
   d. policy and procedures manual

Mark and Caryn both work at the Solé Salon and Spa and their stations are right next to one another. Mark's daughter Maureen was diagnosed with strep throat and was home from school sick for several days. The following week both Caryn and one of Mark's clients, Jane, are also diagnosed with strep throat after seeing Mark for a haircut.

10. Mark appears to be spreading a(n):
- **a.** infectious disease
- **b.** infected disease
- **c.** noninfectious disease
- **d.** contaminated disease

11. What should Mark and his salon be doing to prevent the spread of his daughter's illness?
- **a.** cleaning and sterilizing tools, surfaces, and equipment
- **b.** spraying and wiping the styling station with ammonia
- **c.** cleaning and disinfecting the tools, equipment, and surfaces
- **d.** hosing down the tools, equipment and surfaces

12. Disinfectants used in the salon should be:
- **a.** bactericidal, virucidal, and fungicidal
- **b.** bactericidal, sporicidal, and fungicidal
- **c.** sporicidal, virucidal, and fungicidal
- **d.** bactericidal, virucidal, and disinfectacidal

13. Mark appears to be spreading bacteria called:
- **a.** cocci
- **b.** streptococci
- **c.** diplococci
- **d.** staphylococci

14. How might Caryn have been exposed to the bacteria that caused her strep throat?
- **a.** by having a cup of coffee at work
- **b.** by breathing the same air as Mark
- **c.** by cleaning out her refrigerator at home
- **d.** by taking out the salon's trash

15. Bacteria that are disease-causing are called:
- **a.** pathogenic
- **b.** nonthreatening
- **c.** nonpathogenic
- **d.** threatening

16. Strep throat is:
    a. an organism
    b. a germ
    c. a secretion
    d. an infection

17. When Caryn looks inside her mouth she can see ________, which indicates that she has an infection.
    a. spirilla
    b. mitosis
    c. pus
    d. flagella

18. A disease that can spread from Maureen to Mark to Caryn is said to be:
    a. advantageous
    b. communicable
    c. disadvantageous
    d. communicative

Three of the five nail clients Thomas has seen today have a strange yellow-green spot just under one of their nails. His first client of the day, Marci, has the spot on her large toe, which Thomas noticed while giving her a pedicure. Gina has a similar spot under a nail enhancement on her left hand, and Bonita has a spot on a fingernail on her right hand. Marci is a waitress and likes to take good care of her feet. She has been a loyal pedicure client of Thomas's for the past five years. Gina, a swimming instructor, is a tried and true nail client, coming into the salon every two weeks for a monomer liquid and polymer powder fill-in. She has worn these nail enhancements for the last three years. Bonita, a schoolteacher, is a natural nail client who has a manicure and pedicure about once a month. When Thomas attempts to wipe away the discolored area he is unable to.

19. What is the yellow-green spot that Thomas has detected likely to be?
    a. dirt
    b. infection
    c. fungi
    d. trapped water

20. Why can't Thomas remove the yellow-green spots he sees?
    a. because they are a disease
    b. because they are stained on the skin
    c. because they can never be removed
    d. because they must be cut off the nail

21. How could the fungus have been brought into the salon?
   a. Bonita may have caught it from one of her students.
   b. Gina may have had moisture trapped under a nail.
   c. Marci may have come into contact with spoiled food.
   d. Thomas may have opened an expired bottle of acetone.

22. How could the fungus have spread from one client to another?
   a. improper disinfection of manicure implements
   b. by disinfecting the manicure table
   c. improper storage of the nail enhancements
   d. by using the same nail polish wand on more than one client

Each year Lucille and Frank, who are the co-owners of the Serious Skin Care Center, take many precautions to ward off becoming ill during the cold and flu season. Frank makes it a habit to go to the doctor each year and to get a flu shot, because he knows that if he doesn't he will undoubtedly get a cold or flu at some point during the season. Lucille, on the other hand, makes a concentrated effort to take extra note of the vitamins she takes, to get a little extra sleep and relaxation, and to be sure to wash her hands frequently throughout the day, especially after servicing each client.

23. Both Lucille and Frank are attempting to enhance their _________ to disease.
   a. immunity
   b. availability
   c. susceptibility
   d. contagability

24. Frank's flu shot is considered to be:
   a. a natural immunity
   b. a lost attempt at not getting sick
   c. a viable option for people who don't want to go to the doctor
   d. an acquired immunity

25. Lucille's ability to stave off the flu by taking excellent care of herself is an example of someone with:
   a. a natural immunity
   b. a lost attempt at not getting sick
   c. a viable option for people who don't want to go to the doctor
   d. an acquired immunity

Jason is the new salon manager for the Good Looks Salon and he is very concerned with the cleanliness of the salon and with preventing the spread of disease. In order to assess how the salon is doing in its efforts to control the spread of harmful disease and to make recommendations to his styling staff, Jason is about to review the salon's cleaning and disinfecting practices with the cleaning crew that has been hired to clean the salon each week. Ginger is the crew's supervisor, and she tells Jason that the salon is regularly cleaned and then disinfected with chemical disinfectants. Ginger also mentions that the cleaning crew follows all of the manufacturer's directions for use of each of these cleaning and disinfecting agents and they follow OSHA guidelines.

26. In order to remove the pathogens and other substances that linger on the surfaces of the salon and on implements, the salon must be willing to:
a. decontaminate
b. bathe
c. sterilize
d. contaminate

27. When Ginger's crew disinfects the salon they are using chemical agents to destroy bacteria and viruses on:
a. facial skin and tools
b. surfaces and equipment
c. hair follicles and implements
d. surfaces and clients

28. When Ginger considers the types of products for the crew to use, she must first decide if the product has the correct _________ for getting the job accomplished.
a. audacity
b. efficiency
c. efficacy
d. affection

29. The cleaning crew may use a quat because it is:
a. effective in cleaning the scalp
b. effective for cleaning under the fingernails
c. effective for cleaning the windows
d. effective for disinfecting implements

30. Jason can require the salon's stylists to use a _________ for disinfecting salon tools.
  a. phenol disinfectant
  b. liquid soap
  c. bleach compound
  d. bar soap

31. The cleaning crew's ability to decontaminate is limited mainly to the practice of:
  a. cleaning tools, surfaces, and implements with liquid soap, rinsing them in clean water, and disinfecting them
  b. cleansing countertops with quats and washing them with soap and water
  c. cleaning tables with phenols and immersing them in hospital disinfectants
  d. washing implements with alcohol and allowing them to air dry

32. For multiuse tools and implements the cleaning crew must:
  a. throw them away after use
  b. immerse them in disinfectant immediately after they are used
  c. clean and disinfect them after use
  d. allow the stylist to use them on more than one client before cleaning them

Keith is a busy cutter at Martin's Salon and Spa. In between each client he quickly rinses his combs and brushes with warm water and drops them into a disinfecting solution. Keith allows them to become saturated and then reaches into the jar, pulls the implements out, and wipes them dry with a towel and places them on his roll-about so he can access them easily before the next client is finished being shampooed and is delivered to his station by his assistant.

33. Before immersing his implements into the disinfecting solution, Keith should have:
  a. immersed them in cool water
  b. cleaned them with soap and water
  c. blown dry loose hair from them
  d. immersed them in boiling water

34. To protect himself, Keith should wear _________ when working with disinfecting solution.
  a. sneakers
  b. a cape
  c. a smock
  d. gloves

35. How should Keith mix the disinfecting solution?
  a. according to the salon owner's guidelines
  b. according to the salon manager's guidelines
  c. according to the manufacturer's guidelines
  d. according to the state board's guidelines

36. How long should Keith's implements be immersed in the disinfecting solution?
  a. one hour
  b. until the next client is ready
  c. as long as the directions recommend
  d. four to six hours

37. After the implements have been removed from the disinfecting solution, Keith should:
  a. store them on an empty station until he needs them
  b. rinse, dry, and place them in a clean, covered container
  c. leave them rinsing in the shampoo bowl
  d. wrap them in a towel and put them in his drawer

While cutting his client's hair, Mitch accidentally nicks his finger and his cut begins to bleed. He knows that he must follow the Universal Precautions for an exposure incident.

38. The first thing Mitch should do is:
  a. continue the service and notify his client
  b. call his doctor and notify his manager
  c. stop the service and notify his client
  d. notify OSHA and call his doctor

39. Mitch asks Jan, one of his colleagues, for help. She immediately retrieves:
  a. a paper towel
  b. the salon's first aid kit
  c. the OSHA handbook
  d. the salon's policy manual

40. What should Jan be wearing while she cleans Mitch's cut with an antiseptic wipe and bandages his cut once the bleeding has stopped?
  a. goggles
  b. hairnet
  c. gloves
  d. face mask

41. Mitch should now put on gloves and:
   a. clean and disinfect his styling station with an EPA-registered antiseptic spray
   b. wash and dry his styling station with an EPA-registered disinfectant spray effective against germs
   c. clean and disinfect his styling station with a disinfectant designed for cleaning blood and body fluids
   d. clean and disinfect his styling station with an phenolic spray

42. Mitch will need to discard all of his single-use contaminated implements and materials by:
   a. throwing them into the garbage
   b. double bagging them and putting a biohazard sticker on the bag before putting it into the sterilizing unit
   c. piling them on his station and completing his interrupted service
   d. double bagging them and putting a biohazard sticker on the bag before putting it into a container for contaminated waste

43. Mitch will need to make sure that all multiuse tools and implements that have come into contact with blood or other body fluids are thoroughly cleaned and completely immersed in a(n)________ designed for cleaning blood and body fluids or 10 percent bleach solution.
   a. OSHA-registered decontamination solution
   b. salon-approved disinfecting solution
   c. EPA-registered disinfecting solution
   d. industry-recommended decontamination solution

44. Mitch's multiuse tools and implements must be immersed in the solution for at least _____or for the time recommended by the manufacturer.
   a. 5 minutes
   b. 10 minutes
   c. 15 minutes
   d. 20 minutes

45. Before returning to the client and resuming the service, Mitch should:
   a. wash and dry his hands and rebandage his cut
   b. wash and immerse his cutting apron
   c. wash and disinfect his hands
   d. wash and disinfect his hands and rebandage his cut

Heather has just hired a new pedicurist, Allie, who has finished her training and is eager to start work at her very first salon job. Heather gives Allie a quick tour of the salon and then instructs Allie on where the salon's disinfectants are stored and on how and when to clean and disinfect the foot spas that are used for pedicure clients. Heather gives Allie instructions on how and when to clean and disinfect the foot baths.

46. Heather instructs Allie to __________ after each client.

- **a.** store the foot bath in a dark cool place
- **b.** scrub all visible residue from the inside walls of the basin
- **c.** dry the foot bath with a clean towel
- **d.** spray the foot bath with alcohol

47. Next, Heather explains that Allie will need to disinfect the foot bath with a(n) __________ disinfectant, according to the manufacturer's directions.

- **a.** NCA-registered
- **b.** FDA-registered
- **c.** EPA-registered
- **d.** ANC-registered

48. At the end of each day, Heather tells Allie that she will need to:

- **a.** add a cup of bleach to the water and leave the foot bath running for two hours
- **b.** circulate alcohol through the foot bath for 5 to 10 minutes
- **c.** spray a foot deodorizer into the foot bath and allow it to dry completely
- **d.** remove the screen and clean the debris trapped behind it

49. At the end of the day, Allie should use an EPA-registered liquid hospital disinfectant and circulate through the basin for:

- **a.** one hour
- **b.** fifteen minutes
- **c.** ten minutes
- **d.** one day

50. Heather tells Allie that at least once a week she will need to fill the foot spa tub with an EPA-registered disinfectant solution, circulate it, and then let the solution sit:

- **a.** for two days
- **b.** for one hour
- **c.** overnight
- **d.** for five minutes

CHAPTER 6 General Anatomy and Physiology

Malik has been feeling ill for quite some time when he finally decides to go to a doctor. The doctor performs a number of tests, and diagnoses Malik with a disease that affects his cells' ability to remain healthy and reproduce.

1. Malik's cells contain ________, a colorless, jelly-like substance in which food elements and water are present.
  a. cytoplasm
  b. protoplasm
  c. nucleus
  d. cell membrane

2. The nucleus of Malik's cells plays a vital role in:
  a. replication
  b. repatriation
  c. reproduction
  d. reposition

3. If Malik's cells are unable to repair themselves, the problem most likely lies in the cells':
  a. protoplasm
  b. nucleus
  c. cell membrane
  d. cytoplasm

4. The two phases of metabolism that Malik's cells undergo are:
  a. cannibalism and anabolism
  b. catabolism and mitosis
  c. catabolism and anabolism
  d. anabolism and mitosis

In her training, Robin is studying the body's tissues and their uses. Since tissues are a collection of similar cells that all perform a particular function, Robin, in her work as an esthetician, knows that she will need to be aware of their effect on her clients, especially during services such as facials and massage.

5. The ________ tissue is responsible for supporting, protecting, and binding together other tissues of the body.
  a. nerve
  b. liquid
  c. connective
  d. muscular

6. The tissue that carries food, waste, and hormones through the body is called:
   a. nerve
   b. liquid
   c. connective
   d. muscular

7. As a skin care specialist, Robin will be very interested in the epithelial tissue since it includes the:
   a. feet
   b. senses
   c. skin
   d. scalp

8. When giving a facial massage, Robin will be coming into contact with the ________system:
   a. nerve
   b. liquid
   c. connective
   d. muscular

9. When facial clients realize that they feel relaxed and calm as a result of Robin's facial manipulations, it will be because the _______ tissues are carrying those messages from the brain to the rest the body.
   a. nerve
   b. liquid
   c. connective
   d. muscular

Richard is losing his hair and realizes that for many reasons, especially esthetic reasons, he wants to do whatever he can to naturally slow the process down. He speaks with his dermatologist, who advises him to massage the top of his head, especially the areas where he sees the most hair loss, to eat a balanced diet, and to stop drinking soft drinks and to replace them with plenty of water. His doctor also suggests that Richard begin taking long walks in the park and that he take time to sit in a peaceful place and breathe in clean air. Richard also realizes that because his skin is so dry he should use a moisturizer to avoid skin breakage and cracking.

10. When Richard is advised to massage his scalp, the doctor's intention is to increase Richard's blood circulation, which is a function of the:
    a. brain
    b. skin
    c. heart
    d. liver

11. Drinking plenty of water will allow Richard's body to eliminate waste products through the work of the:
    a. kidneys
    b. eyes
    c. lungs
    d. stomach and intestines

12. Supplying oxygen to the blood is the work of Richard's:
    a. kidneys
    b. eyes
    c. lungs
    d. stomach and intestines

13. Using a cream or lotion will moisturize Richard's skin, which is responsible for:
    a. removing toxins from the body
    b. controlling the body
    c. digesting food
    d. forming an external protective covering for the body

Billy volunteers his time and his talent one day a week by going to a nearby nursing home and helping the residents by servicing their hair and beauty needs. Many of the residents at the home have very serious health problems. While Billy knows he should never try to treat the patients, he is aware of the symptoms of their illnesses and able to notify the nurse on duty to watch out for the patients' well-being. On his schedule today are Mrs. Hammil, Mrs. Boxing, and Mrs. Reyper, all of whom want hair services.

14. While setting her hair, Billy notices that Mrs. Hammil's legs and ankles are swollen, which indicates that her ________ system is not working properly.
    a. circulatory
    b. digestive
    c. endocrine
    d. excretory

15. Mrs. Boxing has difficulty controlling the position of her head during her service; she is experiencing difficulty with her:
    a. digestive system
    b. muscular system
    c. endocrine system
    d. excretory system

16. During her perm Mrs. Reyper sounds like she is having difficulty breathing. This is the work of the:
   a. endocrine system
   b. skeletal system
   c. excretory system
   d. respiratory system

David is a businessman with a very stressful job. He has an appointment with Christy for a haircut and he decides to add on a scalp and head massage before his haircut. David complains of head and neck aches to Christy and tells her that he isn't sleeping as comfortably as he would like to be.

17. In the first part of the massage, Christy will begin at the crown and work her way down to the ________, which is above the nape.
   a. mandible
   b. parietal bone
   c. maxilla
   d. occipital bone

18. The muscle that Christy will be massaging when she works on David's' crown and occipital area is the:
   a. frontalis
   b. occipitalis
   c. origin
   d. insertion

19. The bone that forms David's forehead is called the:
   a. mandible
   b. frontal
   c. maxilla
   d. occipital bone

20. The muscle that allows David to raise his eyebrows is the:
   a. frontalis
   b. occipitalis
   c. origin
   d. insertion

21. The bones that are at David's temples are the:
   a. lacrimal bones
   b. parietal bones
   c. temporal bones
   d. occipital bones

22. To relieve his neck aches, Christy suggests that David sleep with a soft pillow to support the seven bones of his:

a. nasal cavity
b. thorax
c. cervical vertebrae
d. scapula

23. The muscles that allow David to lower and rotate his head are the:

a. aponeurosis
b. masseter
c. platysma
d. sternocleidomastoideus

Betty has been told time and time again by her clients that the best part of the manicure is the hand and arm massage. Today she takes extra time with Pam, an administrative assistant who spends a lot of time on her computer; Betty takes special care of Pam's fingers and wrists.

24. When Betty massages Pam's fingers, the muscles that are responsible for separating the fingers are the:

a. flexors
b. triceps
c. abductors
d. adductors

25. By massaging Pam's fingers Betty will be concentrating on the bones of the:

a. ulna
b. carpus
c. phalanges
d. metacarpus

26. Because of her work, Pam is in danger of having pain in her ______, which is the result of repetitive movement.

a. ulna
b. carpus
c. phalanges
d. metacarpus

27. In order to massage the palm of Pam's hand, Betty would come into contact with the:

a. ulna
b. carpus
c. phalanges
d. metacarpus

28. Betty finishes Pam's treatment by massaging her upper arm, also called the:
   a. ulna
   b. humerus
   c. carpus
   d. phalanges

29. The muscle that allows Pam to rotate her palm outward is the:
   a. supinator
   b. biceps
   c. triceps
   d. extensors

Alma is a middle-aged facial client of the Skin Deep Salon and she asks her esthetician, Cindy, what she can do to help her tone and maintain the muscles of her face. Alma points out that she has noticed her skin starting to wrinkle, especially around her mouth, eyes, and nose and says that she wants to remain looking as young as she can without having cosmetic surgery. Cindy explains that there are several muscles in those areas that could benefit from gentle massage.

30. The muscle in Alma's forehead that is responsible for vertical wrinkles is the:
   a. masseter
   b. temporalis
   c. buccinator
   d. corrugator

31. The muscle between the cheek and upper and lower jaw that compresses the cheeks and gives Alma the appearance of high cheek bones is the:
   a. masseter
   b. temporalis
   c. buccinator
   d. corrugator

32. The muscle around Alma's eye socket, toned to reduce the tiny wrinkles around her eyes, is the:
   a. orbicularis oculi
   b. buccinator
   c. depressor labii inferioris
   d. corrugator

33. The muscle that causes wrinkles across the bridge of Alma's nose is the:

a. orbicularis oculi
b. procerus
c. depressor labii inferioris
d. platysma

34. When she made her comment about looking young, Alma employed her ________ muscle to lower her lower lip and draw it to one side.

a. orbicularis oculi
b. procerus
c. depressor labii inferioris
d. platysma

35. The muscle that would allow Alma to draw her lips in a sexy pout is the:

a. orbicularis oculi
b. procerus
c. depressor labii inferioris
d. levator anguli oris

Sean is a very successful hairdresser who works a lot to accommodate his clients' needs. He has recently read a number of articles about how important it is for truly successful people to take excellent care of their bodies as well as their minds. Sean spent some time thinking about this and evaluating his life, and he decided to commit to a regular exercise routine, going to the gym three times a week and eating a health-conscious diet. Sean's workouts involve lifting weights and working out on machines designed to build his strength. Sometimes the workout routine leaves Sean out of breath and light-headed. For his protection, the gym requires Sean to frequently stop and check his heart rate, which is often elevated. Sean also sometimes experiences leg cramps in his sleep.

36. The system whose activities are responsible for Sean's thought processes about exercise is the:

a. autonomic nervous system
b. peripheral nervous system
c. central nervous system
d. astronomic nervous system

37. When Sean realizes that he feels tired as a result of his workout, the realization is the ________ system at work.
   a. autonomic
   b. peripheral
   c. central nervous
   d. astronomic

38. When Sean's heart rate becomes elevated, it is the response of the ________ system to the workout.
   a. autonomic
   b. peripheral
   c. central nervous
   d. pstronomic

39. The nerves that carry the message from Sean's brain to his muscles, thus allowing him to pick up and move weights during his workout, are called:
   a. afferent
   b. different
   c. motor
   d. mixed

Stress can sometimes run high at the Stop Here Salon, which employs more than 20 stylists and is located in a busy strip mall. In order to relieve some of the tension from the hectic schedule, the salon manager Jo has decided to introduce a new technique called Expression Therapy during a staff meeting. When stylists are feeling the stress of the day, they are encouraged to go to the break room, close the door, and make funny faces into the mirror, then take a deep breath, laugh at themselves, and return to their styling station. They all agree to give it a try. To start, Marty decides to pull his ears away from his face and bend them downward. Next, Anne puts her index finger on the tip of her nose and lifts it up slightly. Missy follows by extending her lower lip and chin into a huge pout. Laughing, Matt raises his eyebrows, as if he has just been shocked or surprised by something terrible. Finally, when Patsy pushes her lower lip and chin out from her face, the whole group can't stop laughing. They all agree that this technique would be a great stress reliever. Jo flashes a huge smile at the staff and then dismisses the meeting.

40. When Marty pulls his ears away from his face and bends them downward, he is affecting the ________ nerves.
   a. nasal
   b. infratrochlear
   c. auriculotemporal
   d. infraorbital

41. When Anne puts her index finger on the tip of her nose and lifts it up slightly, she is affecting the ________ nerve.

a. nasal
b. infratrochlear
c. auriculotemporal
d. infraorbital

42. When Missy extends her lower lip and chin into a pout, she is affecting the ________ nerve.

a. nasal
b. infratrochlear
c. mental
d. infraorbital

43. When Matt raises his eyebrows as if he has just been shocked or surprised, he is affecting the ________ nerve.

a. nasal
b. supraorbital
c. mental
d. supratrochlear

44. When Patsy pushes her lower lip and chin out from her face, she is affecting the ________ nerve.

a. zygomatic
b. temporal
c. buccal
d. mandibular

45. When Jo flashes a huge smile at the staff, she is affecting the ________ nerve.

a. zygomatic
b. temporal
c. buccal
d. mandibular

After running up and down the stairs from the salon's retail and reception area to the stock room where additional retail products are stored, John is completely out of breath and his heart is pumping hard. He just spent the last hour recording what products were depleted and restocking the salon's shelves.

46. The circulatory system consists of John's ________, arteries, veins, and capillaries.

a. spinal cord
b. heart
c. reflexes
d. mandible

47. John's body is employing _______ circulation when it sends blood from the heart throughout the body and back to the heart again.

a. pulmonary
b. valve
c. systemic
d. capillary

48. John's heart is a(n):

a. nerve
b. artery
c. tissue
d. organ

49. In order to purify it, John's heart will employ _______ circulation to send his blood to his lungs for purification.

a. pulmonary
b. valve
c. systemic
d. capillary

50. The thick-walled, muscular, flexible tubes that carry oxygenated blood away from John's heart to the capillaries are called:

a. valves
b. capillaries
c. arteries
d. veins

51. John has _______, which are thin-walled blood vessels that are less elastic than arteries.

a. valves
b. capillaries
c. arteries
d. veins

52. John's veins contain _______ which are situated between the chambers of the heart and allow blood to flow in only one direction.

a. valves
b. capillaries
c. arteries
d. veins

53. John's _______ are minute, thin-walled blood vessels that connect the smaller arteries to venules.
   a. valves
   b. capillaries
   c. arteries
   d. veins

54. John's red blood cells:
   a. carry the body's cells to the heart
   b. carry cells to the blood
   c. carry cells to oxygen
   d. carry oxygen to the body's cells

55. John's white blood cells:
   a. destroy mold
   b. destroy disease-causing toxins and bacteria
   c. destroy useful bacteria-causing toxins and bacteria
   d. destroy oxygen

56. The plasma in John's blood is responsible for:
   a. carrying food to cells
   b. carrying bacteria to cells
   c. carrying nerves to cells
   d. carrying muscle tissue to cells

57. Which of the following is NOT a function of John's lymphatic/immune system?
   a. provide waste to cells
   b. carry nourishment from the blood to the cells
   c. act as a defense against toxins
   d. remove waste from cells

Karen has recently begun to feel sudden and overwhelming rushes of heat which she calls hot flashes. They are so severe at times that she has to stop servicing clients and excuse herself to the restroom until they pass. After an episode, Karen is typically covered in perspiration and her clothes are wet. To help her relax after such an episode, Karen practices deep breathing exercises that are designed to help calm her and return her heart rate to a normal and natural rate.

58. The name of the system that affects the growth, development, and health of the Karen's entire body is the _______ system:
   a. circulatory
   b. endocrine
   c. respiratory
   d. digestive

59. Karen's endocrine glands secrete _______ into her bloodstream, which influence(s) the well-being of her entire body.

a. hormones
b. bile
c. urine
d. carbon dioxide

60. The _______, which is part of Karen's excretory system, is responsible for eliminating waste through perspiration.

a. kidneys
b. large intestine
c. skin
d. lungs

61. When she practices deep breathing exercises, Karen is employing her:

a. kidneys
b. large intestine
c. skin
d. lungs

62. The muscular wall that helps Karen control her breathing is the:

a. lungs
b. skin
c. diaphragm
d. diagram

63. When Karen breathes in and oxygen is absorbed into her blood, the process is called:

a. inhalation
b. excretion
c. exhalation
d. urination

64. When Karen breathes out and carbon dioxide is expelled from the body, the process is called:

a. inhalation
b. excretion
c. exhalation
d. urination

65. Karen's skin, oil and sweat glands, sensory receptors, hair, and nails all belong to which of the following body systems?
a. circulatory
b. integumentary
c. respiratory
d. digestive

After a long day of servicing clients at the salon, Susan realizes that she hasn't eaten and is feeling very hungry. She decides to drive through a fast food restaurant for a burger on her way home from the salon. She arrives at the order window at 9 p.m. and orders a hamburger, French fries, and a large iced tea. She pays for her food and then sits in her car and eats her dinner.

66. The system responsible for changing Susan's burger into nutrients and waste is the _______ system:
a. circulatory
b. endocrine
c. respiratory
d. digestive

67. Susan's _______ will be busy at work changing certain kinds of foods into a form that can be used by the body.
a. digestive insulin
b. digestive adrenaline
c. digestive enzymes
d. digestive estrogen

68. If Susan eats her burger at 9:15 p.m., what time will it be when her body completes the entire digestive process?
a. 10:15 p.m.
b. 1:15 a.m.
c. 3:15 a.m.
d. 6:15 a.m.

CHAPTER 7

Skin Structure, Growth, and Nutrition

Clare has returned from a week-long vacation in the Bahamas and has made an appointment with Donna, an esthetician, for a facial. While examining her skin, Donna notices that Clare has a tan and that, in certain areas on her face and neck, the skin is taut, pink, dry, and painful to the touch. Clare complains that she is beginning to see wrinkles around her mouth and eyes, that the skin on her nose is a bit oily, and there are dark spots imbedded in the skin.

1. During her examination Donna is observing Clare's:
  a. epidermis
  b. papillary layer
  c. dermis
  d. reticular layer

2. Clare's tan is a result of the effect of ultraviolet light that increased the amount of ______ in her skin.
  a. keratin
  b. stratum lucidum
  c. melanin
  d. stratum granulosum

3. The appearance of skin that is taut, pink, and dry indicates that Clare may have a(n):
  a. tan
  b. SPF
  c. sunburn
  d. nerve disorder

4. What is causing Clare's wrinkles?
  a. laughing too much
  b. loss of collagen and elastin
  c. not squinting enough
  d. too much collagen and elastin

5. Which nerves are responsible for the pain Clare feels?
  a. motor nerve fibers
  b. sensory nerve fibers
  c. elastin nerve fibers
  d. secretory nerve fibers

6. Which nerves are responsible for Clare's nose being oily?
   a. motor nerve fibers
   b. sensory nerve fibers
   c. elastin nerve fibers
   d. secretory nerve fibers

7. The dark spots that are imbedded in the skin on Clare's nose are called:
   a. milia
   b. comedones
   c. seborrhea
   d. rosacea

8. These dark spots are caused by:
   a. hardened sebum in a hair follicle
   b. discoloration of the cells
   c. the accumulation of dry skin
   d. loosened debris

9. These dark spots are considered to be a disorder of the:
   a. sweat glands
   b. sudoriferous glands
   c. sebaceous glands
   d. mammary glands

Marlee is a hard-working stylist with three young children to care for. She has just returned from her yearly doctor's visit, where she complained of feeling tired all of the time. Marlee told the doctor that she not only feels tired, but that she thinks she looks tired too. Her skin is always dry, no matter what type of moisturizer she uses on it, her jawline is sagging, and when she gets cuts and scratches it takes a long time for her skin to heal. The doctor asks Marlee how much time she spends in the sun. She tells him that since she lives near the beach, she often takes her children there on the weekends to swim and play while she relaxes and catches up on magazine reading. Her doctor also asks her about her regular diet and water intake. Marlee tells him that she is very busy and quite often eats a lot of fast food and doesn't like to have too many liquids during the day because she wants to avoid having to leave her clients frequently to use the restroom. Her doctor recommends eating a more balanced diet, packed with the essential vitamins and nutrients she needs for overall better health, and drinking plenty of water. Marlee agrees to take better care of herself.

10. In order for her to take better care of herself, Marlee will need to create an eating plan that includes the following six nutrients:

a. carbohydrates, breads, proteins, vitamins, cheeses, and water
b. carbohydrates, fats, proteins, vitamins, minerals, and water
c. fats, cholesterol, proteins, vitamins, lipids, and water
d. water, fats, chicken, vitamins, minerals, and lean meats

11. Marlee does a little research and finds out that there are five basic food groups. Those food groups are:

a. breads, vegetables, fruits, milk, and protein
b. grains, vegetables, fruits, yogurt, and protein
c. grains, vegetables, fruits, milk, and protein
d. grains, roughage, fruits, milk, and protein

12. Which of the following should Marlee *avoid* when trying to eat a balanced diet?

a. a diet that is high in fresh fruits, vegetables, and grain products and low in fats, saturated fat, and cholesterol
b. eating large amounts of salt and sugar, including the sodium and modified sugars that are in prepared food products
c. keeping alcoholic beverages to a minimum
d. balancing her diet with the right amount of physical activity

13. One thing Marlee can do while deciding what items to purchase in the grocery store is:

a. taste the foods before she purchases them
b. weigh the foods before she purchases them
c. read the food's product label before she purchases it
d. read about the food's product category before she purchases it

14. Marlee promised herself that she would drink more water every day. How can she determine how many ounces of water is appropriate for her to drink?

a. by dividing her age by two
b. by multiplying her age by two
c. by dividing her weight by two
d. by multiplying her weight by two

15. If Marlee wishes to enhance her skin's elasticity, she should consider taking:

a. vitamin E
b. vitamin D
c. vitamin C
d. vitamin A

16. If Marlee wishes to enhance her skin's ability to repair itself, she should consider taking:

- **a.** vitamin E
- **b.** vitamin D
- **c.** vitamin C
- **d.** vitamin A

17. If Marlee wishes to enhance her bone health, she should consider taking:

- **a.** vitamin E
- **b.** vitamin D
- **c.** vitamin C
- **d.** vitamin A

18. If Marlee wishes to enhance her ability to protect her skin from UV light, she should consider taking:

- **a.** vitamin E
- **b.** vitamin D
- **c.** vitamin C
- **d.** vitamin A

CHAPTER 8 Skin Disorders and Diseases

Gigi is a runner who has just completed a five-mile run. She has just come across the finish line and is drenched in perspiration and breathing heavily. This was a difficult race for Gigi because it was a very hot day. As a result of running through a wooded area, she also has several mosquito bites on her arms and legs, which she has already been scratching. Under her arms, Gigi notices a mass of small red bumps that burn when she moves her arms back and forth. After a few moments, Gigi takes off her running shoes and notices a foul smell as well.

1. Gigi's perspiration is a function of the:
   a. sebaceous glands
   b. motor nerve fibers
   c. sweat glands
   d. sensory nerve fibers

2. The itchy, swollen lesions caused by Gigi's mosquito bites are called:
   a. cysts
   b. pustules
   c. vesicles
   d. wheals

3. To protect herself from overexposure to the sun while running, Gigi should have worn:
   a. facial moisturizer
   b. capri pants
   c. sunscreen
   d. a baseball cap

4. As a result of scratching the mosquito bites on her legs, Gigi has developed a(n):
   a. crust
   b. excoriation
   c. fissure
   d. keloid

5. The small red bumps that burn when Gigi moves her arms back and forth are called:
   a. eczema
   b. anhidrosis
   c. miliaria rubra
   d. bromhidrosis

6. The foul odor Gigi notices after removing her running shoes is called:
   a. eczema
   b. anhidrosis
   c. miliaria rubra
   d. bromhidrosis

Dr. Tinsley is a dermatologist who sees patients with all sorts of skin disorders.

Today she has several patients waiting to see her. Brent is a construction worker who works in many types of weather conditions. His hands have a tremendous amount of hard, dried skin accumulated on them which sometimes cracks and becomes painful. Pam, another patient, has developed a dark-colored red wine spot on her forehead that only started to appear after a long illness she recently overcame. Mrs. Fagan has noticed a number of small, light brown-colored outgrowths of skin on her neck and wants to make sure they are not harmful to her health. Finally, Maryann has a large, dark raised spot on her chest and has recently noticed a hair growing out of it.

7. As a dermatologist, what kinds of conditions is Dr. Tinsley concerned with?
   a. disorders and diseases of the hair, scalp, and eyebrows
   b. disorders and diseases of the skin, hair, and nails
   c. disorders and diseases of the feet and legs
   d. disorders and diseases of the hands and arms

8. Brent's hands contain:
   a. stains
   b. skin tags
   c. calluses
   d. moles

9. Pam's discolored spot is called a:
   a. stain
   b. skin tag
   c. callus
   d. mole

10. What causes the discolored spot Pam has?
   a. overexposure to the sun
   b. certain medications
   c. there is no known cause
   d. too many trips to the tanning bed

11. Mrs. Fagan's outgrowths of skin are called:
    a. stains
    b. skin tags
    c. calluses
    d. moles

12. When do these outgrowths normally appear?
    a. when a person changes jobs
    b. when a person ages
    c. when a person moves to a warmer climate
    d. when a person colors her hair

13. What is the dark-colored spot on Maryann's chest?
    a. carbuncle
    b. comedone
    c. mole
    d. tumor

CHAPTER 9 Nail Structure and Growth

Robin's client, Cheryl, is in the salon for a haircolor and cut. She made her appointment for today because tomorrow her daughter, Elizabeth, is getting married, and Cheryl wants the "works" because she wants to look her best. As the haircolor is applied, Cheryl tells Robin that she is considering having a manicure as well and asks her to check the manicurist's schedule to see if an appointment is available while her haircolor processes. Robin consults the schedule and the manicurist and realizes that if she begins the service for the manicurist by removing the nail polish and setting Cheryl's hands to soak in a finger bowl, the manicurist will be able to accommodate Cheryl's last-minute request. Robin obliges her client.

1. As Robin removes Cheryl's old nail polish, she finds that her natural nail bed is ______ in color, indicating that Cheryl has healthy nails.
- **a.** peach
- **b.** green
- **c.** lavender
- **d.** pink

2. A healthy nail is made up of _____ percent of water.
- **a.** 0 to 10
- **b.** 15 to 25
- **c.** 30 to 50
- **d.** 85 to 95

3. Robin notices the white, visible part of the matrix, the part that extends from underneath the living skin of Cheryl's nail. This is called the:
- **a.** lunula
- **b.** cuticle
- **c.** nail bed
- **d.** free edge

4. Robin also notices that Cheryl's _____ is quite thick. She explains to Cheryl that this is the dead, colorless tissue attached to the nail plate and is incredibly sticky and difficult to remove from the nail plate.
- **a.** lunula
- **b.** cuticle
- **c.** nail bed
- **d.** free edge

5. Cheryl comments that her nails seem to grow very slowly and asks Robin what the normal growth rate of a nail is. Robin's answer is:
   - **a.** 1/50 inch (0.5 mm) per month
   - **b.** 1/30 inch (0.8 mm) per month
   - **c.** 1/70 inch (0.4 mm) per month
   - **d.** 1/10 inch (2.5 mm) per month

CHAPTER 10 Nail Disorders and Diseases

Ellie has been a nail technician for more than 20 years. In the course of her career, she has had many clients with nail disorders and problems whom she has been able to service and help through regular nail care and maintenance.

1. While recovering from stubbing her finger into a window jam, one of Mrs. Jones's nails developed a dark purplish spot. Ellie recognized the condition as:
   a. bruised nail
   b. corrugations
   c. hangnail
   d. onychophagy

2. Ruben gave his daughter a gift certificate for a manicure with Ellie, in the hopes that it would arrest her onychophagy, a condition in which she ________ her nails.
   a. paints
   b. cuts
   c. bites
   d. pulls out

3. After losing more than 100 pounds (45 kg), Sabrina noticed that her nails were much thinner, whiter, and more flexible than normal. Ellie explained that this is called ________.
   a. bruised nail
   b. eggshell nails
   c. hangnail
   d. nail pterygium

4. Rick has nails that seem to curve into the sides of his fingers. He has:
   a. nail pterygium
   b. ridges
   c. plicatured nail
   d. melanonychia

5. After Sabrina slammed her hand into a table when she fell at home, she noticed a whitish discoloration of her nails. Ellie told her this was called ________ and was caused by injury to the base of the nail.
   a. nail pterygium
   b. plicatured nail
   c. leukonychia
   d. melanonychia

Wendy, a loyal monomer liquid and polymer powder nail enhancement wearer, has been going to Cecilia for maintenance procedures for more than three years. Recently she noticed that a dark greenish spot had appeared on her index finger nail. At first she ignored it, but over time it became darker and eventually she noticed that it had a foul odor.

6. The green spot is:
- **a.** a mold
- **b.** a bacterial infection
- **c.** an old nail tip
- **d.** dirt

7. The green spot is most likely caused by:
- **a.** using acetone that was too strong for the nail polish
- **b.** using contaminated instruments
- **c.** cutting the natural nail too frequently
- **d.** wearing an enhancement that is longer than 1/4" inch (0.6 cm)

Raul, a nail technician, is attending a nail care seminar. One of the classes is conducted by Dr. Reddy, a medical doctor, who is discussing the types of nail diseases. Dr. Reddy uses a slide projector with photo examples of each kind of disease he discusses.

8. Dr. Reddy's first slide shows a nail that is separated from and falling off of the nail bed. This condition is called:
- **a.** onychia
- **b.** onycholysis
- **c.** onychomadesis
- **d.** onychoptosis

9. The next slide depicts a fingernail with a matrix that is inflamed with pus. The nail also is shedding. This is:
- **a.** onychia
- **b.** onycholysis
- **c.** onychomadesis
- **d.** onychoptosis

10. Dr. Reddy shows another slide and explains that the nail has grown into the sides of the finger. This is called:
- **a.** onychia
- **b.** onycholysis
- **c.** onychomadesis
- **d.** onychophosis

11. Dr. Reddy's final slide is of a man's foot with what appear to be red patches between the toes. These are:

- **a.** tinea pedis
- **b.** clubfoot
- **c.** hammer toes
- **d.** stubbed toes

CHAPTER 11 Properties of the Hair and Scalp

Mrs. Brand is a very loyal client of the Hearts Salon. She colors and perms her naturally blond hair and makes a weekly visit to the salon for a wet set and comb out. On her most recent visit, Jean, her regular stylist, notices that Mrs. Brand's hair is very dry and rough looking.

1. When Mrs. Brand has her hair colored or permed, the chemical solution affects which layer of the hair shaft?
- **a.** follicle
- **b.** cuticle
- **c.** cortex
- **d.** medulla

2. If Mrs. Brand's hair looks and feels dry and rough, it is most likely a result of:
- **a.** contracting of the cuticle layer of the hair
- **b.** too much swelling of the hair's cortex
- **c.** contracting of the hair's cortex
- **d.** too much swelling of the cuticle layer of the hair

3. In order for her permanent haircolor to actually change the hair's color, which layer of Mrs. Brand's hair must be affected?
- **a.** follicle
- **b.** cuticle
- **c.** cortex
- **d.** medulla

4. The appearance of Mrs. Brand's hair indicates that:
- **a.** the medulla has never been opened
- **b.** the cortex is completely closed
- **c.** the cuticle has been opened many times
- **d.** the follicle is completely absent

5. Based on the information you have on Mrs. Brand, it is very likely that her hair is missing a:
- **a.** follicle
- **b.** cuticle
- **c.** cortex
- **d.** medulla

6. Mrs. Brand's hair is made up of approximately _______ percent protein.
   a. 19
   b. 73
   c. 90
   d. 100

7. When Mrs. Brand's hair is permed, the bonds that are broken are called:
   a. protein bonds
   b. hydrogen bonds
   c. salt bonds
   d. disulfide bonds

8. When Mrs. Brand's hair is wet set, the bonds that are broken are called:
   a. protein bonds
   b. hydrogen bonds
   c. salt bonds
   d. disulfide bonds

9. Mrs. Brand's natural blond hair is a result of the _______ in her hair's cortex.
   a. keratin
   b. eumelanin
   c. pheomelanin
   d. peptides

Marlene is a new client for John, so before he begins the cut and color service she has booked, he performs a hair analysis. While it is still dry, John looks at Marlene's hair and notes that she has what appears to be thick, curly, dark brown hair. When he touches her hair, it feels hard and glassy but slick and greasy, and he notices that she has a lot more strands of hair on her head than some of his other clients have. Upon further investigation John realizes that Marlene's hair grows in a circular pattern in the back of her head, at the crown. After her shampoo, John gently pulls Marlene's hair away from the scalp and sees that it readily springs back to its original place. John must now note all of his findings on a client record card before he begins to cut or color Marlene's hair.

10. In determining the texture of Marlene's hair, John notes that it is:
   a. fine
   b. medium
   c. soft
   d. coarse

11. Based on his diagnosis, Marlene's hair diameter and structure are characterized as:
   a. large and fine
   b. thin and coarse
   c. large and coarse
   d. thin and fine

12. John must be aware of Marlene's hair texture because it may affect the outcome of:
   a. whether he receives a large tip
   b. the haircolor service
   c. how many referrals Marlene will send to him
   d. the type of combs he will use while cutting

13. Based on what he felt when he touched her head, John would have noted that Marlene's hair density is:
   a. low
   b. medium
   c. moderate
   d. high

14. Marlene's hair density indicates that she has:
   a. only a few hairs per square inch (2.5 cm) on her head
   b. a medium number of hairs per square inch (2.5 cm) on her head
   c. a moderate number of hairs per square inch (2.5 cm) on her head
   d. a lot of hairs per square inch (2.5 cm) on her head

15. Based on Marlene's hair color, how many hairs is she likely to carry on her head?
   a. 140,000
   b. 110,000
   c. 108,000
   d. 80,000

16. Based on John's diagnosis of Marlene's hair, what is her hair's porosity likely to be?
   a. low
   b. normal
   c. average
   d. high

17. Chemical services performed on hair with Marlene's porosity require a(n):
   a. acid solution
   b. oxidative solution
   c. alkaline solution
   d. heated solution

18. Based on John's observations, Marlene's hair elasticity would be categorized as:
- **a.** low
- **b.** abnormal
- **c.** springy
- **d.** normal

19. The growth pattern that is evident on the back of Marlene's hair is called a:
- **a.** stream
- **b.** whorl
- **c.** lake
- **d.** cowlick

20. John must remember Marlene's growth pattern especially when:
- **a.** coloring her hair
- **b.** perming her hair
- **c.** spraying her hair
- **d.** cutting her hair

21. What type of hair and scalp condition does Marlene have?
- **a.** dry hair and scalp
- **b.** normal hair and scalp
- **c.** scaly hair and scalp
- **d.** oily hair and scalp

Bonnie has just taken a new position at a salon that specializes in servicing clients with hair loss. On this particular day she is booked with clients who have various forms of hair loss. Bonnie's first client of the day is Albert, a 70-year-old man whose hairline has receded about two inches (5 cm) but who otherwise has a thick head of healthy hair. Six months after having her baby, Anna, another of Bonnie's clients, is experiencing sudden hair loss and is interested in having her hair cut short to make her daily routine easier and to minimize the appearance of the hair loss. Bonnie's final client of the day, a successful 40-year-old businessman named Martin, has just discovered a small round bald area at his nape and asks Bonnie to be sure to leave the hair above it long enough to cover that spot.

22. As she services Albert and learns about his hair loss, Bonnie realizes that his type of hair loss is categorized as:
- **a.** androgenic alopecia
- **b.** inherited alopecia
- **c.** alopecia areata
- **d.** postpartum alopecia

23. The cause of Albert's hair loss is likely to be his:
   a. styling regimen
   b. age
   c. shampoo
   d. water temperature

24. Anna's hair loss is categorized as:
   a. androgenic alopecia
   b. inherited alopecia
   c. slopecia areata
   d. postpartum alopecia

25. Anna's hair loss is usually:
   a. permanent, with no more hair growth
   b. temporary, with hair growth returning to normal within a year
   c. permanent, with terminal new growth in three months
   d. temporary, with only vellus new growth

26. Martin's type of hair loss is called:
   a. androgenic alopecia
   b. inherited alopecia
   c. slopecia areata
   d. postpartum alopecia

27. Martin's hair loss is caused by:
   a. brushing the hair too strongly
   b. chemicals that were improperly applied
   c. an unpredictable autoimmune skin disease
   d. always wearing a baseball cap

Judy has a full day of clients booked for various services. Her day begins with Mrs. Hines, who is 65 years old and has mostly gray hair with several areas of hair that are striped—both gray and dark. Joe, another of Judy's clients, wears his hair at a medium length but notes that his hair feels knotted and that he is experiencing lots of hair breakage; he is also finding lots of small white flakes when he brushes or combs his hair. Joe's wife, Sandra, is also in the salon today. She is booked for an upper lip waxing because, she complains, she has dark, coarse hair on her face that almost looks like a man's mustache. When Jan arrives for services today, Judy asks one of the salon's assistants to shampoo her long hair and apply a deep penetrating conditioning treatment for 20 minutes to help her combat her splitting ends. On her day off, Judy will go to her son's third-grade class and speak to the students about hair and scalp care, and she will warn them not to swap hats, especially if someone in the class may have head lice.

28. The technical term for Mrs. Hines's gray hair is:
- **a.** canities
- **b.** hirsuties
- **c.** monilethrix
- **d.** trichoptilosis

29. The technical term for Mrs. Hines's striped hair is:
- **a.** canities
- **b.** strained hair
- **c.** monilethrix
- **d.** ringed hair or hypertrichosis

30. The dark hair on Sandra's upper lip is a result of:
- **a.** canities
- **b.** hirsuties
- **c.** monilethrix
- **d.** trichoptilosis

31. The technical term for Jan's split ends is:
- **a.** canities
- **b.** hirsuties
- **c.** monilethrix
- **d.** trichoptilosis

32. The technical term for Joe's knotted and breaking hair is:
- **a.** monilethrix
- **b.** trichorrhexis nodosa
- **c.** trichoptilosis
- **d.** fragilitas crinium

33. The small white flakes Joe finds when brushing or combing his hair are called:
- **a.** tinea capitis
- **b.** scabies
- **c.** carbuncle
- **d.** pityriasis

34. The technical term for head lice is:
- **a.** tinea capitis
- **b.** scabies
- **c.** pediculosis capitis
- **d.** pityriasis

CHAPTER 12 Basics of Chemistry

On his way into the salon for a full day of servicing clients, Jack realizes that he needs to fill his car with gas. He stops at a service station, fills his car's tank, purchases a small bottle of water and some chewing gum, pays for all of these, and then heads to the salon. When he arrives, he finds that the sprinkler has just completed a cycle and the front of the salon is drenched with water. He steps over the puddles and walks into the salon. His first two clients are already there waiting for him—Mr. Ramirez, who will be having his hair cut and colored, and Ms. Crespa, who will be having a steam facial, a perm, and styling. With no time to waste, Jack gets to work.

1. The gasoline that Jack put into his car is considered to be:
   - **a.** healthy
   - **b.** organic
   - **c.** unhealthy
   - **d.** inorganic

2. Jack's gasoline is considered organic because it contains:
   - **a.** power
   - **b.** carbon
   - **c.** oxygen
   - **d.** energy

3. Jack's car, made of metal and steel, is considered:
   - **a.** healthy
   - **b.** organic
   - **c.** unhealthy
   - **d.** inorganic

4. The bottle of water that Jack bought is an example of:
   - **a.** organics
   - **b.** matter
   - **c.** carbon
   - **d.** inorganics

5. Jack's pack of chewing gum exists in what form?
   - **a.** liquid
   - **b.** element
   - **c.** gas
   - **d.** solid

6. The haircolor that Jack will apply to Mr. Ramirez is considered to be:
   - **a.** an organic substance
   - **b.** an example of matter
   - **c.** an inorganic substance
   - **d.** an example of carbon

7. The permanent wave solution that Jack will apply to Ms. Crespa's hair is considered to be:
   - **a.** an organic substance
   - **b.** an example of an emulsion
   - **c.** an inorganic substance
   - **d.** an example of carbon

8. Ms. Crespa's steam facial is an example of water in what form?
   - **a.** liquid
   - **b.** element
   - **c.** gas
   - **d.** solid

9. When Jack evaluates Mr. Ramirez's natural hair color level he is determining its:
   - **a.** chemical properties
   - **b.** chemical composition
   - **c.** physical properties
   - **d.** physical composition

10. When Jack assesses the change in curl from before Ms. Crespa's perm to after it, he is assessing its:
    - **a.** chemical properties
    - **b.** chemical composition
    - **c.** physical properties
    - **d.** physical composition

11. When Mr. Ramirez's hair is cut, the change is considered to be:
    - **a.** chemical
    - **b.** physical
    - **c.** gaseous
    - **d.** elemental

12. When Mr. Ramirez's hair is colored, the change is considered to be:
    - **a.** chemical
    - **b.** physical
    - **c.** gaseous
    - **d.** elemental

Nancy is booked for a full facial and makeup application and then a conditioning treatment and blowdry at her favorite salon. She arrives at the salon and her esthetician, Sierra, takes her right in and begins to perform the facial. First, Sierra takes a powder from a bag and mixes it with water and applies it to Nancy's face and lets it sit on the skin for three minutes. After removing this mixture Sierra applies a facial scrub that is both smooth and rough because it contains small, hard particles smattered throughout. Next she applies a cold cream to Nancy's skin, which cools and soothes her face. Throughout the service, Sierra rinses her tools several times in water. When the facial is completed, Sierra shampoos Nancy's hair and applies the deep conditioning treatment. Once the hair is rinsed, dried, and rolled on hot rollers, Sierra removes bottles and tubes of cosmetics and begins the makeup application with foundation. The foundation that she chooses looks like it has separated in the bottle. Sierra shakes it vigorously and then applies it to Nancy's face as a base.

13. The water that Sierra uses to rinse her tools is an example of a:
- **a.** chemical compound
- **b.** physical compound
- **c.** solvent
- **d.** suspension

14. The foundation that Sierra used on Nancy's face during the makeup application is an example of a:
- **a.** chemical compound
- **b.** physical compound
- **c.** solvent
- **d.** suspension

15. When Sierra blended the powder and the water for application to Nancy's skin, she made a:
- **a.** problem
- **b.** mixture
- **c.** solution
- **d.** liquid

16. The powder that Sierra blended into the water is referred to as a:
- **a.** solvent
- **b.** chemical compound
- **c.** solute
- **d.** suspension

17. The liquid into which Sierra blended the powder is considered to be a:
   a. solvent
   b. chemical compound
   c. solute
   d. suspension

18. The fact that the water and powder mixed together without separating implies that they are:
   a. united
   b. miscible
   c. opposed
   d. immiscible

19. Since the foundation that Sierra used had to be shaken every time it was used because the two ingredients kept separating, it is an example of a(n) _______ substance.
   a. united
   b. miscible
   c. opposed
   d. immiscible

20. The facial scrub that Sierra applied to Nancy's skin is an example of a _______ because it contains solid particles distributed throughout a liquid form.
   a. solvent
   b. chemical compound
   c. solute
   d. suspension

21. The hair conditioner that was applied to Nancy's hair is an example of a(n):
   a. water-in-oil emulsion
   b. color-in-water emulsion
   c. water-in-color emulsion
   d. oil-in-water emulsion

22. The cold cream that was applied to Nancy's skin is an example of a(n):
   a. water-in-oil emulsion
   b. color-in-water emulsion
   c. water-in-color emulsion
   d. oil-in water emulsion

Mike is creating an order list of products the salon needs to replenish for when Allie, their distributor sales consultant, comes into the salon next week. Every day Mike adds to the list, and he has asked all of his fellow stylists to add on items as they notice them becoming depleted. The list currently contains the following: rubbing alcohol, chemical hair relaxer, three jars of hand and skin cream for the manicure tables, and hair spray.

23. Mike's colleagues like using an alcohol that evaporates quickly for their needs in the salon. This type of alcohol is called:
- **a.** violent
- **b.** peaceful
- **c.** volatile
- **d.** passive

24. Which of the items on Mike's list is a form of ammonia?
- **a.** hair spray
- **b.** alcohol
- **c.** sun block
- **d.** chemical hair relaxer

25. Which of the items on Mike's list contains glycerin?
- **a.** hair spray
- **b.** alcohol
- **c.** hand cream
- **d.** chemical hair relaxer

26. Which of the items on Mike's list contains silicones?
- **a.** hair spray
- **b.** alcohol
- **c.** hand cream
- **d.** chemical hair relaxer

27. Which of the items on Mike's list contains volatile organic compounds (VOCs)?
- **a.** hair spray
- **b.** alcohol
- **c.** sun block
- **d.** chemical hair relaxer

It's another busy day in Marco's salon. He already has two clients in the reception area waiting their turn for services. The first, Barbra, has an appointment for a shampoo, condition, and updo, and Mandy, his second appointment of the day, is booked for a chemical hair straightening. As Marco reviews his scheduled appointments he sees that he has a 1 p.m. appointment with Andrea for haircolor and a 2:30 p.m. appointment with Renee for a perm. Since he has so many chemical services to perform today, Marco takes a moment to remind himself of the issues surrounding pH and to picture the pH scale in his head.

28. When shampooing Barbra's hair, Marco will use pure (distilled) water, which has a pH of:
- **a.** 3
- **b.** 5
- **c.** 7
- **d.** 9

29. The pH of the water Marco will use is considered to be:
- **a.** acidic
- **b.** alkaline
- **c.** potential
- **d.** neutral

30. The pH of Barbra's hair and skin is:
- **a.** 3
- **b.** 5
- **c.** 7
- **d.** 9

31. The pH of Barbra's hair and skin is considered to be:
- **a.** acidic
- **b.** alkaline
- **c.** potential
- **d.** neutral

32. Pure (distilled)water is _______ than Barbra's hair and skin:
- **a.** 100 times less acidic
- **b.** 100 times more acidic
- **c.** 100 times less alkaline
- **d.** 100 times more alkaline

33. The chemical hair relaxer treatment that Mandy will receive will have a pH that indicates it is:
- **a.** acidic
- **b.** alkaline
- **c.** potential
- **d.** neutral

34. An alkaline pH is useful in straightening Mandy's hair because it will:
- **a.** harden and contract the hair
- **b.** soften and condition the hair
- **c.** harden and break the hair
- **d.** soften and swell the hair

35. When Marco performs his perm service later in the day for Renee, the perm will have a pH that indicates it is:
- **a.** acidic
- **b.** alkaline
- **c.** potential
- **d.** neutral

36. An acidic pH is useful in permanent waving hair because it will _______ Renee's hair:
- **a.** harden and contract
- **b.** soften and condition
- **c.** harden and break
- **d.** soften and swell

37. After relaxing Mandy's hair, Marco will use a normalizing lotion that will neutralize the relaxer by creating a(n):
- **a.** relaxer-neutralizer reaction
- **b.** perm-neutralizer reaction
- **c.** acid-alkaline reaction
- **d.** oxidation-reduction reaction

38. When Marco's haircolor client, Andrea, has her service, he will witness a(n):
- **a.** relaxer-neutralizer reaction
- **b.** permanent neutralizer reaction
- **c.** acid-alkaline reaction
- **d.** oxidation-reduction reaction

39. If, when perming Renee's hair, an element is combined with oxygen, _______ will be produced.

a. curl
b. straightness
c. heat
d. odor

40. If heat is released during her perm, Renee's hair is experiencing a(n) _______ reaction.

a. endothermic
b. combustible
c. exothermic
d. oxidizing

CHAPTER 13 Basics of Electricity

Carlene has just parked her car in the salon's parking lot and realizes that, because it has begun to rain, she will need to run to the salon's door to protect her beautiful new silk blouse from rain droplets. As she gets to the doorway, she realizes that she is the first person to arrive at the salon and will need to unlock the door. Once the door is opened she steps into the salon's lobby and fumbles for the light switch in the dark. Finally, she gets the lights on, closes the door, and gets ready for the day. The first thing Carlene does is plug in her battery-operated curling iron so she can use it on her clients without worrying about it losing its power, and then she plugs her straight irons into the wall outlet. Next she makes sure that her cordless electric clipper is in its charger, and then, finally, she goes into the back room to make a pot of coffee.

1. Carlene's car employs a constant, even-flowing current generated by a battery, which is called:
   - a. in and out current
   - b. constant current
   - c. direct current
   - d. alternating current

2. The form of energy Carlene was fumbling to activate when she entered the salon is called:
   - a. reactions
   - b. electricity
   - c. electrotherapy
   - d. light therapy

3. An ________ is what accounts for the lights coming on when Carlene flipped the switch.
   - a. electric switch
   - b. electronic handle
   - c. electric current
   - d. electronic current

4. Supporting the switch that Carlene turned on is a(n) ________, which conducts electricity.
   - a. insulator
   - b. nonconductor
   - c. conductor
   - d. converter

5. Carlene's silk blouse is a:
   a. complete circuit
   b. nonconductor
   c. conductor
   d. converter

6. When Carlene plugs her battery-operated curling iron into the wall outlet she is using an apparatus known as a:
   a. rectifier
   b. converter
   c. complete circuit
   d. nonconductor

7. When Carlene plugs her straight irons into the wall outlet, she is using:
   a. in and out current
   b. constant current
   c. direct current
   d. alternating current

8. Carlene's cordless electric clippers are an example of a:
   a. rectifier
   b. converter
   c. complete circuit
   d. nonconductor

Manuel intends to buy the Special Days Hair Salon, but before the deal is finalized he has a walk-through with an electrical inspector, Andy, to be sure the salon is wired properly and able to handle the special electrical needs that a salon requires. They first inspect the outlets where the styling stations will be and where most of the hair drying and curling will take place. Next, they move to the facial rooms and discuss the special needs when providing esthetic services. Finally, they move into the laundry room to inspect the area and outlets for a washing machine and dryer, and Andy explains the fuse box and circuit breaker.

9. Manuel learns that the normal wall sockets that power hair dryers and curling irons are ________ volts.
   a. 120
   b. 220
   c. 320
   d. 420

10. Outlets that can accommodate the correct amount of power for washing machines and dryers are ________ volts.
    a. 110
    b. 210
    c. 310
    d. 410

11. Andy explains that, due to its ________ rating, a hair dryer cord must be twice as thick as an appliance with a lower rating in order to avoid overheating and starting a fire.
    a. volt
    b. amp
    c. ohm
    d. watt

12. To create an atmosphere that is relaxing in the facial room, Manuel will use a 40- ________ bulb.
    a. volt
    b. amp
    c. ohm
    d. watt

13. Manuel's 2,000-watt blowdryer will use ________ watts of energy per second.
    a. 2
    b. 20
    c. 200
    d. 2,000

14. If a fuse gets too hot and melts, Manuel will know that:
    a. an appropriate amount of the current was prevented from passing through the circuit
    b. an excessive current was allowed to pass through the circuit
    c. a deficit of current was prevented from passing through the circuit
    d. an excessive current was prevented from passing through the circuit

15. If too many appliances are operating on the same circuit and they all suddenly stop working, Manuel will know that the ________ has shut off to protect the salon from a dangerous situation.
    a. fuse
    b. amp
    c. circuit breaker
    d. watt

16. Manuel realizes that his salon has several appliances that have a three-prong plug and that this is evidence of _____.
    a. fusing
    b. grounding
    c. amping
    d. breaking

Karen is booked for a series of facial treatments with Gale, an experienced esthetician at the Red Tree Spa. Karen has some oil and comedones trapped in the skin on her nose and some dry patches on her cheeks and temple area. Karen would like to improve the muscle tone of her face and neck, increase the blood circulation, and relieve her skin's congestion. Gale explains to Karen that she will be using various forms of electrotherapy in her treatments, including galvanic current and faradic current, both of which are perfectly safe and useful in treating Karen's problems when administered carefully by Gale. Karen agrees and they begin the treatment.

17. Gale has prepared an electrode which is a(n) ________ for use in treating Karen.
    a. applicator
    b. charger
    c. outlet
    d. plug

18. Gale determines that the positive electrode she will use, called the ________, is red.
    a. cathode
    b. charger
    c. anode
    d. plug

19. The first modality Gale will use is called ________ current, which is a constant and direct current.
    a. cathode
    b. galvanic
    c. plug
    d. faradic

20. If Gale wants to force acidic substances into Karen's skin, she must use:
    a. iontophoresis
    b. cataphoresis
    c. anaphoresis
    d. disincrustation

21. If Gale wants to force liquid into Karen's tissues, she must use:
   a. iontophoresis
   b. cataphoresis
   c. anaphoresis
   d. disincrustation

22. If Gale wants to introduce water-soluble products into Karen's skin, she must use:
   a. iontophoresis
   b. cataphoresis
   c. anaphoresis
   d. disincrustation

23. To increase glandular activity, Gale may use a ________ on Karen.
   a. steamer
   b. heater
   c. vibrator
   d. conditioner

24. To relieve any redness or inflammation that Karen may be experiencing from mild acne, Gale could use a:
   a. tesla high-frequency current
   b. tesla low-frequency current
   c. microcurrent
   d. desincrustation

After a couple of days off, Debbie has spent the day running around in the bright, hot sun completing errands and has just entered the salon she owns with her partner, Larry. Larry comments that she has gotten a bit of a tan and that it makes her look very healthy. He asks Debbie if she is ready for their meeting with Beth, their distributor sales consultant. They are going to discuss adding tanning services to their salon menu by putting a tanning bed in a small, unused room off the skin care area of their salon. Both Debbie and Larry have some concerns about the safety of tanning and are prepared to discuss them with Beth, who has just been to a training session and should have the answers they need to make the best decisions. Beth explains that tanning beds are safe, as long as clients follow the manufacturer's instructions and guidelines and that tanning beds provide both UV and infrared light. Beth also suggests that Debbie and Larry consider using specialized light bulbs for treating some scalp and skin conditions.

25. The bright sunlight that Debbie saw while running her errands is called:
   a. a wavelength
   b. invisible light
   c. therapeutic light
   d. visible light

26. Since Debbie has a slight tan, she has been exposed to:
  a. UV rays
  b. blue light
  c. infrared rays
  d. white light

27. Beth explains that infrared rays:
  a. produce the least amount of heat
  b. have the shortest wavelengths
  c. penetrate the deepest
  d. are the coolest

28. Beth explains that using ________ light is useful for reducing bacteria on the skin.
  a. white
  b. yellow
  c. blue
  d. red

29. When Larry asks her about improving collagen and elastin production in the skin, Beth recommends using ________ light in combination with oils and creams.
  a. white
  b. yellow
  c. blue
  d. red

CHAPTER 14 Principles of Hair Design

Andie has just returned from a terrific hair show where she attended several educational classes, and she is excited to use some of the techniques she learned there with her clients. One of the classes she attended was all about the elements of designing a great hairstyle that uniquely fits the client's needs and characteristics. In another class—a haircolor class—ways to use haircolor to enhance the client's face shape and hairstyle were described. A third class explored how wave patterns in the hair can be added or subtracted to further emphasize the shine and beauty of the hair.

1. Andie's excitement over what she learned at the hair show and her desire to try out some of the techniques is considered to be:
   a. inspiration
   b. depression
   c. inertia
   d. disinterest

2. When designing a style for hair that forces the eye to look up and down, Andie is creating a hairstyle with:
   a. horizontal lines
   b. vertical lines
   c. diagonal lines
   d. curved lines

3. Cathy, one of Andie's clients, is a single mom with three children who is looking for a very simple hairstyle that requires the least amount of care, so Andie must consider a:
   a. single line hairstyle
   b. repeating line hairstyle
   c. contrasting line hairstyle
   d. transitional line hairstyle

4. To create the illusion of a more slender face for her client Joan, Andie could use haircolor that is a:
   a. light color
   b. warm color
   c. dark color
   d. cool color

5. To create a hairstyle that reflects the most light for her client Meredith, Andie should consider a style with a ________ wave pattern.
   a. wavy
   b. curly
   c. very curly
   d. straight

Since she was a teenager, Kim has worn the same hairstyle—long, dark, wavy hair that falls to just above the shoulders. Because she really wants to create a new look for herself, Kim makes an appointment with her stylist, Courtney, for a makeover. When she arrives, Kim talks with Courtney and explains what she sees as her problem areas. Kim complains that her face is too wide, that she has a large forehead, that her eyes are set too closely together, and that she has a wide, flat nose. Kim also feels that her hair is too wavy and that for her to keep it tamed she has to wear her hair flat against her head, which she is bored with. Kim explains to Courtney that she wants to have a new style to accentuate her best features and minimize her flaws.

6. Based on Kim's description of her face, she has a(n) ________ face shape.
   a. oval
   b. triangular
   c. round
   d. square

7. To help this face shape to appear longer and thinner, the best hairstyle is one that:
   a. is flat at the top of the head
   b. creates volume at the jaws and temples
   c. is close to the head all around, with no volume at all
   d. creates volume at the top and is close at the sides

8. To minimize the appearance of Kim's forehead, Courtney should style her hair:
   a. away from the forehead
   b. across one side of the forehead
   c. back and off the face
   d. forward over the sides of the forehead

9. To combat her close set eyes, Kim's hair should be:
   a. directed back and away from the temples
   b. directed forward and pointing to the eyes
   c. left long and hanging in front of the ear
   d. fringed over the ear and sculpted onto the face

10. What type of part is best for a face with a wide, flat nose?
- **a.** left side
- **b.** no part
- **c.** center part
- **d.** right side

11. To bring more definition to Kim's jawline, which type of line should be used?
- **a.** rounded
- **b.** wavy
- **c.** straight
- **d.** curved

12. When restyling Kim's hair, Courtney will need to make sure her wavy hair is ________ at the temple area and ________ at the top.
- **a.** close; high
- **b.** shaved; spiked
- **c.** high; close
- **d.** curled; straight

Donny greets his final client of the day, Jason. Jason is middle-aged and balding. To combat the thinning of his hair on top, Jason combs the hair from one side of his head all the way across his forehead to the other side. He recently decided to stop trying to camouflage his thinning hair and has asked Donny for some advice on a new look. Donny considers the options.

13. Donny asks Jason if he would be comfortable wearing a beard. What style might Donny suggest?
- **a.** a long beard that comes to a point below the chin
- **b.** a short beard, keeping the hair closely trimmed to his face
- **c.** a long beard with bushy sideburns
- **d.** a soul patch

14. When reviewing Jason's eyebrow length, Don suggests:
- **a.** arching them
- **b.** keeping them long and combed upward
- **c.** keeping them long and combed downward
- **d.** trimming them so they are full, but not too bushy

CHAPTER 15 Scalp Care, Shampooing, and Conditioning

Nestor is taking a course on scalp massage with a product manufacturer. He knows that his clients certainly enjoy having a scalp massage when they get their hair shampooed, but he has some clients who could benefit from scalp treatments as well. He is unsure of how to know when it is appropriate to suggest one or what kinds of products to use. Nestor has made some notes and he has gone into the class with several questions.

1. The instructor explains that there are two requirements for a healthy scalp. They are:
   - **a.** professional shampoos and conditioners
   - **b.** pH-balanced service products and neutralizing agents
   - **c.** cleanliness and stimulation
   - **d.** manipulations and aromatherapy oils

2. Scalp treatment products and massage may be given before the shampoo if:
   - **a.** a scalp condition is apparent
   - **b.** a client is running late for his appointment and time needs to be made up
   - **c.** the client is in need of relaxation
   - **d.** a client is early for her appointment and she needs to be entertained until her stylist can begin her service

3. Scalp treatment products and massage may be given during the shampoo if:
   - **a.** a scalp condition is apparent
   - **b.** a client is running late for his appointment and time needs to be made up
   - **c.** the client is in need of relaxation
   - **d.** a client is early for her appointment and needs to be entertained until her stylist can begin her service

4. Nestor learns that the only difference between a relaxation and treatment massage is:
   - **a.** the length of time the massage takes
   - **b.** the manipulations used during the massage
   - **c.** the products used during the massage
   - **d.** the length of time between massages

5. The purpose of a general scalp and hair treatment is:
   a. to increase the natural oil on a dry scalp and hair
   b. to reduce the natural oil on an oily scalp and hair
   c. to maintain the cleanliness and health of normal scalp and hair
   d. to suppress the growth of a fungus called malassezia

6. Nestor also discovers that ______ is crucial to maintaining a healthy hair and scalp.
   a. hair brushing
   b. hair drying
   c. thermal styling
   d. hair wrapping

7. Hair brushing is important because it:
   a. stimulates the blood circulation to the scalp
   b. helps remove dust, dirt, and hair spray buildup from the hair
   c. gives hair added shine
   d. all of the above

8. Hair brushing is mandatory before which of the following services?
   a. single-process and double-process haircolor
   b. chemical texture services
   c. none of the above
   d. all of the above

Alexia is a receptionist at the Bubbles Salon and is frequently asked to explain the various shampoos and conditioners and their uses to the salon's clientele. She is surrounded by shelves full of products for retailing, and she answers questions and makes product recommendations all day long.

9. Barton is a 15-year-old client who frequently uses a lot of thick styling glue to get his hair to stand up in long spikes. He notices that his hair sometimes feels gooey even after shampooing. Alexia recommends a(n) ________ shampoo for him.
   a. acid-balanced
   b. conditioning
   c. medicated
   d. clarifying

10. Mrs. Kames is a long-time haircolor client and needs a shampoo that will enable her to keep her color looking fresh between retouch visits. She should try a(n) ________ shampoo.
   a. acid-balanced
   b. color-enhancing
   c. medicated
   d. clarifying

11. Alexia usually suggests that a client with ________ hair purchase a moisturizing shampoo.
   a. short
   b. permed
   c. roller set
   d. naturally curly

12. For Norman's oily scalp, Alexia suggests a ________ shampoo.
   a. balancing
   b. color-enhancing
   c. medicated
   d. clarifying

13. For Joyce, who washes, blowdries, and flat irons her hair everyday, Alexia recommends a ________ conditioner.
   a. rinse-through
   b. treatment
   c. light leave-in
   d. repair

14. For Janice, who has a full head of bleached hair, Alexia recommends an in-salon conditioning service and a ________ conditioner for at-home use.
   a. rinse-through
   b. treatment
   c. leave-in
   d. color-enhancing

Donna, a new assistant at the Tranquil Escape salon, has retrieved Ashley's haircolor client from the waiting area and has walked her to a shampoo bowl. Also in the shampoo area is Bob's next haircutting client, who is waiting to be shampooed, and Lakeesha, who is already in the midst of having her hair relaxed. Donna helps to seat her client, folds her collar under and into her blouse, puts a paper neck strip and cape over her, and begins her shampoo.

15. How should Donna have draped Ashley's haircolor client?
   a. exactly as she did
   b. using two capes and a neck strip
   c. using two neck strips and a cape
   d. using two towels and a cape

16. How should Bob's haircutting client be draped for her shampoo and service?

a. using one cape and a neck strip
b. using two capes and a neck strip
c. using two neck strips and a cape
d. using two towels and a cape

17. How should Lakeesha have been draped for her relaxer service?

a. with one cape and a neck strip
b. with two capes and a neck strip
c. with two neck strips and a cape
d. with two towels and a cape

CHAPTER 16 Haircutting

Johnny is a master haircutter at a posh, upscale salon in town. He has spent many years perfecting his cutting skills and getting to know the human head form. Today Johnny is booked solid—he has several clients to service and he is ready to get cutting!

1. Erin, Johnny's first customer, wants to wear an old haircutting favorite—the wedge. Johnny will use her occipital bone as his ________ for the entire cut.
   a. fringe
   b. reference point
   c. guideline
   d. cutting line

2. To determine if the wedge haircut is suitable for this client, Johnny needs to review the width of her _____.
   a. parietal ridge
   b. apex
   c. occipital bone
   d. four corners

3. When cutting Erin's hair, Johnny is careful to observe the ________ for unusual growth patterns such as cowlicks.
   a. top of the head
   b. nape area
   c. sides of the head
   d. crown area

4. To cut Sandra's long hair along the face and to connect the bangs and the nape, Johnny will use a ________ cutting line.
   a. straight
   b. vertical
   c. horizontal
   d. diagonal

5. When Johnny cuts Marianne's hair into a one-length bob, he uses a ________ cutting line.
   a. straight
   b. vertical
   c. horizontal
   d. diagonal

6. When using the line mentioned above to cut Marianne's hair into a one-length bob, Johnny uses ________ degrees of elevation.
   a. 0
   b. 45
   c. 90
   d. 180

7. Marianne's bob will be uniform if Johnny makes sure to continuously use his initial ________ guideline when cutting.
   a. stationary
   b. moving
   c. traveling
   d. layered

8. Darla has very long, one-length hair that she wants shorter and uniformly layered so, in order to create the layers she seeks, Johnny cuts her hair using a _____ guideline.
   a. stationary
   b. moving
   c. traveling
   d. layered

9. Mindy has very long hair that she wants to be layered, but she also wants to keep all of the length at her nape. In order to accomplish this Johnny will have to ______ the hair as he cuts the layers.
   a. blunt
   b. overdirect
   c. thin
   d. texturize

Pat is looking over his appointment book today and sees that his first three clients are coming in for haircuts. Lucy has very thick, coarse, straight hair; Frank has a good amount of hair that is easy to handle and moderately soft to the touch; and Susan has thin, fine hair that usually lies limp no matter what style Pat cuts into it.

10. Lucy is the first client to sit in Pat's chair and she complains that her hair is always too "fluffy" on top and doesn't look good on her. Pat must first determine her ______ to know whether or not the silhouette of her style is right for her.
   a. natural hair color
   b. face shape
   c. cutting line
   d. cutting elevation

11. Lucy asks Pat what he thinks about her having her hair cut really short so it can just lay flat against her face. Pat explains that a cut like that will cause her hair to:

a. fall out
b. stand up away from the scalp
c. become oily
d. dry out

12. Which tool should Pat NOT use when cutting Lucy's hair?

a. sectioning clips
b. haircutting shears
c. razor
d. thinning shears

13. What type of haircut should Pat recommend for Lucy, based on her specific hair texture and face shape?

a. short, layered haircut
b. short, textured haircut
c. long, one-length haircut
d. medium length, layered haircut

14. Based on Frank's hair type and texture, what kinds of styles would work for him?

a. extremely short haircuts
b. cuts with lots of texturizing
c. neither of the above
d. both of the above

15. Frank likes to wear his hair short at the nape and sides and fuller on top with a messy look. To achieve this, Pat will need to use ________ on the top.

a. sectioning clips
b. haircutting shears
c. a razor
d. thinning shears

16. To get a clean line at the nape, Pat will employ a(n):

a. razor
b. clipper
c. straight razor
d. edger

17. To create the impression of thicker hair, Pat needs to create _________ in Susan's style.
    a. layers
    b. weight
    c. partings
    d. thinning

18. The best cut for Susan's hair is the:
    a. graduated cut
    b. blunt cut
    c. layered cut
    d. long-layered cut

19. The best cutting tool for Pat to use on Susan's hair is a:
    a. sectioning clip
    b. haircutting shear
    c. razor
    d. thinning shear

20. The type of comb that Pat will use for each of his haircuts will be the:
    a. wide-toothed comb
    b. barber comb
    c. tail comb
    d. styling comb

Pam is about to graduate from beauty school and has decided that it is time to buy a new pair of haircutting shears. She has saved her money and has thought about how often she will use her shears and has created a list of questions to ask the salesperson at her local distributor's store. She is on her way to make her big purchase.

21. Pam begins by asking the salesperson to show her several brands of haircutting shears. The one she is most interested in has an ideal Rockwell hardness of:
    a. 32
    b. 46
    c. 57
    d. 66

22. Pam begins to pick a couple of shears she likes. The salesperson explains that _____ shears are thought to be the most durable.
    a. cast
    b. wired
    c. forged
    d. plated

23. Pam asks the salesperson how she should care for a new pair of shears and is told that in addition to daily cleaning, lubrication, and __________, once per week the blades of the shears should be loosened and cleaned and lubricated.
   a. tension adjustment and balancing
   b. balancing of the tension rod
   c. adjusting of the handle and cutting blade
   d. tightening of the cutting blade and tang

24. The sales person asks Pam what type of blade edge she is interested in. Pam explains that she wants a _____ for the smoothest cut and sharpest edge possible.
   a. concave edge
   b. convex edge
   c. beveled edge
   d. bi-leveled edge

25. After making her purchase, Pam asks the salesperson how often she should have her shears sharpened. The salesperson informs Pam that with proper care, sharpening is only needed every ______.
   a. two months
   b. four months
   c. eight months
   d. twelve months

Manny attends the ABC Beauty School and is enrolled in a cutting class for curly hair. Today, he and his classmates will cut and style three clients with varying amounts of curly hair. Manny's first client, Jen, has very curly hair that falls down in ringlets. Jen wants her blunt cut trimmed about an inch (2.5 cm) shorter. Sandy, Manny's next client, has medium length wavy hair and wants her new style to be shorter and spiky. Finally, Renee, his third client, wants to show off her curly hair, so she is looking for a mid-length style to showcase the curl.

26. To give Jen the trim she wants, Manny will need to:
   a. pull the hair taut to cut a straight line
   b. cut it straight across the bottom with no tension at all
   c. use an elevated guideline
   d. create layers with a 90-degree angle

27. To achieve the appearance of having cut Jen's hair 1 inch (2.5 cm), Manny will actually need to cut off about:
   a. 1 inch (2.5 cm)
   b. ¼ inch (.6 cm)
   c. 2 inches (5 cm)
   d. ½ inch (1.25 cm)

28. Cutting 1 inch (2.5 cm) of hair will make Jen's finished style appear ________ when it is dry.

a. longer
b. angled
c. shorter
d. diagonal

29. When Manny begins cutting Sandy's hair, he must be aware that her curly hair will need to be elevated ________ to achieve the desired look.

a. more
b. the same as straight hair
c. less
d. the same as color-treated hair

30. To give Sandy's hair the spiky look she desires, Manny will need to texturize her hair using the ________ technique.

a. thinning
b. point cutting
c. notching
d. slicing

31. To give Renee the mid-length style she desires Manny will need to cut the hair at a ________-degree angle all around the head.

a. 0
b. 45
c. 90
d. 180

32. To remove bulk and add movement to Renee's cut, Manny will use a technique called:

a. thinning
b. point cutting
c. notching
d. slicing

CHAPTER 17 Hairstyling

Gayle has been styling hair for the movies for a number of years and has recently been asked to work on a movie whose story takes place in the 1920s and 1930s. She will be responsible for styling the hair for the two lead characters, Esther and Johanna. The director explains to Gayle the look he is after for each of the characters. For Esther, he wants Gayle to create a real flapper look, with many wide but uniformly sized dark waves around the head. The hair should be close to the head when dry, perfectly curled into the wave formations, and set so that no matter how much dancing or movement the character experiences, the hair remains in place. The second character, Johanna, will need to wear her hair in a more flamboyant manner, so it should be light blond in color and the hair should sweep forward at the temples and onto the face. Johanna's hair requires lots of volume but the style should also be very controlled and perfectly coifed so that it stays in place. Gayle begins working on her designs and the supplies she'll need.

1. The list of supplies Gayle will need to have handy for styling the two characters includes:
- **a.** scissors, comb, and hair spray
- **b.** blowdryer, rollers, and comb
- **c.** scissors, blowdryer, and clips
- **d.** clips, combs, and rollers

2. In terms of styling aids, Gayle will need to purchase:
- **a.** setting lotion, styling lotion, and hair spray
- **b.** setting lotion, mousse, and pomade
- **c.** styling lotion, hair spray, and leave-in conditioner
- **d.** styling mousse, spray wax, and hair spray

3. To achieve the close-to-the head waves the director wants Esther to wear, Gayle will need to create:
- **a.** a wet set
- **b.** a layered cut
- **c.** a finger wave
- **d.** a pin curl

4. To ensure that Esther's hair lays appropriately for the style, Gayle should use:
- **a.** a left-hand part
- **b.** a part down the middle
- **c.** her natural part
- **d.** no part

5. The best type of comb for Gayle to use when creating Esther's style is a:
   a. tail comb
   b. styling comb
   c. wide-toothed comb
   d. barber comb

6. When Gayle completes styling Esther's hair, the waves should look like a continuous letter:
   a. B
   b. M
   c. S
   d. X

7. How should Gayle dry Esther's hair prior to combing it out?
   a. with a blowdryer
   b. with a heat lamp
   c. with a Marcel iron
   d. with a hooded dryer

8. To create Johanna's style, Gayle will use:
   a. a blowdryer, rollers, and pin curls
   b. a hooded dryer, round brush, and curling iron
   c. a blowdryer, round brush, and flat iron
   d. a hooded dryer, rollers, and pin curls

9. To create the most volume she can on the top of Johanna's head, Gayle will place:
   a. rollers on base
   b. rollers off base
   c. rollers at half base
   d. rollers without a base

10. In order for Johanna's hair to sweep forward at her temples, Gayle will place pin curls into a ________ shaping.
    a. A
    b. B
    c. C
    d. D

11. In order to get a tight, long-lasting curl without too much mobility, Gayle will use:
    a. no-stem pin curls
    b. full-stem pin curls
    c. half-stem pin curls
    d. part-stem pin curls

12. To achieve a smooth, directed shape Gayle will need to use a(n) ________ base pin curl at the temple area of Johanna's style.
   a. rectangular
   b. triangular
   c. arc
   d. square

13. When combing out the finished style, Gayle will certainly need to ________ the hair on the top of Johanna's head to achieve the height she desires and to ensure the shape lasts as long as needed.
   a. back out
   b. backcomb
   c. back cut
   d. backshape

Marcia has decided that, after many years with the same styling tools and implements, she needs to purchase new, better quality ones. In preparation for going to her distributor's store to purchase her new equipment, Marcia thinks about her various clients and their hair needs and makes a list of the new tools she will need to purchase. Marcia also decides to look for some new styling lotions as well.

14. The foundation tool for all of Marcia's styling begins with her:
   a. styling comb
   b. lotions and gels
   c. blowdryer
   d. round brush

15. Marcia's blowdryer must have a(n) ________ attachment that allows the hair to be dried as if it were being air dried.
   a. nozzle
   b. concentrator
   c. diffuser
   d. adaptor

16. For her clients with mid- to longer-length hair, Marcia will need a ________.
   a. classic styling brush
   b. paddle brush
   c. vent brush
   d. large round brush

17. For clients with fine hair or for adding lift at the scalp area, Marcia will need a:
  a. classic styling brush
  b. paddle brush
  c. vent brush
  d. large round brush

18. For clients who need a strong-hold styling preparation, Marcia picks up:
  a. styling foam
  b. styling mousse
  c. styling gel
  d. styling pomade

19. For clients who want to add weight to their hair and achieve a piecy, textured look, Marcia purchases:
  a. styling foam
  b. styling mousse
  c. styling gel
  d. styling pomade

20. To add gloss and shine to a finished style, Marcia will need:
  a. hair spray
  b. styling mousse
  c. silicone shiners
  d. styling pomade

Brandis has an appointment with Shereen for a shampoo and styling. Brandis has medium length, layered hair and likes to wear it straight, close to the head, and curled under around the face and at the neckline. Brandis is an African-American client who does not chemically straighten her hair.

21. In order for Shereen to style Brandis's hair, she will need to determine:
  a. how long it is
  b. how much curl to add to it
  c. how clean it is
  d. how much curl to remove from it

22. To remove 100 percent of Brandis's curl, Shereen will need to use a:
  a. soft press
  b. medium press
  c. hard press
  d. double press

23. Before pressing, Shereen should add ________ to Brandis's hair and scalp.

a. pressing dressing
b. dry shampoo
c. pressing oil
d. cholesterol cream

CHAPTER 18 Braiding and Braid Extensions

Darlene is interested in having her hair extended through braids and has made an appointment with Tameka for the service. She is told by the receptionist that she will need to be in the salon for several hours so she plans accordingly. Darlene arrives at the salon on time and Tameka begins the service with a client consultation, hair and scalp analysis, and then a discussion about the type and length of the braid and extensions Darlene is looking for. Tameka also takes the time to inform Darlene how to wear and care for her braids before beginning the actual service.

1. Tameka informs Darlene that she uses natural hairstyling techniques, which means:
   a. she will change only the color of Darlene's hair
   b. she will use chemical products to alter the texture of Darlene's hair
   c. she will not use any chemicals in providing Darlene's services
   d. she cannot change the color of Darlene's hair because her hair is too curly

2. Tameka explains that a complicated braid style can last for up to:
   a. 3 days
   b. 30 days
   c. 60 days
   d. 90 days

3. One of the most important aspects of Tameka's client consultation will be to assess the ________ of Darlene's hair.
   a. porosity
   b. density
   c. color
   d. texture

4. Tameka determines that Darlene would look best in a braid style that is full on top and at the neckline, but close to her head at the temples because she has determined that she has a(n) ____________ facial type.
   a. round
   b. oval
   c. triangular
   d. diamond

5. In addition to the combs, brushes, and blowdryer Tameka will need for the service, she also sets up her station to include the extension materials, ________________.
   a. comb and clips
   b. cape and hackle
   c. drawing board and hackle
   d. drawing board and clips

6. Since Darlene intends to wash her hair once a week and let it dry naturally without the use of heat or irons, and since she desires a shiny, reflective finished look, the material Tameka considers using is:
   a. human hair
   b. kanekalon
   c. nylon
   d. lin

7. Tameka decides to use an underhand technique for braiding, which means that:
   a. the side sections will go over the middle section
   b. the middle section goes under the left, then under the right section
   c. the side sections go under the middle section
   d. the middle section goes over the left, then over the right section

8. Darlene explains that she wants a braid that looks like two strands of hair are wrapped around one another. This style of braid is called a(n):
   a. inverted braid
   b. rope braid
   c. fishtail braid
   d. extroverted braid

It's prom time and there are several teen-aged clients waiting for their "special" hair styles in the Braided Up Salon reception area. One client, Maria, has very long, one-length hair and is looking for a braided style to which she can add flowers or a hair accessory. Another client, Stephanie, is hoping to try something different—she wants to wear a chignon with a couple of braids accentuating it. And finally, Marcus is waiting for a braiding style that will provide a neat, clean look and some extra length for prom night.

9. With Maria's long, one-length hair and her desire to add an accessory to the hair, a _______ braid may be the best choice.
   a. rope braid
   b. fishtail braid
   c. simple braid
   d. complex braid

10. Stephanie is planning to wear a very traditional updo to the prom but wants to add a braid design to the finished style. Which of the following techniques might work best for her?
   a. invisible braid
   b. double braid
   c. visible braid
   d. single braid

11. What type of braid will provide Marcus with the clean-cut look he seeks?
   a. invisible braid
   b. double braid
   c. cornrow
   d. single braid

12. In order to get the additional length that Marcus is looking for, his stylist will need to give him:
   a. an invisible braid with extensions
   b. a double braid with extensions
   c. a cornrow with extensions
   d. an single braid with extensions

CHAPTER 19 Wigs and Hair Additions

Carlotta has had a number of clients ask her about wigs lately and so she has decided to create a special area within her salon that is dedicated to these items. Clients who are interested in being fitted for a wig or who want to experiment with various wigs will be welcomed to try them out in her salon. Carlotta has several clients who are interested in using the wigs as fashion accessories and others who are experiencing hair loss, so she orders a number of different items from her local distributor.

1. For clients who want the highest quality wigs to cover 100 percent of their hair, Carlotta orders:
   - **a.** synthetic wigs
   - **b.** caplets
   - **c.** human hair wigs
   - **d.** blocks

2. If a client is interested in a product that is ready-to-wear, that comes in fantasy colors, and whose color will not fade, Carlotta should recommend a:
   - **a.** synthetic wig
   - **b.** caplet
   - **c.** human hair wig
   - **d.** block

3. For a client who is interested in a wig that has spaces for air to flow through and is less structured, Carlotta should suggest a:
   - **a.** synthetic wig
   - **b.** capless wig
   - **c.** cap wig
   - **d.** block

4. For a client who may have significant hair loss, a ____ wig would be a good suggestion.
   - **a.** hand-tied wig
   - **b.** capless wig
   - **c.** cap wig
   - **d.** block

5. Carlotta learns that hand-tied wigs are made:
   - **a.** by inserting individual strands of hair into mesh foundations and knotting them with a needle.
   - **b.** by machines
   - **c.** by inserting wefts of hair into a block and gluing them to a cap
   - **d.** by using natural hair strands that are knotted together

6. Semi-hand-tied wigs contain:
   a. 100 percent human hair
   b. synthetic hair only
   c. both synthetic and human hair
   d. machine-made hair

7. To measure a client for a wig, Carlotta will need a:
   a. hard ruler
   b. block
   c. soft tape measure
   d. weft of hair

8. To practice working with wigs, Carlotta should work with the wig while it is:
   a. on the client's head
   b. on a block
   c. on her own head
   d. on a mannequin

9. A hairpiece that has openings in the base through which the client's own hair is pulled to blend with the hair of the hairpiece is called a(n):
   a. fashion hairpiece
   b. natural hairpiece
   c. integration hairpiece
   d. disintegration hairpiece

Judy has had short hair most of her life and has always wanted to try having long hair but has difficulty letting her fine, thin hair grow long. She discusses this with her stylist Larissa, who recommends that she consider having a hair extension service. Larissa explains that hair extensions come in various forms and amounts and are secured to Judy's existing hair to lengthen the overall style and appearance. Judy books an appointment for the extension service.

10. Before attaching any hair extensions, Larissa will need to ascertain from Judy whether or not to:
    a. change her natural hair color
    b. add length or fullness, or both
    c. tweeze her eyebrows
    d. perm the hair

11. When attaching an extension, it should be placed:
    a. at the front hairline
    b. about 3 inches (7.5 cm) from the scalp
    c. just behind the ear
    d. about 1 inch (2.5 cm) from the hairline

12. Since Judy has fine, thin hair, Larissa will need to:
    a. let her hair grow 2 inches (5 cm)
    b. give the natural hair a perm
    c. be careful to hide the base of the hair weft
    d. recommend a full wig

13. Larissa will have several options for attaching the extension to Judy's hair. Which of the following is NOT an option?
    a. the braid and sew method
    b. the bob and weave method
    c. the bonding method
    d. the fusion bonding method

14. The best method Larissa can use for attaching the hair weft to Judy's fine hair is the ________ method.
    a. track and sew
    b. linking
    c. tube shrinking
    d. fusion bonding

CHAPTER 20 Chemical Texture Services

Nick checks his appointment book and sees that he has three perms scheduled for the day. Ava has short, thick, coarse hair and is booked for a tight perm so she can wear her hair curly and let it dry naturally. Maureen has medium-length, colored hair that is extremely dry. She wants to create additional body in her hair so that it is easier to style and will hold the style a bit longer once she has blown it dry and curled it. Reva has very long, straight, one-length virgin hair that she is bored with. Instead of cutting her length, Reva wants to try a long and very curly style. To get prepared, Nick stocks his rollabout and retrieves each client's record card.

1. Ava's hair texture indicates to Nick that her hair may:
  a. require less processing time
  b. have too much elasticity
  c. require more processing time
  d. have too little elasticity

2. Since Maureen's hair is colored, Nick must take special care to notice her hair's:
  a. porosity
  b. elasticity
  c. density
  d. texture

3. When wrapping Ava's hair, Nick will employ the ________ technique in order to achieve a tighter curl at the ends and a looser curl at the scalp.
  a. spiral
  b. off-base
  c. croquignole
  d. on-base

4. In order to achieve a uniform curl throughout the entire hair strand, Nick will wrap Reva's long hair using the ________ technique.
  a. spiral
  b. off-base
  c. croquignole
  d. on-base

5. To achieve a tighter curl in the center of each strand and a looser curl on the outer edges, Nick will use ________ rods when wrapping Maureen's hair.
   a. round
   b. concave
   c. long
   d. straight

6. To protect the many layers in Maureen's haircut while perming, Nick will employ the ________ wrap.
   a. flat
   b. double-flat
   c. single-flat
   d. bookend

7. To perm Ava's thick, coarse hair, Nick should select a(n) ________ wave.
   a. exothermic
   b. true acid
   c. thio-free
   d. ammonia-free

8. To perm Maureen's extremely damaged hair, Nick should select a(n) ________ wave.
   a. exothermic
   b. true acid
   c. thio-free
   d. ammonia-free

9. To perm Reva's virgin hair, Nick should select a(n) ________ wave:
   a. alkaline/cold
   b. true acid
   c. thio-free
   d. ammonia-free

Mrs. Carr, who was in the salon two weeks ago for a perm service, has come back into the salon today to tell her stylist Jill that the perm "fried" her hair; she also complains that her hair is curly at the scalp and about halfway down the strand but the bottom half of the strand is straight, dry, and frizzy. Jill finds Mrs. Carr's record card and reviews the perm she selected and the procedure.

10. Based on Mrs. Carr's description of her hair, her hair is:
    a. underprocessed
    b. neutralized
    c. overprocessed
    d. acidic

11. The perm solution that Jill chose was most likely too:
   a. weak
   b. acidic
   c. strong
   d. neutralized

12. Mrs. Carr's hair doesn't have enough strength left to:
   a. straighten out
   b. remain moisturized
   c. hold the desired curl
   d. grow out naturally

13. Mrs. Carr's hair cannot hold its curl because too many _____ bonds were broken during the perm processing.
   a. sulfur
   b. disulfide
   c. amino
   d. peptide

14. Jill realizes that because the perm solution she used was too strong, the damage to Mrs. Carr's hair occurred in the _____ minutes of the service.
   a. first two to three
   b. first five to six
   c. first two to eight
   d. first five to ten

15. Mrs. Carr asks Jill for another perm. Jill explains that another perm at this time will:
   a. make the hair very curly
   b. change the hair's color
   c. make the hair even straighter
   d. make the hair healthier

Melinda has two clients arrive at the salon for appointments. Both Charlotte and Brenda have extremely curly hair that they want to have relaxed. Charlotte wants to wear her hair perfectly straight in a chin-length blunt style. Brenda wants her hair to be layered, and she wants the curl reduced but not completely taken out so that she can wear her hair wavy. After reviewing their record cards, Melinda realizes that Charlotte had some scalp irritation as a result of her last haircolor appointment. Melinda prepares for the services.

16. To completely straighten Charlotte's hair, Melinda will use a:
   a. permanent wave solution
   b. chemical hair relaxer
   c. soft curl permanent
   d. neutralizer

17. To remove some of the curl from Brenda's hair, Melinda will use a:

a. permanent wave solution
b. chemical hair relaxer
c. soft curl permanent
d. neutralizer

18. What can Melinda do to minimize the potential reaction Charlotte's scalp may have to the service?

a. a scalp examination
b. use a no-base product
c. a test curl
d. use a protective base

19. A relaxer containing which of the following active ingredients is most appropriate for Melinda to use on Charlotte's hair, given her sensitive scalp?

a. sodium hydroxide
b. lithium hydroxide
c. potassium hydroxide
d. guanidine hydroxide

20. What strength relaxer is best used on Charlotte?

a. mild
b. regular
c. moderate
d. super

21. Brenda's soft-curl perm will:

a. lighten her hair color
b. make her hair completely straight
c. reformulate the amount of curl she has
d. darken her hair color

22. How many services are required for Melinda to complete the soft-curl perm procedure on Brenda's hair?

a. 1
b. 2
c. 3
d. 4

23. Which of the following is involved in Melinda performing the soft-curl perm on Brenda's hair?

a. wrapping the hair on perm rods
b. relaxing the hair and then re-curling it
c. relaxing the hair, perming the hair, re-relaxing the hair
d. perming virgin hair, relaxing the hair, soft-curl perming the hair

CHAPTER 21 Haircoloring

Danny is a master colorist at the Suprema Salon. He has a long list of color clients who see him each day. Today, he notices that he has three color correction services planned. The first is Mary, who wears light-blond highlights and is a swimmer. After swimming in a chlorinated pool every day for the past three months, her hair has a greenish tinge which is unsightly and needs to be corrected. Danny's next client, Amber, colored her own hair at home but was unhappy when her hair turned a brassy orange color. Amber wants to return to her natural color, a deep brown without so much red in it. And, finally, Zeena, who recently had her hair lightened from root to ends, wants Danny to change her color because she feels it is too "lemony looking."

1. To counteract the greenish tinge to Mary's haircolor, Danny will need to select a shade that has a ________ base color.
- **a.** blue
- **b.** yellow
- **c.** red
- **d.** violet

2. To prevent Mary's highlighted hair from becoming too dark during the correction procedure, Danny must be careful not to select a shade with too much ________ in it.
- **a.** blue
- **b.** yellow
- **c.** red
- **d.** violet

3. The color Danny will use to correct Mary's hair color is a(n) ________ color.
- **a.** primary
- **b.** secondary
- **c.** elementary
- **d.** tertiary

4. To return Amber's haircolor to the desired shade, Danny will need to use a ________ tone.
- **a.** warm
- **b.** brassy
- **c.** light
- **d.** cool

5. Typical colors in the tone range Danny will use on Amber's hair have a(n) ________ base.
   a. yellow
   b. orange
   c. red
   d. blue

6. The color Danny will use to correct Amber's brassy tone is a(n) ________ color.
   a. duplicate
   b. complementary
   c. tertiary
   d. identical

7. Once achieved, Amber's deep brown haircolor will be a level:
   a. 10
   b. 7
   c. 5
   d. 3

8. If Zeena wanted her lightened hair to have a cooler, more platinum look instead of the lemony color it is now, Danny would need to select a shade that has a ________ base.
   a. green
   b. yellow
   c. red
   d. violet

9. If Zeena wanted her lightened hair to have a strawberry blond color instead of the lemony color it is now, Danny would need to select a shade that has a ________ base.
   a. green
   b. yellow
   c. red
   d. violet

10. A strawberry blond shade would indicate that Zeena preferred a ________ tone in her hair.
   a. warm
   b. brassy
   c. light
   d. cool

11. Once Zeena's lightened hair has achieved a platinum shade, her haircolor will be a level:
    a. 10
    b. 7
    c. 5
    d. 3

Another colorist at the Suprema Salon, Sarah, also has a busy day ahead. She has her first client, Gina, booked for a color service. Gina has about 25 percent gray hair and wants something close to her natural medium brown color to blend and cover her gray. Maya is another of Sarah's clients; she is a natural redhead who wants to have a few chunky blond highlights around her face. And Katie, who loves to wear her hair short and funky and who has been lightening her hair, is booked for a full head lightener retouch on a two-inch (5 cm) regrowth area.

12. Since Gina has about 25 percent gray hair, what is the overall situation Sarah will encounter when coloring Gina's hair?
    a. Gina has less pigmented hair than gray hair.
    b. Gina has more pigmented hair than natural-colored hair.
    c. Gina has more pigmented hair than gray hair.
    d. Gina has less pigmented hair than natural-colored hair.

13. To effectively blend Gina's gray hair, Sarah should use a:
    a. temporary color
    b. semipermanent color
    c. demipermanent color
    d. permanent color

14. The type of color product Sarah uses on Gina should:
    a. add highlights
    b. remove color
    c. deposit color
    d. remove ash tones

15. When formulating Gina's color, to assure proper coverage, Sarah should:
    a. select a shade two levels darker than the desired shade
    b. use a shade the desired level straight out of the bottle
    c. mix the color formulation with 40-volume peroxide
    d. select a shade two levels lighter than the desired shade

16. To achieve the chunky highlights that Maya desires, Sarah will need to use a(n):
- **a.** on-the-scalp bleach
- **b.** cream bleach
- **c.** oil bleach
- **d.** off-the-scalp bleach

17. Since Maya's natural hair color is a bright shade of red-orange, her hair will go through ________ degrees of decolorization to achieve the yellow base shade she desires for her highlights.
- **a.** 3
- **b.** 4
- **c.** 5
- **d.** 6

18. Since Maya has so much red pigment in her hair naturally, Sarah may opt to use a ________ technique to achieve a pleasing finished tone to the highlighted hair.
- **a.** single-process coloring
- **b.** temporary coloring
- **c.** double-process coloring
- **d.** one-step coloring

19. To lighten Katie's regrowth area, Sarah will use a(n):
- **a.** on-the-scalp bleach
- **b.** one-step coloring
- **c.** off-the-scalp bleach
- **d.** double-process coloring

20. To boost the lifting power of the cream bleach, Sarah will use a(n):
- **a.** intimidator
- **b.** activator
- **c.** motivator
- **d.** crystallizer

21. Before applying the toner to Katie's hair, Sarah may choose to use a(n) ________ to protect and condition the previously bleached hair.
- **a.** activator
- **b.** color filler
- **c.** booster
- **d.** conditioner filler

22. After her hair is lightened to the desired level, Sarah should formulate and tone Katie's hair using a ________ -volume developer to simply add color and lessen the amount of damage done to the hair.

a. 10
b. 20
c. 30
d. 40

23. Which of Sarah's clients require a patch test before she begins their services?

a. none of them
b. Maya only
c. Gina only
d. all of them

CHAPTER 22 Hair Removal

Joanie is a fashion-conscious businesswoman who deals with the public all day long. She is very careful to present a professional and attractive appearance. Joanie has always had a problem with superfluous facial and body hair. Once a week she shapes her eyebrows at home with a pair of tweezers, and every other week she books an appointment for removal of unsightly facial hair on her upper lip, chin, and neck. Joanie has noticed that sometimes her face is irritated by waxing. Joanie usually shaves the hair on legs and underarms every other day but her skin often feels bumpy from shaving. Joanie wants to investigate some other options for hair removal that may make her personal grooming routine easier and less bothersome. She discusses her options with Amy, her esthetician.

1. Before determining the appropriate methods of hair removal, a positive answer to which of the following questions would indicate to Amy that she should not be providing hair removal services for Joanie?
   a. Do you suffer from oily skin patches?
   b. Have you ever had a mud mask?
   c. Do you currently use Retin-A?
   d. Are you a frequent tanning salon client?

2. When Joanie shapes her own eyebrows with a pair of tweezers, she is using a method called:
   a. permanent hair removal
   b. photoepilation
   c. sugaring
   d. temporary hair removal

3. If Joanie wanted to learn more about permanent hair removal methods, Amy would suggest:
   a. electrolysis, tweezing, and epilation
   b. photoepilation, shaving, and depilatories
   c. laser hair removal, electronic tweezers, and waxing
   d. electrolysis, photoepilation, and laser hair removal

4. A quick and easy method of temporary hair removal Amy could suggest to Joanie for removing the hair on her legs that would leave the skin smooth but requires a patch test is:
   a. a depilatory
   b. photoepilation
   c. sugaring
   d. tweezing

5. A milder but equally effective way of removing Joanie's facial hair could be to:
   a. wax
   b. tweeze
   c. shave
   d. sugar

6. To minimize the irritation to Joanie's underarms, Amy suggests the use of:
   a. hot wax
   b. shaving
   c. depilatories
   d. cold wax

CHAPTER 23 Facials

Rebecca, an esthetician, is asked by a high school counselor to visit a class of graduating students to discuss skin care with them. She arrives with product samples and begins to explain about the skin, its function, and how best to care for it. When she opens the floor to questions, she receives many from three students—Jane, Anne, and Andrea—about types and uses of skin care products available on the market and how best to use them. Rebecca is happy to answer the questions and reduce confusion.

1. Anne asks Rebecca about the difference between a foaming cleanser and cleansing milk. Rebecca tells her that:
   - **a.** a foaming cleanser removes makeup, a cleansing milk does not
   - **b.** a cleansing milk is usually best used on very oily skin
   - **c.** a foaming cleanser is not useful for people with acne
   - **d.** a foaming cleanser is useful for people with oily skin, a cleansing milk is best for dry skin

2. Jane explains that she has some acne, and asks what she should use to cleanse her face. Rebecca suggests a:
   - **a.** bar of soap
   - **b.** foaming cleanser
   - **c.** cleansing cream
   - **d.** cleansing lotion

3. For Andrea's sensitive but oily skin, Rebecca recommends using a(n) ________ after cleansing.
   - **a.** alcohol
   - **b.** tonic
   - **c.** toner
   - **d.** astringent

4. Jane complains that her skin appears bumpy and lumpy. Rebecca recommends that she use a(n) ________ two to three times a week.
   - **a.** cleansing cream
   - **b.** tonic
   - **c.** astringent
   - **d.** exfoliant

5. Andrea tells Rebecca that her esthetician suggested an enzyme peel but that she wasn't sure what it was. Rebecca responded by explaining that it is a(n):
   a. exfoliating procedure using fruit acids
   b. cleansing procedure using banana peels
   c. acne treatment using a nourishing cream
   d. exfoliating procedure using keratolytic enzymes

6. Jane asks Rebecca if there is anything she can use on her skin daily to reduce dryness. Rebecca suggests:
   a. massage cream
   b. night cream
   c. moisturizer
   d. treatment cream

Trisha has booked a facial at her favorite salon and can't wait for the soothing massage to begin. She arrives, changes into a facial gown, and waits patiently for her esthetician, Alyssa, to arrive. The lights are dim and there is a soft music playing in the background. Before entering the room Alyssa reviews Trisha's client record card and notices that the last time she was in Trisha commented that she wanted to tone her muscles and improve her circulation and general health. Alyssa enters the room and discusses these notes with her client. Once they have agreed on a course of action, Alyssa begins the service.

7. Alyssa begins by using a technique that involves a light, continuous stroking movement called:
   a. pétrissage
   b. effleurage
   c. fulling
   d. chucking

8. To offer deep stimulation to Tricia's muscles, Alyssa employs:
   a. pétrissage
   b. effleurage
   c. friction
   d. chucking

9. To increase Trisha's circulation and glandular activity, Alyssa uses a(n) ________ technique.
   a. pétrissage
   b. effleurage
   c. friction
   d. chucking

10. Alyssa uses ________ on Trisha's neck to tone her muscles.
   a. wringing
   b. effleurage
   c. tapotement
   d. chucking

11. Alyssa is always careful to massage from the:
   a. origin to the outset
   b. outset to the inset
   c. insertion to the origin
   d. origin to the insertion

George sells electric facial machines that help enhance the effectiveness of facial treatments. He has a meeting with Joyce to review her needs for additional equipment and special appliances. When George arrives, Joyce is ready and waiting for him with a list of questions.

12. Joyce asks if there is any electrotherapy treatment that will help to liquefy sebum stuck in the hair follicles on the face of a client. George explains that the application of ________ will do just that.
   a. galvanic current
   b. faradic current
   c. sinusoidal current
   d. high-frequency current

13. To stimulate blood flow and help products to penetrate, Joyce is a interested in using:
   a. galvanic current
   b. light therapy
   c. faradic current
   d. high-frequency current

14. Joyce asks George to explain how the use of microdermabrasion can help her clients. George explains that microdermabrasion is a ________ and leaves the skin looking_____.
   a. chemical exfoliant, calmer
   b. mechanical exfoliant, redder
   c. chemical exfoliant, less wrinkled
   d. mechanical exfoliant, younger

CHAPTER 24 Facial Makeup

Amanda has booked a makeup appointment with Sandra for the morning of her wedding. She has discussed with Sandra the color of her wedding gown—off-white—and her belief that she looks best in orange or coral tones. Sandra notes that Amanda has deep auburn-colored hair, light pale skin, and large green eyes. The morning of her wedding, Amanda arrives at the salon with a freshly cleansed, toned, and moisturized face but she has a blemish on her forehead and some dark circles under her eyes. Sandra starts the application.

1. From the information that Sandra has received about Amanda's color preferences and from analyzing her skin, she determines that Amanda's skin tone is:
- **a.** cool
- **b.** cold
- **c.** hot
- **d.** warm

2. Before any other product goes on Amanda's face, and to even out her skin tone and create a base for the makeup application, Sandra applies:
- **a.** concealer
- **b.** foundation
- **c.** face powder
- **d.** cheek color

3. To cover Amanda's blemish and reduce the discoloration around her eyes, Sandra should apply a concealer whose color is:
- **a.** lighter than the skin tone
- **b.** the same as the skin tone
- **c.** heavier than the skin tone
- **d.** darker than the skin tone

4. To set the foundation and concealer and to give the face a matte finish, Sandra pats on a:
- **a.** concealer
- **b.** foundation
- **c.** face powder
- **d.** cheek color

5. To keep Amanda's makeup matte-looking, Sandra adds ________ cheek color.
  a. gel
  b. cream
  c. powder
  d. liquid

6. To harmonize with Amanda's coloring, she should wear a ________ color on her cheeks.
  a. pink
  b. mauve
  c. coral
  d. burgundy

7. To keep Amanda's lip color from feathering, Sandra applies:
  a. lip color
  b. concealer
  c. foundation
  d. lip liner

8. Sandra fills in Amanda's lips with:
  a. lip color
  b. concealer
  c. foundation
  d. lip liner

9. The best lip color to apply to Amanda is:
  a. warm-toned
  b. blue-red
  c. cool-toned
  d. light pink

10. To make Amanda's green eyes a focal point, Sandra should select a ________ color:
  a. deep blue
  b. silver-gray
  c. plum
  d. green

11. Sandra highlights Amanda's eyes with a color that is:
  a. lighter than the skin tone
  b. the same as the skin tone
  c. heavier than the skin tone
  d. darker than the skin tone

12. To make Amanda's eyes appear larger and more open, Sandra should apply:
   a. eyeliner across the top
   b. mascara on the top lashes only
   c. eye color in the crease
   d. mascara on top and bottom lashes

Linda is a makeup artist who works for a very high-end cosmetics line that is sold exclusively through salons and spas. Today, a distributor is hosting an educational conference where Linda will be the guest educator. The topic of today's class will be corrective makeup techniques and Linda will be demonstrating these techniques using the cosmetics line she represents. Instead of hiring models, the conference participants will analyze and perform the corrective techniques on one another. Kelly, one of the class participants, is first. She has a wide forehead and cheek area but a rather narrow jawline, with small eyes, and she also has a very long, thin neck. Carmen, another participant, has a very full, round face, with a wide and somewhat flat nose, protruding eyes, and a rather thick chin and neck area. Rita has a very low forehead and a thin upper lip.

13. What face shape does Kelly have?
   a. diamond
   b. triangle
   c. square
   d. inverted triangle

14. To make Kelly's face appear more oval, Linda will need to:
   a. offset the hard edges at the chin and jawline
   b. minimize the width of the forehead and increase the width of the jawline
   c. create width at the forehead and slenderize the jawline
   d. create the illusion of a wider cheek bone area

15. To make Kelly's small eyes appear larger, Linda will:
   a. apply shadow to the outer corners of the eye only
   b. apply shadow in the crease
   c. blend the eye shadow over the upper lid
   d. extend shadow above, beyond, and below the eyes

16. To create more fullness to Kelly's neck and jawline area, Linda decides to apply a ________ to the area.
   a. dark concealer
   b. translucent powder
   c. light foundation
   d. bronzing lotion

17. To make Carmen's round face appear slimmer, Linda will need to:
   a. offset the hard edges at the chin and jawline
   b. create width at the forehead and slenderize the jawline
   c. create the illusion of a wider cheek bone area
   d. slenderize and lengthen the face

18. To correct Carmen's wide, flat nose Linda will:
   a. apply a light foundation on either side of the nostrils
   b. apply a line of extra light foundation down the center of the nose
   c. apply a dark foundation on either side of the nostrils
   d. apply a line of extra dark foundation down the center of the nose

19. To minimize Carmen's protruding eyes, Carmen should:
   a. use a light, pearly color on the entire eye lid
   b. blend a deep shade of shadow over the upper lid and to the eyebrow
   c. use a highlight color in the crease and upper eyelid
   d. blend a medium-toned shadow into the crease line

20. To slenderize Carmen's neck and jawline area, Linda will apply a ________ to the area.
   a. dark foundation
   b. translucent powder
   c. light foundation
   d. bronzing lotion

21. To give the appearance of a more balanced face, Rita can offset her low forehead with eyebrows that have:
   a. a high arch
   b. a medium arch
   c. a low arch
   d. no arch

22. How can Linda correct Rita's thin upper lip?
   a. by using a dark color on the upper and lower lips
   b. by using a lip pencil to make the curve of the bottom lip proportionate to the chin
   c. by using a lip pencil to make the curves of the upper lip proportionate to the nostrils
   d. by using a light, frosted shade on the upper and lower lips

CHAPTER 25 Manicuring

Josie is a new nail technician at the Helpful Hands Nail Salon. On her first day, she sets up her manicure station with all of her tools and implements and gets ready for her first client, Wanda. Wanda arrives and requests a natural nail manicure and gives Josie a bottle of bright-red nail polish she has selected from those provided by the salon.

1. Before beginning the manicure, Josie and Wanda should:
- **a.** wash their hands
- **b.** file their nails
- **c.** exchange polish color ideas
- **d.** set up the manicure table

2. Once at the table, the first thing that Josie does is:
- **a.** file the nails
- **b.** cut the cuticle
- **c.** remove the old nail polish
- **d.** place the hands into the fingerbowl

3. To shape Wanda's nails, Josie will use a(n):
- **a.** cuticle nipper
- **b.** wooden pusher
- **c.** cotton pledget
- **d.** nail file

4. Wanda explains that she would like her nails shorter, so Josie uses a _________ to shorten them to the desired length.
- **a.** nail buffer
- **b.** cuticle nipper
- **c.** wooden pusher
- **d.** nail clipper

5. Josie recommends that Wanda consider using a _________ daily to correct and prevent brittle nails and dry cuticles.
- **a.** cuticle oil
- **b.** base coat
- **c.** penetrating nail oil
- **d.** dry nail polish

6. Once the manicure is completed and before the polish is applied, Josie begins the hand and arm:
   a. cleansing
   b. washing treatment
   c. massage
   d. hot oil treatment

7. The manipulation in which Josie's hands glide over Wanda's hand and arm is called:
   a. effleurage
   b. pétrissage
   c. tapoment
   d. friction

8. The manipulation that involves lifting, squeezing, and pressing the tissue is called:
   a. effleurage
   b. pétrissage
   c. tapoment
   d. friction

9. _____is a rapid tapping or striking motion of the hands against the skin.
   a. Effleurage
   b. Pétrissage
   c. Tapoment
   d. Friction

10. Vibration is a continuous __________movement applied by the hand without leaving contact with the skin.
   a. trembling or shaking
   b. shaking or twisting
   c. pulling or trembling
   d. kneading or shaking

11. ________incorporates various strokes that manipulate or press one layer of tissue over another.
   a. Effleurage
   b. Pétrissage
   c. Tapoment
   d. Friction

12. Before applying the base coat and polish, Josie applies a ________ to strengthen the nails and prevent them from splitting or peeling.
   a. nail color
   b. cuticle cream
   c. nail dryer
   d. nail hardener

13. How should Josie remove excess nail polish from around Wanda's nails?
   a. by removing all of the polish and painting the nail again
   b. with a cotton-tipped wooden pusher dipped in polish remover
   c. by spraying nail dryer on the nail, then removing all of the polish from the nail
   d. with a cotton pledget while the nail polish is still wet

Mariel lives in a cold climate and during the winter months, when the temperatures fall below freezing, her hands frequently become dry and even chapped. She also experiences stiffness in her hands and only a warm hand bath seems to help alleviate her symptoms. While in the Nails Forever Salon, Mariel tells her nail technician James about her situation and he says he may be able to recommend a service that can help.

14. What type of service could James be thinking of?
   a. an aromatherapy manicure
   b. a paraffin wax treatment
   c. a cuticle treatment
   d. a new fast-drying polish application

15. What is the benefit of this type of treatment for Mariel?
   a. It will make her long, natural nails look even longer.
   b. It will call attention to the color of polish she wears.
   c. It will trap moisture in the skin.
   d. It will keep additional moisture from penetrating the skin.

16. James and Mariel decide to do the treatment before her manicure that day because it will:
   a. pre-soften rough or callused skin
   b. eliminate the need for a massage
   c. pre-treat her brittle nails
   d. cause delays at the end of the service

17. Before beginning the service, James asks Mariel to:
   a. remove her nail polish
   b. file her nails
   c. wash her hands
   d. clean her jewelry

18. Since she has never had this treatment before, James performs a:

a. pre-manicure test
b. oil manicure
c. natural nail cleansing
d. patch test

19. James checks the temperature of the wax, which is a perfect ____ degrees.

a. 85 to 90 (29 to 32 C)
b. 90 to 95 (32 to 35 C)
c. 115 to 120 (46 to 49 C)
d. 125 to 130 (52 to 55 C)

20. Before applying the wax, James checks Mariel's hands for:

a. open sores, wounds, or abrasions
b. closed sores, warts, and bumps
c. open sores, abrasions, and beauty marks
d. wounds, closed sores, and warts

21. Once he has determined that he can proceed, James applies _____ to Mariel's hands.

a. hot oil
b. penetrating cuticle remover
c. moisturizing lotion
d. hand antiseptic

22. James prepares Mariel's hand for dipping into the paraffin by placing the palm facing down with the wrist slightly bent and the fingers:

a. bent and closely together
b. straight and slightly apart
c. straight and tightly together
d. bent and loosely apart

23. James dips Mariel's hand into the wax, up to the wrist ______ times.

a. one to three
b. three to five
c. five to seven
d. seven to ten

24. Once each hand is dipped into the wax, James places Mariel's hands into:

- **a.** an armrest
- **b.** woolen mitts
- **c.** a curing unit
- **d.** plastic mitts

25. Once the treatment is over, James peels the wax from Mariel's hands and ________.

- **a.** puts it back into the wax machine to melt and use again
- **b.** disposes of it
- **c.** gives it to Mariel to microwave and use at home
- **d.** keeps it for use on her next treatment

CHAPTER 26 Pedicuring

Carla is a retail store manager who spends over 40 hours a week on her feet. For her birthday, Carla's husband Leonard has booked an appointment for her to have a pedicure with Joya, a pedicurist at their local salon. When she arrives for the appointment, Carla explains to Joya that she is eager to have her feet massaged. Joya begins the service.

1. The first step of the service involves Joya instructing Carla to:
   a. place her feet into heated socks
   b. place her belongings onto a chair
   c. place her feet into the bath
   d. remove Carla's feet from the foot bath.

2. Carla's feet should be left soaking for about _____ minutes.
   a. two
   b. five
   c. eight
   d. ten

3. Once the first foot is removed from the foot bath and dried, Joya must:
   a. remove any toenail polish
   b. clip and file the toenails
   c. file down rough skin
   d. insert toe separators

4. In the next step of the pedicure, Joya should clip the toenails ______ across the top and even with the end of the toes.
   a. in a rounded manner
   b. straight
   c. in a diagonal manner
   d. curved

5. Joya will use her nail rasp to:
   a. dig out an ingrown toenail
   b. file and roughen the edges of the nail plate
   c. clean under the free edge of a toenail
   d. file and smooth the edges of the nail plate

6. Joya uses a professional strength ________ to soften and smooth thickened tissue on Carla's heels and over other pressure points.
   a. callus softener
   b. hot oil
   c. moisturizing lotion
   d. cuticle softener

7. Joya will use a foot _____ to reduce Carla's thickened calluses.
   a. file
   b. rasp
   c. wooden pusher
   d. curette

8. To gently remove cuticle tissue from the nail plate, Joya will use a:
   a. liquid soap and a cotton-tipped wooden pusher stick
   b. foot lotion and a nail rasp
   c. a diamond nail file and cuticle cream
   d. cuticle remover and a cotton-tipped wooden pusher

9. To complete the pedicure Joya will use a ________, a small, scoop-shaped implement used for more efficient removal of debris from the nail folds, eponychium, and hyponychium.
   a. file
   b. rasp
   c. cream
   d. curette

10. Joya begins the foot and leg massage by applying moisturizing lotion and rotating the foot at the ________.
    a. toes
    b. knee
    c. ankle
    d. heel

11. The only place on the foot and/or leg where a friction movement should be performed is on the_____of Carla's foot.
    a. outstep
    b. top
    c. instep
    d. heel

12. To begin the leg massage, Joya will grasp Carla's leg from behind the ankle and perform ______movements up the leg, to just below the knee.
    a. friction
    b. vibration
    c. pétrissage
    d. effleurage

13. Joya will perform these manipulations _____ times on the front, sides, and back of Carla's legs.
    a. three to five
    b. five to seven
    c. seven to ten
    d. eleven to thirteen

CHAPTER 27 Nail Tips and Wraps

Roberta has been a nail technician for many years and has a thriving clientele. Roberta's clients, like many nail clients, love long nails and so aren't shy about wearing nail extensions and enhancements. Today she will be seeing a long-time client, Kaila, who is scheduled for tips and wraps.

1. After Kaila has washed and dried her hands thoroughly and is seated at Roberta's manicure table, she is asked:
- **a.** how much extra width she would like added
- **b.** how much extra thickness she would like added
- **c.** how much extra length she would like added
- **d.** how much extra color she would like added

2. To add extra length to Kaila's natural nails, Roberta will use nail tips, which are made of:
- **a.** glass
- **b.** plastic
- **c.** styrofoam
- **d.** nylon

3. Roberta will use ____ to put the tips on to Kaila's natural nails.
- **a.** super glue-adhesive
- **b.** fast-drying glue
- **c.** nail adhesive
- **d.** craft glue

4. After the nail extensions have been applied, a(n) _____ must be applied over the natural nail and nail tip for added strength.
- **a.** underlay
- **b.** layer of adhesive
- **c.** overlay
- **d.** layer of plastic

5. In order to determine the best type of wrap for Kaila, Roberta will need to ask her which of the following questions?
- **a.** What color polishes do you most like to wear?
- **b.** Do you plan on having nail art over the finished nails?
- **c.** How rough are you on your hands and nails?
- **d.** Would you like to have a pedicure while you're here?

6. Kaila explains that she is a landscape artist and she works outdoors planting and gardening all day long. Based on this, Roberta recommends that she wear_____ wraps for their durability.
   a. silk
   b. fiberglass
   c. linen
   d. paper

7. Roberta recommends this type of wrap material because it is the:
   a. most natural-looking
   b. prettiest
   c. strongest
   d. weakest

8. Roberta begins to pull out the products she needs to perform this service for Kaila. The products she gathers include:
   a. gel adhesive
   b. wrap resin
   c. jar of polymer powder
   d. tub of manicuring cream

9. Before applying tips or wraps onto Kaila's nails, Roberta must wipe the natural nail with ____ to remove any moisture from the nail's surface.
   a. nail fungal product
   b. spray adhesive
   c. wrap resin accelerator
   d. nail dehydrator

10. As she prepares to apply the fabric to Kaila's nails, Roberta ____ the fabric to fit her nail size and shape.
    a. glues
    b. cuts
    c. folds
    d. files

11. Before applying the fabric to Kaila's nails, Roberta applies a layer of wrap resin to _____ and then begins applying the fabric wrap.
    a. three of her nails
    b. half of her nails
    c. seven of her nails
    d. all of her nails

12. Roberta uses a small piece of thick plastic to:
- **a.** shape the nail
- **b.** smooth the fabric onto the nail
- **c.** shorten the nail
- **d.** adhere the fabric onto the nail

13. After the second coat of wrap resin is applied to all of the nails, Roberta sprays ______ onto Kaila's nails to speed their drying time.
- **a.** wrap resin decelerator
- **b.** polish drying solution
- **c.** wrap resin accelerator
- **d.** top coat

14. Roberta will apply wrap resin and wrap resin accelerator ___ more time(s) before the nails are completed.
- **a.** one
- **b.** two
- **c.** three
- **d.** four

15. Kaila asks Roberta about maintaining her new nails. Roberta explains that every two weeks she will need to have her nails maintained, and the maintenance will follow this schedule:
- **a.** a hot oil manicure every two weeks
- **b.** wrap resin only applied two weeks after a fresh wrap is applied, with additional fabric needing to be applied every four weeks
- **c.** rewrapped with resin and fabric every two weeks
- **d.** rewrapped every two weeks and glued every four weeks

CHAPTER 28 Monomer Liquid and Polymer Powder Nail Enhancements

Martine specializes in monomer liquid and polymer powder nail enhancements and has done so for years. She is about to begin servicing Jamie, a new client to her salon.

1. If Jamie wishes to have her nails extended past the length of her natural nails, Martine has two options. She can use _____ or _____.
   a. files, tips
   b. nail tips, nail files
   c. nail tips, nail forms
   d. nail forms, nail files

2. Jamie wears sculptured nails, so when Martine does Jamie's nails, she uses:
   a. nail forms and primer
   b. a monomer liquid and polymer powder
   c. a monomer liquid and nail form
   d. a catalyst and nail tips

3. To aid in the adhesion and to prepare the nail surface for attachment with the monomer liquid and polymer powder material, Martine will use _____ on Jamie's nails.
   a. monomer
   b. polymer
   c. catalyst
   d. primer

4. When Martine combines the monomer liquid and polymer powder on her application brush, a(n) ____ forms.
   a. nail
   b. overlay
   c. tear
   d. bead

5. Martine knows that if she uses twice as much monomer liquid as she does polymer powder the bead is considered:
   a. medium
   b. dry
   c. drippy
   d. wet

6. Curing is the process by which the monomer liquid and the polymer powder:
   a. liquefy
   b. harden
   c. change color
   d. whiten

7. Martine knows that she must play close attention to the ____ of the nail, because this is where the strength of the nail enhancement lies.
   a. sidewall
   b. apex
   c. free edge
   d. base

8. Once applied, monomer liquid and polymer powder overlays should be _____ every two weeks and the shape of the nail should be _____ each time monomer liquid and polymer powder is used.
   a. maintained, rebalanced
   b. filed, changed
   c. refilled, cut
   d. maintained, trimmed

CHAPTER 29 UV Gels

Jen is preparing for a full day of nail clients. Her first client is Falon, who has booked a full set of UV gel nails. Jen has already applied tips to Falon's nails and is ready to begin the application of the gel.

1. In addition to the materials in her basic manicuring setup, Jen will need a _____ to complete the service for Falon.
   a. UV gel trimmers
   b. UV gel light-unit
   c. UV gel clipper
   d. UV gel lamp

2. Jen will first apply a _____ to improve adhesion of the UV gel to the natural nail plate.
   a. cleaning gel
   b. bonding gel
   c. self-leveling gel
   d. building gel

3. When applying this UV gel, Jen should firmly brush UV gel onto the _____ nail.
   a. free edge
   b. lunula
   c. natural
   d. sidewalls

4. To create the right arch in Falon's nail, Jen will apply a _____.
   a. cleaning gel
   b. bonding gel
   c. self-leveling gel
   d. building gel

5. After the building gel is applied, Jen may choose to apply a _____, which will create a smooth finish on the nail and requires less filing.
   a. cleaning gel
   b. bonding gel
   c. self-leveling gel
   d. building gel

6. Curing the gel means:
   a. allowing it to run over the eponychium
   b. maintaining its clear white color
   c. healing it of imperfection
   d. allowing it to harden

7. The inhibition layer left on the nail after the UV gel has cured is:
   a. tacky
   b. wet
   c. dry
   d. brittle

8. This layer must be:
   a. left on the nail
   b. cleaned with a cotton ball
   c. able to change color
   d. cleaned from the nail

9. Jen must remove the inhibition layer from Falon's nails:
   a. after each gel is cured
   b. before polishing the nails
   c. after the building gel is cured
   d. before the light unit's timer sounds

CHAPTER 30 Seeking Employment

Samuel has just received notice from his state board of cosmetology that he is scheduled to take his licensing exam in two weeks. He is happy but also nervous about taking the exam. He wants very badly to pass the test on his first try, but test-taking always makes him nervous. Samuel pulls out his textbook and study materials and begins to schedule his study and preparation time.

1. Samuel should begin studying:
- **a.** the day before the exam
- **b.** the evening before the exam
- **c.** the morning of the exam
- **d.** several weeks before the exam

2. In order to get ready for his written exam, Samuel should:
- **a.** practice his finger-waving technique
- **b.** take time to party with his buddies right before the exam
- **c.** have a drink of alcohol the morning of the exam to help him relax
- **d.** review past quizzes, tests, and homework assignments

3. The evening before the exam Samuel should plan to:
- **a.** study all night long
- **b.** get about four hours of sleep
- **c.** go out and forget about the exam
- **d.** get a full night's sleep

4. Once he is given the exam, Samuel should:
- **a.** begin answering the questions in the order they are presented
- **b.** answer all multiple-choice questions by selecting option "A"
- **c.** read through the exam and all of the directions before beginning the test
- **d.** answer all multiple-choice questions by selecting option "C"

5. If Samuel is stuck on a question, he can _____ and then determine which are possible correct answers.
- **a.** skip to a question he can answer
- **b.** eliminate answers he knows are incorrect
- **c.** look at another person's sheet
- **d.** opt to take only the practical exam

Amira has graduated from beauty school and received passing grades on her exams. She wants to find a good salon job and begins looking in various local newspapers for job openings. She makes a list of salons that have openings and then schedules several appointments with salons that have run help-wanted ads in the newspapers. She dresses well in a beautiful outfit with matching shoes and handbag, has her hair and makeup done expertly, and washes her car so that she presents a great-looking appearance to her prospective salon manager.

6. When she arrives at the first salon, the salon manager asks Amira for her credentials. Amira should hand the manager a:

a. photo of herself doing hair
b. resume
c. reference letter
d. business card

7. What kinds of information will the salon manager need to ascertain about Amira before determining if she is right for the open position?

a. her marital status
b. her job history
c. her product preferences
d. her favorite clothing designer

8. Another tool Amira should consider creating to take with her on interviews is a(n):

a. photo album of hairstyles from popular magazines
b. picture book of herself and the styles she has worn over the years
c. employment portfolio showing before and after photos of past clients
d. picture book of the type of salon and layout she prefers to work in

9. In order to validate her claim that she has been a responsible employee while working for others, Amira should provide:

a. letters of commendation from her school
b. a trophy she won in high school
c. letters of reference from past employers
d. old pay stubs

10. If Amira has the opportunity to ask questions of the interviewer, which of the following would NOT be appropriate?

a. What are you looking for in a stylist?
b. When will the position be filled?
c. Does the salon offer continuing education opportunities?
d. Will someone be fired when I am hired?

11. One question that Amira's interviewer is legally prohibited from asking her is:

a. What is your date of birth?
b. Do you have any disabilities?
c. Do you smoke cigarettes?
d. Do you take drugs?

12. After having met and spent some time with the salon manager, Amira should send:

a. a bouquet of flowers
b. a state board inspector into the salon
c. a basket of muffins
d. a thank you note for the interview

13. If she is offered the position, Amira will have to decide _____ before taking the job.

a. if the salon has enough shampoo bowls to accommodate all of the salon's needs
b. if the stylists she'll be working with are candidates for possible friendship
c. if the salon has the kind of image, culture, and values that she has
d. if the color palette the designer used to decorate the salon is suitable for her tastes

CHAPTER 31 On the Job

Today is Marshall's first day at the Jolie Salon, and he is excited. He will meet the entire staff this morning at the weekly staff meeting, and then he'll meet with Sara, the salon manager, to go over the rules and regulations of the salon and to discuss the details of his financial remuneration. Marshall also has a few questions he wants to ask Sara and a couple of issues he would like her to clarify.

1. Sara tells Marshall that the salon operates very much like a(n) _____ in that all of the employees are aware of their own duties but are also ready and must be willing to aid their coworkers in whatever needs to be accomplished.
   - **a.** booth rental situation
   - **b.** team
   - **c.** individual salon
   - **d.** private salon

2. Sara explains that payday is on Friday and that Marshall will make a _____, which is a percentage of his service dollars and an hourly wage.
   - **a.** commission
   - **b.** salary
   - **c.** tip
   - **d.** salary plus commission

3. Sara explains that after his first 90 days of employment Marshall will have a(n)_____, which will be an opportunity for her to assess his progress and performance and for Marshall to discuss his thoughts and ideas about the salon.
   - **a.** hair service
   - **b.** employee evaluation
   - **c.** in-salon training class
   - **d.** management workshop

4. Marshall asks Sara if she can help him to determine what his paychecks might be for the first three months of employment so that he can make a _____ to track his expenses, such as loan repayments and his rent.
   - **a.** salon budget
   - **b.** pie chart of client retention
   - **c.** personal budget
   - **d.** tipping sheet

5. Sara assigns Marshall to Joyce, a senior stylist who will be responsible for answering his questions, giving him guidance, and helping him when he has difficulty. Joyce will be his:
   a. friend
   b. coworker
   c. manager
   d. mentor

Chantal has just learned that her salon will be retailing a product line that she has used in the past and has wanted to sell to her clients for some time. She is excited because many of the salon's clients can really benefit from the products and the new services their use will introduce to the salon. Chantal's first client is Noreen, who has had her hair colored and chemically straightened and who uses a hot iron to flatten and style her hair about once a week. As a result of the intense chemicals and heat, Noreen's hair is very brittle, dried, and damaged and Chantal feels that any additional pulling or styling may cause Noreen's hair to break.

6. When Noreen comes in for her haircut and styling appointment, Chantal should:
   a. get reacquainted with Noreen and proceed with the service
   b. offer Noreen a cup of coffee and walk her to the styling station
   c. fill Noreen in on all of the latest gossip since her last visit
   d. review Noreen's record card and discuss the condition of her hair

7. While discussing her hair Noreen mentions that she is having difficulty with her hair being so dry and looking dull. Chantal will want to use this as an opportunity to:
   a. describe the new line of retail products to Noreen and how they can benefit her
   b. tell her what a mistake it is to chemically straighten the hair
   c. talk her into leaving her hair curly and natural
   d. suggest that she wear a wig for a while

8. Since Noreen's hair is very dry and damaged, Chantal suggests adding a deep-conditioning treatment to today's service. This is called:
   a. upping the service
   b. ticket upgrading
   c. adding up the ticket
   d. selling unneeded services

9. Once Noreen has had her service and sees the benefit of the treatment, Chantal can use a _____ approach to recommending additional retail products for at-home use, because Noreen already feels their benefit.
   a. hard-sell
   b. fast-sell
   c. soft-sell
   d. slow-sell

Cassie is worried. She has a great clientele who are very loyal to her, but she knows that if she moves to a bigger salon and rents more space that her expenses will go up and she wonders what she can do to increase her income. She decides to take some time and write out her plan for how to increase her income to cover her expenses by increasing her client base. Cassie gets to work.

10. To obtain important demographic information on her clients, Cassie will need to refer to her:
   a. appointment book
   b. client intake form
   c. client service record card
   d. salon manual

11. Cassie notes that she can use her business cards to:
   a. get speaking engagements
   b. promote a referral program with current clients
   c. obtain free entrance to hair shows
   d. impress new clients with her professionalism

12. As a reward for her loyal clients and to promote the purchase of additional services and products, Cassie can prepare a _____ and include it in a thank you or birthday card mailing.
   a. free bottle of nail polish
   b. CD of the music played in the salon
   c. discount coupon
   d. gift certificate for a lunch at a nearby restaurant

13. To make herself visible to new groups of potential clients, Cassie could:
   a. work harder at keeping her current client base
   b. steal clients from other stylists in her current salon
   c. make herself available to speak at local organizations
   d. stake out neighboring salons and hand out flyers to their clients

14. Cassie could make use of her relationships with other local merchants by:
    a. going to their place of business and secretly handing out her business card
    b. agreeing to cross-promote with merchants who are willing to do so
    c. working part-time in their establishment
    d. discouraging her clients from using local merchants

15. Cassie realizes that one of the simplest ways to keep her business steady is to:
    a. double her prices
    b. book clients for their next appointment before they leave the salon
    c. use a less expensive brand of shampoo and conditioner
    d. purchase haircolor and perm solution in bulk

CHAPTER 32 The Salon Business

Don has been a stylist for more than six years and has built a loyal clientele at his current salon. He has thought about opening his own salon for several months and has decided to explore the various options open to him. He calls his friends, Emily, Scott, and Matt, who work at different salons in the area, and they agree to get together to discuss options and share ideas with Don.

1. Emily tells Don that she is a ________, which means that she pays rent to a salon owner for the space she works in and that she supplies all of her own materials and products. She has complete control over her work schedule and appointments.
   a. partner
   b. co-owner
   c. booth renter
   d. sole proprietor

2. Scott is a _______of the Scott Salon. He is responsible for determining all the policies of the salon and hiring and paying all of the employees. He also assumes all of the responsibilities of expenses and the profits of the salon.
   a. partner
   b. co-owner
   c. booth renter
   d. sole proprietor

3. Matt explains that he is a __________ with his wife, Anne. They share all of the duties of owning the business and all of the rewards as well. Since Matt is a cosmetologist, he manages the salon while his wife, who is an accountant, manages the finances and operations of the salon.
   a. partner
   b. sole owner
   c. booth renter
   d. sole proprietor

4. Scott advises Don to be aware of the area he will be working in. He explains that ________, _______, __________, and _________ are important factors in determining where to open a new salon and whether or not it will be successful.
   a. color palette, decor, furniture, and drapery
   b. demographics, visibility, parking, and competition
   c. style magazines, hair posters, reception literature, and retail stations
   d. cutting tools, rollabouts, mirrors, and styling implements

5. Don's friends advise him to develop a __________, which will help him clarify his vision and determine which type of opportunity is best for him.
   a. job description
   b. business plan
   c. will
   d. letter of resignation

After careful consideration, Don has decided to open his own salon as a sole proprietorship. He writes an extensive business plan, outlining his vision for his business, and creates a budget to determine what his expenses will be to open and run the salon. Don takes his business plan and budget to his local bank and meets with John Burke, a small business loan officer, to see about getting a loan to open his new salon.

6. John asks Don how much __________ he is seeking to run the salon for the first two years.
   a. space
   b. investment
   c. capital
   d. interest

7. John asks Don what percentage of the overall salon revenue he expects to spend on rent for the space and for advertising.
   a. approximately 3 percent
   b. approximately 13 percent
   c. approximately 16 percent
   d. approximately 26 percent

8. To make informed decisions about the salon's financial success, Don explains to John that he will keep _______and ________ records to control expenses and waste.
   a. inventory and service
   b. service and nonservice
   c. purchase and inventory
   d. purchase and service

9. Don mentions that _______ supplies such as hair spray and styling products will be on hand to sell to salon clients so that they can maintain their styles at home and that these sales will increase the salon's profitability.
   a. consumption
   b. back room
   c. service
   d. retail

10. John asks to see a copy of the projected _________so that he can assess whether the salon will have the correct flow and be conducive to the many services and demands of the clients who will patronize it.
    a. newspaper ads
    b. service menu
    c. salon layout
    d. price list

11. Don knows that when he interviews prospective employees for his salon, the following three items are very important:
    a. communication, public relations, and public speaking skills
    b. haircutting, haircoloring, and hair relaxing skills
    c. level of technical skill, overall attitude, and communication skills
    d. overall attitude, haircutting, and communication skills

CHAPTER 1 History and Career Opportunities

Marsha is about to graduate from cosmetology school and in her last three weeks of class, her instructor, Ms. Smith, asks her to research the various career opportunities available to a licensed cosmetologist and to create a career plan for herself. Marsha takes advantage of the career fair her school is sponsoring to gather information about the various career options available to her. At the career fair, Marsha speaks to April, a haircolor specialist; Anderson, a texture specialist; Morris, a cutting specialist; Alfredo, a salon trainer; and Barry, a distributor sales consultant.

1. April is a haircolor specialist, which means she:

d. *trains herself and others to perform haircolor services in the salon*

A haircolor specialist does many things, including working for a product manufacturer, in which case she will be expected to train others in how best to perform color services according to the company's guidelines and product instructions.

2. A texture specialist like Anderson would most likely spend his days:

c. *performing texture services for salon clients*

A texture specialist would most likely work in a salon and/or for a manufacturer and he or she will be expected to train others on how best to perform texture services according to the company's guidelines and product instructions.

3. Morris would have to __________ to be an effective cutting specialist.

a. *have a dedicated interest in learning various cutting styles and techniques*

After perfecting his own skills and developing his own method of cutting (everyone develops his or her own unique way of cutting hair), Morris may then choose to study with some of the greatest haircutters in the business to learn and adopt their systems and techniques. This training would allow him to perform top-quality haircutting in his own salon as well as teach those around him how to hone their skills.

4. As a salon trainer, Alfredo is primarily responsible for:
   b. *developing the skills of salon staff and personnel*
   Many companies such as manufacturers and salon chains hire experienced salon professionals and train them to train others. This kind of training can take many forms, from technical training to management and interpersonal relationship training. A salon trainer can work with small salons as well as large organizations and trade associations to help develop the beauty industry's most valuable resource—salon staff and personnel.

5. As a distributor sales consultant (DSC), the most important thing that Barry takes care of is:
   b. *the relationship between the salon and the distributor*
   The distributor sales consultant (DSC) is the most important link between a distributor and his or her salon accounts. Salons rely on the DSC to learn about new products, new trends, and new techniques to stay abreast of what is occurring in the marketplace. The DSC is the salon and salon staff's link with the rest of the industry, and this person constitutes the most efficient method manufacturing companies have to reach the salon stylist.

6. While discussing his job, Barry mentions that a manufacturer educator will be in town in the coming months and that Marsha may want to speak with her. A manufacturer educator's primary function is to:
   a. *train stylists and salon staff to understand and use a company's hair care, haircolor, and chemical-service products*
   Manufacturers hire their own educators to train stylists and salon staff to understand and use that company's hair care, haircolor, and chemical-service products. Mastery of the company's product lines is a must for manufacturer educators. An accomplished educator who is a good public speaker can advance to field educator, regional educator, or even platform educator, appearing on stage at shows in the U.S. and around the world.

7. Marsha has had an example of a very viable cosmetology career option all the time she was in beauty school. Who might that have been?
   b. *her cosmetology instructor*
   A career as a cosmetology instructor can be very rewarding. Many instructors had successful careers in salons before dedicating themselves to teaching new professionals the tricks of the trade. If this career path interests you, spend some time with your school's instructors and ask them why they went into education.

8. Marsha, who feels she has a sharp business mind, also considers becoming a:

   d. *a salon manager*

   A salon management position is the perfect job for someone who feels that business is her calling. There are many diverse management opportunities in the salon and spa industry. They include being an inventory manager, department head, educator, special events manager (promotions), assistant manager, and general manager. With experience, you can also add salon owner to this list of career possibilities. To ensure your success, it is wise to enroll in business classes to learn more about managing products, departments, and—above all—people.

CHAPTER 2 Life Skills

John has always dreamt of becoming a very successful professional. He has carefully thought through and imagined who he wants to be. John has taken a position with a very prestigious salon, where he has been working for five years. John drives an expensive automobile and rents a pricey apartment in a chic neighborhood. His wardrobe consists of designer and name-brand clothing and fashionable shoes and accessories, and he is always impeccably dressed. John spends a lot of time and money on his appearance and he wishes he were better compensated for his work because he has difficulty paying his other expenses—his car and rent—each month. However, he is reluctant to reduce his expenses because he is concerned that the salon's well-to-do clients won't patronize him if he doesn't live up to their standards of living. Because John works about 70 hours per week, he doesn't have a lot of time to devote to activities other than his work. John hardly ever sees his friends and family and rarely takes any time to enjoy sports or music, his favorite pastimes.

1. John's self-esteem appears to be based on:

b. *his ability to possess things*

True self-esteem is based on inner strength and trusting your ability to reach your goals. Since John's is based on his ability to possess things, his self-esteem will be dictated by how many things or belongings he has. This is not a true assessment of who John is or what his value and worth are.

2. John has used the technique of visualization to:

a. *picture himself as a complete success*

Visualization is a technique John can use to see himself in a certain light in his mind's eye, which makes it easier for him to manifest the image into reality because he is adept at seeing it, feeling it, and being comfortable with it.

3. Truly successful people do not:

c. *allow business to be the only focus of their life*

A truly successful person works hard but also takes time to enjoy the fruits of his or her labor—friendship, family, rest and relaxation, and quiet time to reflect and think about his life.

4. John's lifestyle requires him to spend all of his time:

d. *working*

John has created a very rigid lifestyle that does not allow him to do any of the things he may really enjoy, such as visiting with family and friends, exercising, or exploring hobbies.

5. John's definition of success includes:
   d. *keeping up appearances*
   A balanced view of success includes not only financial success but also the ability to have time for both work and pleasure, continuing to learn, having time daily for exercise, and caring for the physical as well as emotional body.

6. Whose definition of success is John attempting to achieve?
   c. *his clients'*
   John feels that in order to be respected by and patronized by this elite clientele he must be seen by them as one of them. He thinks his equality is based on the possession and acquisition of material things.

Ramona is a busy person. She has a part-time job and a small child; she attends cosmetology school and has many other tasks and responsibilities to take care of each day. Now that she is about to graduate and begin looking for a job in a salon, Ramona knows that she has to get better organized but she is always feeling frustrated by how much she has to do and how little time she has to do it. Ramona has good intentions but often gets so caught up in the day's activities and events that she forgets important errands she needs to run or appointments she has made. Ramona has resolved to use her time more efficiently.

7. The first thing Ramona must do is:
   b. *prioritize the list of tasks that need to be done*
   With a list of tasks that need to be accomplished arranged in order of priority, Ramona can be sure that the most important ones are being attended to and that they are not superseded by less important tasks.

8. Ramona needs to have some specific time with her young child each day. She can accomplish this by:
   b. *designing a schedule for herself that includes blocks of unstructured time*
   If Ramona created a time-management structure to follow daily, she could be sure that those things that are of the greatest importance receive the kind of time they need and deserve. This way important tasks and appointments aren't short-changed.

9. Which of the following will NOT save Ramona time in her busy schedule?

c. *Relying on others to problem-solve and uncover solutions she can use.*

Ramona will waste a lot of time if she waits for others to solve her problems or if needs to check and double-check decisions with others before she acts. By using a priority list and a time-management system, Ramona can be well aware of her needs and the options available to her so that she can act quickly and expediently.

10. When Ramona is feeling overwhelmed by the circumstances of her hectic life she could try a technique called:

b. *deep breathing*

By taking a moment or two to calm herself down, Ramona can concentrate on the demands at the moment and open herself to the many possibilities for a solution to her dilemma. Deep breathing or meditating is one way to stop the mind from wandering and to get focused.

11. To aid Ramona in remembering important notes and reminders she should carry:

a. *a memo pad or day planner*

Many people find it very helpful to have a dedicated place to jot down notes and reminders as they think of them. By always keeping your notes in the same place (e.g., a purse or a backpack) you can reduce the incidence of losing an important note or reminder.

12. Ramona might consider scheduling her time in _____ intervals to study for a major exam.

d. *60-minute*

By scheduling one-hour increments of time for studying, Ramona will allow herself enough time to settle into studying, to make notes, and review material without interruption or without spending so much time that she becomes bored or anxious.

13. To make the most of her time, Ramona should schedule activities that require alert, clear thinking during times when she is:

c. *highly energetic and able to focus*

Trying to accomplish tasks at the end of the day when she is tired, or after a great amount of physical or mental energy has been expended on something else, is a time waster. Ramona should know what type of energy level is needed for her various tasks and schedule them at those times during the day that are most conducive to the task.

14. Which of the following is NOT a healthy way for Ramona to reward herself for a job well done?

d. *smoking a cigarette*

Ramona should reward herself for doing a good job, but the method she uses should be one that enhances her mental, physical, and spiritual self instead of doing something that is potentially harmful or dangerous to herself and her well-being.

15. Another activity Ramona must consider scheduling to promote clear thinking and planning is:

a. *exercising*

By planning some physical exercise every day—by walking, running, or going to a gym—Ramona is taking good care of her physical well-being and doing what she can to maintain a healthy and strong body.

16. Which of the following tools would best help Ramona keep focused on the tasks she needs to complete each day?

c. *a to-do list*

A to-do list will help Ramona to stay on track and keep abreast of the tasks that need to be accomplished each day. A to-do list is especially useful for her to carry around with her and to check throughout the day when she has some additional time and can possibly complete one or two of the tasks.

Hector is a dedicated student who wants very badly to progress through school and become a licensed professional. While he is happy to be in school, he has difficulty staying focused during lectures and studying for and taking exams. He usually ends up cramming the night before an exam, even for important tests that cover many topics. Hector is frustrated and wants to have an easier time with this part of his schooling. He knows that he is a capable and serious student, and he is willing to try some new techniques to lessen his fears and anxieties about test-taking.

17. What is missing from Hector's educational background?

b. *good study skills*

Hector may not have learned some of the basics of how to study, such as staying focused on the task at hand and resisting distractions during those times that he has set aside for study. These are tools he can learn now to make studying easier for him.

18. When Hector feels overwhelmed by his courses and upcoming tests, he can focus on _____ to feel better about himself and his progress.

c. *accomplishing small tasks, one at a time*

Trying to do something new and then becoming proficient and successful at it can be very difficult and frustrating. Hector should break down each task into several smaller tasks and focus on accomplishing them one at a time. Sooner or later he will have the entire goal accomplished and realize that he is able to do whatever he sets his mind to doing.

19. Instead of cramming the night before an exam, Hector should:

d. *study the day's lessons each day and then review all the material before the exam*

By using a time-management system while he is in school and by scheduling an hour or so each day for reviewing the day's lessons and readings, Hector will slowly build up his knowledge of the material he is studying as well as his self-confidence as a student and learner.

20. Which of the following techniques will help Hector to stay focused when his mind begins to wander in class?

c. *Write down key words and discuss them with the instructor.*

In a classroom with many people where many activities are happening simultaneously, it is easy to become distracted and to lose focus on the lesson at hand. Hector can make notes of things he wants to discuss further, words or phrases he didn't understand, or techniques he would like to see demonstrated again, and use these notes to check in with his instructor. By letting these missed opportunities slip by without further discussion, Hector risks missing chunks of information or concepts that other material will build upon.

21. If Hector decides to form or join a study group, what should he look for in the group?

b. *Students who are willing to be helpful and supportive.*

Too many people join study groups because they want to enjoy the company, friendship, or camaraderie of a group of peers. While friendship can certainly be a pleasant bonus of a study group, one should choose a group that has the resources to provide an environment for learning and for enhancing the learning experience.

22. If Hector were to find a "study buddy," what would this person's job be?

c. *to help him to stay focused on studying*

A study buddy is someone who would work with Hector and help him to focus on the lessons of the day, week, and semester. This person should be someone with whom Hector could discuss ideas and concepts and who would make it a priority to work with Hector to aid him in concentrating on his studies.

Hakim and Jackie are senior stylists and assistant managers at La Bella Luna Salon and Spa. Both have excellent technical skills and are attractive-looking professionals who are intelligent and capable. Hakim's behavior is hallmarked by a sense of calm; he manages his fellow coworkers with honest and open communications, he is respectful of clients, and he never gossips. However, when he has problems at home, he often calls in sick for the day with little notice to the salon. Jackie, the other senior stylist, is quick to complain about other people, is sometimes bossy and uncaring about the feelings of others, and acts as if the salon's rules and policies do not pertain to her, yet Jackie is always at work on time and she rarely ever takes unscheduled time off. Adam, the salon's owner, has a salon manager opening to fill and Hakim and Jackie are the two candidates he has to choose from.

23. In making his decision, Adam must choose the person who is best at:

c. *speaking honestly to stylists*

Keeping a salon staff happy and keeping a salon running smoothly require the skills of a person who is open and able to communicate and relate to others honestly. A good manager, while not perfect, does his or her best to balance all of the responsibilities of the job.

24. In assessing Hakim and Jackie, which of the following does NOT indicate a high standard of professionalism?

b. *avoiding all conflict*

While dealing with conflict may be the least pleasant thing a manager has to do, it is also among the most important. All too often, in an effort to avoid the unpleasantness of conflict, people simply do not address situations and resolve them in a timely manner, which only creates an opportunity for bigger problems the longer they remain unresolved.

25. As a service provider, Hakim must be able to practice:

b. *self-care*

Hakim, like any service provider—doctors, nurses, therapists—will only be able to give excellent care if he feels perfectly taken care of himself. This means that he must be sure to tend to his physical, psychological, and emotional needs and to know himself and his limits well enough to know when he needs to be recharged.

26. When determining Jackie's and Hakim's sense of integrity, Adam will need to assess:

b. *if their behavior and actions match their values*

Many people can use catch words and popular phrases, or can say what they think another person will want to hear, but the true test of a person's integrity is observing their behavior and their actions—these things indicate what they really value.

27. For Jackie to display a good sense of integrity she would have to behave in the following manner:

d. *recommend products and services that will benefit the client*

While selling in and of itself isn't a bad thing, professionals have to remember that they have trained and worked hard to achieve their position as a trusted resource for their clients, and to betray that trust in any way is to trade in their long-term success and happiness for a short-lived commission.

28. When Jackie gossips with other stylists about a client's personal situation she is lacking:

c. *discretion*

When Jackie became a cosmetologist, she became a person that her colleagues and clients alike began to confide in. People told her private and confidential information about themselves and their preferences. Along with the information she received, she made an unspoken promise to not use the information in any way that could be hurtful and damaging to the person who confided in her. When Jackie gossips about others, she lacks good judgment.

29. Which of the following indicates that Hakim is using ethical behavior in his communication with customers and the other people he works with?

c. *being direct*

So much miscommunication can occur when people do not say what they actually mean. Being direct with people can go a long way toward having an experience that is honest and focused. Being coy or indirect usually confuses the situation and causes hard feelings.

Tishla is the receptionist at the Salon Omega. One of her most important duties is to schedule clients effectively and efficiently so that neither the stylists nor the clients are waiting for long periods of time. Tishla has scheduled Mr. Everett for a haircut and scalp massage with Jane for 6 p.m. At 6:20 Mr. Everett calls from his cell phone to say that he is stuck in traffic and would like to change his appointment to 7 p.m. Tishla looks at Jane's schedule and sees that she has 7 p.m. and 7:30 p.m. appointments, so there is no way that she can reschedule Mr. Everett for this evening. Annoyed, Tishla says to him, "Well, if you had called immediately, I may have been able to move a later appointment up. You should have called sooner to reschedule, like when you first got stuck in the traffic jam! There's nothing I can do now, Jane has no openings until next week."

Mr. Everett explains, "I thought the traffic would clear up sooner and that I'd make it in time. I'm sorry if I caused any problems. I'd like to make another appointment."

Tishla says, "Okay but Jane is sitting here waiting for you while two other clients have walked in and she could have been servicing them!" Tishla looks at the appointment calendar and says that she can make an appointment for Mr. Everett for the following week but, she warns, "You have to be sure you're going to make it on time and if you can't be on time, you have to call me right away and let us know." Mr. Everett says he would like to take the appointment; Tishla marks his name in the calendar and then completes the call.

30. From her response, what kind of attitude does Tishla have about people who are late?

c. *She is impatient and distrusting.*

One of Tishla's most important jobs is to keep the flow of the salon moving; however, hectic lives inevitably mean that clients will sometimes need to change appointments. While she may be annoyed that Mr. Everett inconvenienced her and the stylist, she must also remember that their salon can only be successful if they accommodate their clients' needs.

31. How would you rate Tishla's ability to handle the situation with Mr. Everett tactfully?

c. *Fair—she wasn't very sympathetic but managed to reschedule the client.*

While Tishla was able to reschedule the appointment, she did not represent the salon in a very friendly or sympathetic manner to the client. While Mr. Everett may keep his next appointment, the burden now falls more heavily on the stylist to repair anything that may have been lost in the delicate relationship between the client and the salon.

32. How should Tishla have handled the conversation with Mr. Everett?

d. *She should have let him know that missing his appointment was a problem and asked him if he'd prefer to be the last client of the day to give him ample time to get to the salon.*

A useful technique for clients who are chronically late or for those who have to drive a long distance in traffic is to give them the last appointment of the day so that if they are late or if they have to cancel altogether the effect on the stylist's schedule is minimized.

33. How sensitive was Tishla to Mr. Everett?

d. *not sensitive at all*

Tishla's attitude and responses to Mr. Everett conveyed that she was more concerned about her own inconvenience and that of the stylist than the needs of the client.

34. Based on Tishla's response to this situation, what do think her values and goals are?

d. *accusation and blame*

Since Tishla is in a position that can be stressful, and since every missed or mishandled appointment can have a financial impact on the salon, it's easy to see how Tishla may want the stylist and her salon manager to know that she was not to blame for the incident with Mr. Everett. However, becoming accusatory and blaming will only serve to alienate a good client from the salon.

35. What will likely be the effect of Tishla's communication on Mr. Everett?

d. *He will feel guilty.*

While Mr. Everett may keep his appointment, it is almost a certainty that he will feel embarrassed, reprimanded, and even angry because a simple situation was made much larger than it had to be. Even if the client agrees to continue to come to the salon, there is likely to be a negative residue overshadowing the experience for quite some time to come.

CHAPTER 3 Your Professional Image

Maggie is always rushed and is frequently late for work. To save time in the morning, she sometimes showers in the evening before going to bed so that the time she spends getting ready for work in the morning is lessened. Maggie awakens a half an hour before she needs to leave her house, quickly washes her face, brushes her teeth, puts on her makeup, dresses, and runs out the door to get to the salon. Several days a week after working at the salon, she goes to her evening job as a waitress, often without freshening her clothes, her body, or her makeup. Maggie's clients and colleagues noticeably pull away from her when she is speaking to them and coming in close contact with them. Behind her back, some of Maggie's colleagues make fun of her and call her names like "sloppy" and "disheveled" because she is always late, seemingly forgetful, and never looks well put together or freshly bathed. Maggie is always tired and she is becoming increasingly unhappy.

1. Based on the reaction from Maggie's colleagues, how would you rate her personal hygiene?
   d. *fair*
   We all know how unpleasant an experience it can be to be in contact with someone who has body odor or bad breath. If the condition is so bad that people are actually pulling away from her when in conversation, a simple solution is available to Maggie, such as using freshening towelettes and breath mints throughout the day.

2. Which of the following should Maggie NOT do to improve her personal hygiene between jobs?
   d. *douse herself with perfume*
   Sometimes when people are in a rush, they may opt to take what they consider to be the easiest solution. In this case dousing oneself with perfume or cologne will not really resolve the body odor issue but will probably make it more pronounced. Instead of covering up, all Maggie needs to do is freshen up.

3. What is most likely the cause of coworkers and clients pulling away from Maggie when she is speaking to them?
   c. *bad breath*
   Most likely Maggie has bad breath. If she is aware of her propensity for it, she can keep some toothpaste and a toothbrush in her handbag or tucked away in her station so that she can freshen up during the day when she needs to.

4. What does Maggie's disheveled appearance say about her professionalism?
   d. *That she is feeling stress and cannot manage her time.*
   Maggie's appearance says that she is overwhelmed by her life and her working conditions and that she is not taking proper care of herself and her health, and therefore not acting in a manner befitting a professional person.

Paige is in her early twenties and loves to wear her short, cropped hair messy with styling glue; she describes her style as the "bad-girl-meets-the-beauty-biz." She also often wears sleeveless or short-sleeved shirts to show off her numerous tattoos. Paige loves to wear dark, colorful makeup applied in a "gothic" fashion. Since she really needs a job, Paige has decided to apply at the luxury spa that has just opened a few blocks from her home. A couple of days before her interview, Paige goes into the spa and observes that the spa employees are all wearing simple black clothing with white smocks over them. She notices that their hair is styled into simple and classic looks and their makeup is very subtle, employing natural colors and techniques. Paige decides that in order to have a shot at the job she wants so desperately she will dress in accordance with the other spa staffers during her interview and then slip into her own style once she has gotten the job.

5. How should Paige go about finding the best place for her to work?
   a. *Visit several salons and determine which one is most in line with her own sense of style.*
   While Paige probably needs a job very badly, the worst thing she can do is to make herself into someone she is not to get a job offer. She should visit several salons in her area to find those that most align with the kind of tastes and preferences she has and then decide which of those she would like to work in.

6. From the description, what seems to be the energy and image of the spa Paige is interviewing at?
   c. *a high-end spa with an exclusive clientele*
   A luxury spa is definitely an environment that caters to affluent clients who are willing to spend their money on luxury products and services and who will expect to be serviced by a certain type of professional whose personal style mirrors the spa's and their own.

7. What type of salon seems most appropriate for someone with Paige's sense of style to work in?
   b. *A moderately priced salon that caters to young clients who have a sense of adventure.*
   To be successful in the long term, Paige needs to work in a salon whose style reflects her own and that caters to clients who can appreciate her sense of style.

8. Is Paige's approach to getting this job ethical?
   c. *No, because she isn't being honest about who she really is.*
      A major component of being ethical is being honest in all aspects of every interaction. By dressing and acting like the other stylists in the salon and then intending to resume her preferred style after she gets the job, Paige is not being honest with the spa owners, or with herself.

Peter loves to have a good time. Almost every day after working at the salon, he meets up with his buddies to hang out. They go to one another's apartments and order pizza and drink and watch television until late into the night. Often, because Peter is so tired, he sleeps on his friend's couch and then gets up the next day and goes directly to work. His salon coworkers always know when Peter has been out with his friends the night before because he is barely awake, is unshaven, and is wearing the same clothes he wore the day before. Peter gets teased by some of the other salon employees for being a "free spirit," but Allie, the salon manager, isn't as able to dismiss his messy appearance becausehe is often so disheveled that he is off-putting to salon clients. Allie decides to have a conversation with Peter about his appearance and general hygiene.

9. The best time for Allie to approach Peter would be:
   c. *When they are alone in the salon.*
      Allie needs to discuss a very personal issue with Peter. The best time to speak to him is when they are alone so that he is not embarrassed or distracted by others. In this way, she will have the best chance of being able to get through to Peter.

10. What should Allie discuss with Peter?
    a. *His personal appearance and its effect on the salon's clients.*
       Allie must keep the conversation focused and professional and not allow her personal feelings or judgments to get interjected. Allie is responsible for the smooth operation of the salon, so it is perfectly acceptable for her to discuss the effects of Peter's behavior and appearance on clients.

11. What could Peter do to make sure he is fresh for work even on nights when he doesn't sleep at home?
    c. *keep clean clothing in his car and freshen up before arriving at the salon*
       No matter what else is happening in Peter's life, he should make his professional appearance and demeanor a priority. By keeping fresh clothing in his car or by awakening early enough to go home and get dressed in clean clothing he can handle the issue directly.

12. The image that Peter is projecting to clients suggests that he is:
   b. *between apartments and sleeping wherever he can*
   Peter is not portraying himself as a serious or dedicated professional; rather, he looks like someone who is sloppy and careless. No client will want to subject him-or herself to someone like Peter more than once or twice. Not only will Peter lose clients, but so will the salon.

Marilyn is both a hairstylist and nail tech who works about eight hours a day servicing clients. When she is standing, she very often leans on one hip or the other, shifting her weight from one side to the other, and when she is seated she's usually leaning forward with her legs either crossed or tucked underneath her body. At the end of the day Marilyn is often in pain–her legs and back are cramping and her arms, shoulders, and neck feel tired and strained. By the time she arrives home at night she hardly has enough energy to do routine chores before plopping in front of the television set for the evening.

13. What does Marilyn's physical presentation indicate?
   b. *poor posture*
   Marilyn's posture, the way that she holds herself, is being compromised by her lack of attention to how she is contorting her body while at work. She probably wants to be comfortable during her work hours, but she doesn't realize that she is hurting herself by holding her body in this manner.

14. To achieve and maintain a good work posture, what position should Marilyn's neck be in?
   c. *elongated and balanced directly above shoulders*
   She should keep her head level with the floor to ensure that she doesn't strain her neck or back by leaning too far forward or backward.

15. To relieve the tension in her shoulders, Marilyn should:
   b. *level and relax them*
   This technique not only relaxes the shoulders but also allows the muscles to be lightly stretched and then relaxed, causing the tension to dissipate.

16. When standing, what position should Marilyn's back be in?
   d. *straight*
   To prevent unnecessary and painful damage to her back, Marilyn should try to keep her spine as straight as possible throughout the day.

17. A sitting posture that would alleviate Marilyn's back and neck pain would include:

c. *keeping her back straight*

Keeping her back straight even when sitting may be tricky as nail techs tend to become so involved in the service they are performing that they forget to be aware of their posture, but it will be the only real way to prevent back pain and damage.

18. How can Marilyn make her work environment more ergonomically correct for herself?

b. *She can adjust the client's chair.*

Adjusting the client's chair to suit the needs of the stylist or nail tech is exactly the reason that client chairs are adjustable. The client should be seated in the chair and an assessment of adjustments can be made. Then the client should stand up so the adjustments can be made, and then be seated again. Never make adjustments to a chair while the client is seated in the chair.

CHAPTER 4 Communicating for Success

Tyrone is a distributor sales consultant who is calling on Eva, a salon owner. Eva placed an order two weeks ago but it still has not been delivered. Eva is angry because she has missed several opportunities to make retail sales and to service clients because she can't get the products she needs. When Tyrone walks in to the salon for his monthly sales call, Eva quickly and loudly complains about her order situation to Tyrone. Frustrated because Eva is the fourth salon owner he has called on this week with the same complaint, Tyrone slams his sales book shut and tells Eva, "I've told you already that the products are back-ordered from the manufacturer and there's nothing I can do about it. If you aren't interested in seeing this new brush line, then I guess there's nothing else I can do for you!"

1. Tyrone's reaction to Eva indicates that he was:

c. *unprepared for her complaints and took them personally*

Since Eva was not the first client to lodge this complaint and since he apparently already looked into the problem at his company, Tyrone has no excuse for not being prepared for this. He took her impatience as a personal insult when she was simply frustrated and disappointed in the customer service she was receiving.

2. If Tyrone had a strong sense of his abilities, how would he have behaved with Eva?

d. *He would have called her with a delivery date and proposed some alternative options.*

Since Tyrone had plenty of time either to get a date for when the items would be delivered or to have come up with a backup plan to accommodate his client, he should have been better able to handle her needs. If he was unsure about how best to serve the client, Tyrone could have checked in with his sales manager for advice and more options to offer Eva.

3. Had Tyrone really been listening to Eva's complaint, what opportunity might he have been presented with?

a. *the chance to sell her a new product line to try*

An adept salesperson is someone who is always ready to offer solutions to a customer's problems. In this scenario, Tyrone became a part of the problem instead of part of the solution, and in doing so he missed an opportunity to help the client and to make an additional sale.

4. What would have been the best way for Tyrone to attend to Eva's needs?
   c. *agreeing with her complaint and asking what he could do to help her in the short term*
      Eva needed to vent her frustration, so, as her sales consultant, it was appropriate for him to allow her to complain a bit. Once she was allowed to do some of that, Tyrone should have redirected the conversation into more constructive and useful directions as he has been trained.

5. From Tyrone's reaction to Eva, what can you infer about his job satisfaction?
   d. *He is unhappy at work and is not handling his frustrations in a positive manner.*
      If Tyrone is unhappy, frustrated, or angry about the circumstances under which he works, he needs to find a mature way of handling his feelings and resolving his problem before he can really be of service to his own customers.

Victoria is out shopping when she sees a salon and decides to go in for some advice. Abe, the stylist who happens to be sitting behind the reception desk, asks if he can help her. "Yes," says Victoria, "I need some help with my hair."

Abe smiles and says, "Sure, what kind of help do you need?"

Victoria thinks for a moment and then points to her wilted style and replies, "Well, I don't know, I'm not really happy with it right now." Abe asks her if she is unhappy with the length or the style. She shakes her head no and then replies "I guess I need something that will help me get and keep body in my hair."

"You want something that will help you get and keep body in your hair?" asks Abe.

Victoria nods her head and says, "Yes, an hour after drying and curling my hair, it's flat again."

Abe grabs a couple of hair magazines from the counter and asks Victoria to find a photo that is closest to the finished look she desires. Once he sees her selection he says, "I see, you want a bit of height on top but not too much width at the temple area?" Victoria nods her head in agreement and Abe hands her a bottle of styling gel, which he explains is useful when styling her wet hair, and a can of super-hold hair spray, to use once her hair is dry to keep the look she desires perfect all day.

Victoria thanks him for listening to her and taking the time to recommend products for her specific needs. Victoria pays for the products and takes one of Abe's business cards before leaving the salon.

6. When Victoria first walked into the salon, what had she neglected to do?
   c. *collect her thoughts*
   Victoria entered the salon on impulse and hadn't really thought about what she would say or ask for. She hadn't gathered her thoughts and translated them into a question; rather, she felt an emotion—"I hate my hair"—and acted on the feeling without being ready to verbalize her needs.

7. When Victoria told Abe that she needed help with her hair, how did Abe help her to articulate her thoughts more clearly to him?
   d. *by asking her questions*
   An effective communication tool is to ask questions, especially if the person with whom you are communicating needs more time to gather her thoughts. By asking her questions, Abe was able to help Victoria pinpoint her thoughts, and then they were able to have an open and useful conversation.

8. How did Victoria clarify her desires to Abe?
   b. *by showing him a photo in a magazine*
   Sometimes the old adage is correct—a picture is worth a thousand words. By using the photo in the magazine, Victoria was able to quickly and clearly articulate to Abe what she was trying to achieve, and the result was a concise understanding.

9. When Abe describes the attributes of the style she has selected back to Victoria, he is using a technique called:
   c. *reflective listening*
   Using the reflective listening technique is a valuable tool for professional cosmetologists because it allows the two people in the communication exchange an opportunity to hear and get clarification on what is being said by the other.

10. Based on the exchange between Abe and Victoria, what is the outcome likely to be?
    d. *Victoria will return to the salon and request Abe's services.*
    Employing good communication skills is one of the best ways for a stylist to convey to a client that he or she is interested in the client's needs and willing and able to understand and accommodate those needs.

11. By going the extra mile to fully understand Victoria's needs, Abe was attempting to build a strong_____.
    a. *relationship*
    The outcome of any good communication exchange is either to begin a new relationship or to strengthen an existing one. Successful cosmetology careers are built on strong relationships between clients and their stylists.

Dennis is in the planning stages of opening a new, full-service salon that will offer hair, nail, and skin care service. As he works with his contractor to make the space usable for his needs, Dennis plans a consultation area that is separate and private from the styling and service areas of the salon. Once Dennis leaves his meeting with the contractor he begins to make a list of the things he will need to provide for the consultation space so he can prepare for the salon's opening.

Dennis has opted to use the intake form on the following page for all of his salon's client consultations. Use the form as a basis for answering the following questions.

12. Having clients fill in all of the questions pertaining to their address and other personal information allows Dennis's salon to:

b. *correctly identify each client*

Many people share the same last name and, since they may not be related or share the same household, having clients fill in all of the pertinent information is an easy way to differentiate them.

13. Knowing when the client last visited a salon will help the stylists in Dennis's salon to:

b. *assess the client's commitment to his or her style upkeep*

This is a crucial element to clients remaining satisfied with their look and ultimately their choice of salon. Stylists can use the record card and a client's style history to make recommendations for streamlining or adding to a client's routine to make the experience a positive and pleasant one.

14. Asking clients which services they have had in the previous year allows the salon to:

d. *determine clients' history and hair condition*

This is especially important for clients interested in having a chemical service on top of other chemical services they may have had previously. A stylist will want to know what other treatments a client has had so that she or he can best advise the client.

15. Why is it useful for Dennis to ask clients about the medications that they take?

c. *So he can assess the effect of the medication on their beauty regimen.*

Many times the medications a person takes won't have any effect on the cosmetology services being performed, but in some instances certain treatments may need to be altered or watched carefully. A person with high blood pressure, for example, should not be left under the hair dryer for an extended period of time.

16. Dennis requires clients to answer questions about their skin and nail care because:

a. *he is opening a full-service salon*

It is best for a salon to get all of the pertinent information about clients the first time they come into the salon and fill in their intake form. Since Dennis is opening a full-service salon, the likelihood that clients may have more than one type of service in the salon is great, so asking questions about their total cosmetology history is appropriate.

17. Why is it important for Dennis to know how often clients wash and condition their hair?

b. *So he can determine their hair care routine and suggest services that will work for them.*

Stylists become partners with their clients in the care of their hair, and in so doing, earn the right to know about clients' habits in order to recommend services and products that may be helpful and useful to them.

18. Asking clients about their allergies allows Dennis to:

c. *protect clients from products or services that may harm them*

Knowing about clients' allergies is vital information in the fight to keep clients safe from ingredients that could seriously harm them.

19. Which of the following is exactly the type of information Dennis's stylists should include in the Service Notes section of the intake form?

d. *any notes pertaining to the client's hair or its reaction during the service*

It is crucial for a stylist to note any and all reactions a client's hair and skin may have during a service. This information not only protects the client from any harm but may also protect the salon from liability.

Angie has been referred to Marshall by a friend who is one of Marshall's long-time clients. Angie loves the way he cuts and styles her friend's hair and she is eager to meet Marshall and have him cut and style her hair. Angie shows up on time for her appointment. When she arrives at the salon, she finds a lot of people and confusion in the reception area, and, since she has never visited this salon before, she is unsure of what to do. Angie approaches the reception desk and tells the person seated behind the desk her name and the name of the stylist she has an appointment with. The receptionist nods her head and turns her back to Angie to answer the telephone. Angie sits down and waits for Marshall. A few minutes go by and a young woman comes down to the waiting area, picks up a slip of paper and calls Angie's name, then turns and goes toward the shampoo area. Angie stands up but the young woman is already gone. Angie again approaches the reception desk and asks what she should do. The receptionist tells her to follow the woman, who is Marshall's assistant, to the shampoo station so she can be shampooed and prepared for Marshall. Angie rushes across the styling floor and finally sits down in a shampoo chair. After her hair is shampooed, Angie is led to a styling station and told to sit down. Another couple of minutes pass when finally a young man walks over to Angie. He begins to towel-dry her hair and says "What can I do for you today?" Angie, confused, asks if he is Marshall. He smiles and sarcastically replies, "Well, I was when I got in here this morning!"

20. Based on this scenario, Angie's first impression of the salon staff is likely to be that they are:

b. *disorganized and too confused to make a new client feel comfortable*

It is easy for a stylist who has been working in a salon for a long time to forget what it is like to be a newcomer, just as Marshall did here. He was so caught up in the day's activities that he overlooked the feelings of a new client, and he didn't take an important opportunity to welcome her to the salon and make her feel comfortable.

21. How should Marshall's assistant have greeted Angie?

b. *with a smile and a handshake*

Marshall's assistant was representing Marshall and the salon when she approached the new client, so she should have greeted Angie and made her feel welcomed and important.

22. When Angie arrived at the salon and checked in, what should the receptionist have offered to do?

c. *give her a tour of the salon*

Even though she was busy, once she had handled whatever task she was working on at the reception desk when Angie walked in, the receptionist should have turned her attention to the new client. The receptionist should have greeted Angie, welcomed her, and then offered to give her a tour of the salon.

23. Although the salon was obviously busy, what could Marshall's assistant have done to help direct Angie?

b. *waited for Angie to get up and accompany her to the shampoo area*

First, the assistant should have been told that Angie was a client new to the salon and that the receptionist had not had the opportunity to greet her properly or show her around. Then, with that insight, the assistant should have taken it upon herself to properly introduce Angie to the salon, its layout, and the staff, and, at the very least, wait for and accompany her to the shampoo area.

24. What should have been the first thing that Marshall said to Angie when he approached her?

a. *"Hi, my name is Marshall. Welcome to the salon."*

Marshall should have begun the conversation with Angie exactly the way he would begin any conversation—by introducing himself to her and by being genuinely happy to meet her.

It's a particularly busy day at the Newmark Salon, where Susan works as a nail tech. Today a loyal salon client, Kim, has several appointments scheduled, beginning with a manicure appointment at 1 p.m. After the manicure she is scheduled for an eyebrow waxing at 1:45 p.m. and a haircut at 2 p.m. Susan is booked with appointments all day long, and at 1:20 Kim still hasn't arrived. Susan decides to start her next client, Mrs. Trevino. At 1:30 Kim comes into the salon. When she is told by the receptionist, Patti, that she is late for her nail appointment, Kim argues that she made the appointment for 1:30 and is on time.

25. Patti should handle the scheduling mix up by:

d. *apologizing for the mix up and offering to reschedule the appointment*

Whether the client is correct or not, Patti's priority is to make the client feel important and to accommodate her needs. The best way to do this is to end the conversation about who is right and move on to when best to get the services scheduled.

26. If Kim insists that she needs her nail appointment today, what can Patti do to accommodate her request?

b. *check with Susan and reschedule Kim for an appointment at the end of the day*

When a client has an urgent need, it is best to find a way to accommodate her as quickly as possible to avoid hard feelings. Even if the nail tech has a long day or plans after her shift is scheduled to end, knowing that a client needs her may be enough incentive to make some changes that accommodate the client and end the problem.

27. In regard to Kim's remaining appointments, the salon should:

a. *be able to accommodate Kim's eyebrow waxing and haircut appointments as scheduled*

Kim's other appointments should be honored exactly as they were scheduled, and, if possible, may present an opportunity to switch times to accommodate the manicure appointment that was missed.

28. If Kim is upset about not being able to have her nail service immediately, Patti should refer her to:

d. *the salon's late policy*

It's always better for the sake of the client–salon relationship to handle a scheduling mix-up as quickly as possible, but if there continues to be an issue with the appointment, Patti can mention the salon's policy about missed appointments and then, again, offer to resolve the issue as soon as is feasible.

29. What could the salon easily do to confirm appointments for clients the evening before their appointments?

b. *call clients and confirm appointments*

It's an excellent policy to call clients the evening before their appointment to remind them of the type of service they have booked and the time the appointment is scheduled for. This also reminds clients to call the salon in case they have to cancel or reschedule the appointment.

Teneka has just cut Mrs. Mendez's hair for the first time. She felt that she really understood Mrs. Mendez's directions and requests but, now that she has completed the cut and blowdry service, her client is very unhappy about the service and has begun to cry. Teneka is understandably nervous and upset but she knows that she must address Mrs. Mendez's concerns quickly so as not to upset other salon clients.

30. Where is the best place for Teneka to have the conversation with Mrs. Mendez about what is wrong?

d. *in the consultation area*

Finding a private place to discuss the issues surrounding Mrs. Mendez's concerns is the best way to calm the client down and to allow the stylist a moment to regroup. The consultation area is also a private area and conducive to having an emotionally charged conversation out of earshot of the other clients in the salon.

31. Which of the following questions most closely resembles a question that Teneka should be asking Mrs. Mendez?

c. *"What specifically don't you like about the style?"*

Teneka needs to get clarification from Mrs. Mendez about her thoughts and feelings regarding the style and the best way to do this is by asking her client specific questions about the style.

32. If Teneka is able to determine from Mrs. Mendez that she would prefer more layers cut into the style, what should Teneka do?

d. *schedule Mrs. Mendez for the next available appointment and re-cut her hair*

At the earliest possible opportunity, Teneka should make the time to re-cut Mrs. Mendez's hair and use that time to mend the miscommunication and attempt to salvage the client-stylist relationship.

33. In the areas around the head where the hair is already too short and more layers can't be cut into the style, Teneka must:

c. *honestly tell the client that they cannot be reshaped*

It is very important for Teneka to be as polite and as sympathetic to Mrs. Mendez as she can be, but she must also be completely honest with her about every aspect of the haircut as well. If Teneka has any chance of mending her relationship with this client, she will need to be as open and up front as she can be.

34. If Teneka is not able to determine the source of Mrs. Mendez's dissatisfaction and they are not able to come to an amiable resolution, Teneka should:

a. *call upon her manager or a senior stylist for help and advice*

Sometimes when there is a dispute between a client and a stylist, it's best to get an objective person to help and advise both parties. If Teneka is unable to please Mrs. Mendez, then calling upon her manager or a senior stylist may be just what it takes to calm the client and allow the manager or senior stylist to aid her in satisfying Mrs. Mendez and rebuilding the relationship.

35. How can Teneka use this experience to grow as a professional stylist?

a. *She can use the feedback to improve her service for the next client.*

Although difficult and even unpleasant, Teneka should discuss this situation with her salon manager and/or mentor and ask them for honest and constructive feedback. Every stylist has encountered a similar situation in his or her career and can very likely offer Teneka good advice.

Sandy has just joined the Master Hair Salon where Bonnie and Stacy have been working for more than a year. Recently while Stacy was on vacation, Bonnie serviced one of her long-time clients and gave her some advice about her haircolor that differed from the advice Stacy had given her and that satisfied the client more with her color service than she had been previously. Now the client has become a regular client of Bonnie's, and Stacy has accused Bonnie of deliberately trying to steal her clients away. The argument has turned ugly in that each is gossiping about the other to their salon coworkers and clients, and the stress of this ongoing feud has caused a lot of tension in the salon. As the new person, Sandy has been approached by each stylist and now must decide how to proceed in this environment.

36. Sandy's best course of action is to:

b. *treat both stylists respectfully and fairly*

While there may be lots of reasons why certain stylists do or do not get along, Sandy needs to stay out of the argument and remain neutral. By showing both Bonnie and Stacy respect and by treating them fairly and without judgment, Sandy makes a statement about her integrity.

37. When asked whose side Sandy believes she should:

d. *remain neutral*

Sandy's best answer would have to be something like, "Since I wasn't involved in the situation, I really have no opinion one way or the other." This makes the statement that she is serious about remaining neutral.

38. If pushed into the conflict, what should Sandy say to Bonnie and Stacy?

d. *"I like you both and don't want to be involved in your argument."*

If she is really pushed into it, Sandy must take a clear and concise stand on where she is with her feelings about getting into the middle of someone else's argument. She needn't judge either of the stylists, and answering their question in this manner states that simply yet effectively.

39. If Sandy continues to feel pressured about taking a side, her best course of action is to ask _____ for help in resolving the matter.

b. *her salon manager*

Anything that happens in the salon, especially something such as an argument where people are pressured into taking sides, is the responsibility of the salon manager. If Sandy cannot resolve this issue on her own, she always has a resource in her salon manager.

40. If Sandy is feeling victimized about the pressure to get involved in the salon conflict, she may feel tempted to discuss it with other salon staff which would be:

b. *detrimental to maintaining a professional relationship at work*

Gossiping or discussing private details of any situation at work is a bad idea, even in a case such as this one. If Sandy is feeling like she needs someone to talk with, she should choose to confide in someone other than a salon staffer—such as a friend or mentor—to get some of her frustrations out so that her feelings don't have an impact on her work life.

It's October and Bruce realizes that he will be having a meeting with his manager Jackie for his annual employee performance evaluation. He hopes to hear that he is doing well at the salon and to discuss some thoughts and ideas he has with Jackie as well. One thing on Bruce's mind is the construction that is occurring in front of the salon and how he feels that it is discouraging the salon's walk-in business. Another issue he hopes to discuss is the flex-time policy the salon has adopted, because he isn't sure how it should be affecting the late-evening shift that he usually ends up working alone. And finally, he wants to talk with Jackie about the possibility of working toward a promotion to assistant manager of the salon.

41. In preparation for the evaluation meeting, Bruce should think about and make a list including:

c. *problems and possible solutions*

Bruce will want to be open with his salon manager when he has a performance evaluation, but he must remember that she cannot solve every problem each person has. Therefore, Bruce should think about possible solutions to the problems he sees. This approach shows Bruce to be a proactive and motivated employee.

42. When discussing the issue of the construction outside of the salon and its effect on the salon's walk-in business, Bruce should:

d. *suggest some ideas for how to work around the inconvenience of the construction*

The issue of the construction is likely to be a problem for the entire salon. If Bruce can suggest some possible solutions for working around it, he proves that he is a thinker, a leader, and someone who is worth looking to when an opportunity for management opens up.

43. When discussing the flex-time policy and the fact that he is often left at the salon alone in the evening, Bruce needs to:

d. *ask for an explanation of the policy and how it affects the evening shift*

While Bruce may feel taken advantage of by other stylists who may abuse the flex-time policy, it would be detrimental to his relationship with his manager and coworkers, and to his opportunity for promotion, to simply go into his meeting and tattle on the other stylists. Instead he should get clarification on the policy and then, if he is working with someone who he feels is abusing the policy, speak with him or her about it directly first before involving the salon manager.

44. When discussing any opportunities there may be for promotion, Bruce will need to be prepared to hear:

b. *the areas that he will need to improve on order to be considered for a promotion*

Anyone who is interested in becoming a manager must also be willing to improve his or her own skills and must be able to demonstrate that willingness to the salon staff. Since, as a manager, Bruce may be responsible for giving other employees feedback, he will only be able to do this compassionately if he also learns how to receive feedback in order to be a good example to his coworkers.

45. If Bruce is serious about working toward a promotion, he will want to ask Jackie:

a. *when they can come together again to discuss his progress*

If it's really important to Bruce, he will be motivated to follow-up with his manager and to work on improving in those areas she outlines to him. While she may be willing to work with and train him for management, his progress will not be her most important priority, so Bruce will need to do his own follow-up.

46. Once the evaluation is completed, Bruce should _____ Jackie.

a. *thank*

Preparing an employee evaluation and fairly delivering that evaluation is as much work as being evaluated, if not more, so it would be polite for Bruce to express his gratitude to Jackie for her time and help.

CHAPTER 5 Infection Control: Principles and Practices

Adam is a new employee at the Spiral Curl Salon. Adam will begin as an assistant and, once he is licensed, he will graduate to a junior stylist. On his first day of work his salon mentor, Mary, takes him on a tour of the salon, pointing out the various areas that will be his responsibility as they walk through the salon. Adam will have many duties; the most important of these will be to help keep the salon cleaned, disinfected, and safe for both the clients and the stylists.

1. Mary explains to Adam that _____, a federal agency, regulates and enforces safety and health standards to protect employees in the workplace.

c. *OSHA*

The Occupational Safety and Health Administration (OSHA) was created as part of the U.S. Department of Labor to regulate and enforce safety and health standards in order to protect employees in the workplace. Regulating employee exposure to potentially toxic substances and informing employees about the possible hazards of materials used in the workplace are key points of the Occupational Safety and Health Act of 1970.

2. Adams asks what is specifically addressed in these standards.

b. *issues relating to the handling, mixing, storing, and disposing of products used in cosmetology services*

OSHA standards address issues relating to the handling, mixing, storing, and disposing of products; general safety in the workplace; and your right to know about any potentially hazardous ingredients contained in the products you use and how to avoid these hazards.

3. Adam sees a binder on the counter in the salon dispensary labeled *MSDS* and asks Mary what that is for. Mary explains that MSDS are:

c. *Material Safety Data Sheet*

Both federal and state laws require that manufacturers supply a Material Safety Data Sheet (MSDS) for all products sold.

4. Mary further explains that MSDS contain information on:
   a. *product safety*
   The MSDS contains information compiled by the manufacturer about product safety, including the names of hazardous ingredients, safe handling and use procedures, precautions to reduce the risk of accidental harm or overexposure, and flammability warnings. The MSDS also provides useful disposal guidelines and medical and first aid information.

5. Adam asks Mary where MSDS come from. She responds that they come from:
   b. *product manufacturers who provide them for free*
   Federal and state laws require salons to obtain MSDSs from the product manufacturers and/or distributors for each professional product that is used. MSDSs often can be downloaded from the product manufacturer's or the distributor's Web site. Not having MSDSs available poses a health risk to anyone exposed to hazardous materials and violates federal and state regulations.

6. Mary tells Adam that if a state inspector comes into the salon he or she will look for a _____, which verifies that all of the salon employees have read the information on the MSDS.
   d. *sign-off sheet with employee signatures*
   All employees must read the information included on each MSDS and verify that they have read it by adding their signatures to a sign-off sheet for the product. These sign-off sheets must be available to state and federal inspectors upon request

7. Adam is reminded that there are two types of disinfectant products and that they:
   a. *destroy all bacteria, fungi, and viruses (but not spores) on surfaces*
   Disinfectants are chemical products that destroy all bacteria, fungi, and viruses (but not spores) on surfaces. The two types that are used in salons are hospital disinfectants and tuberculocidal disinfectants.

8. Adam reads the label on the two types of disinfectants in the salon dispensary and is reminded that, in case someone is accidentally cut and blood is present, a _____ must be used to clean the styling station and tools.
   c. *hospital disinfectant*
   Hospital disinfectants are effective for cleaning blood and body fluids. They can be used on any nonporous surface in the salon.

9. Mary explains to Adam the daily cleaning and disinfecting procedure the salon uses. Mary tells him that each time he cleans and disinfects an area of the salon, he needs to enter it into the salon:

   b. *logbook*

   Salons should always follow manufacturers' recommended schedules for cleaning and disinfecting tools and implements, disinfecting foot spas and basins, scheduling regular service visits for equipment, and replacing parts when needed. Although your state may not require you to keep a logbook of all equipment usage, cleaning, disinfecting, testing, and maintenance, it may be advisable to keep one. Showing your logbook to clients provides them with peace of mind and confidence in your ability to protect them from infection and disease.

Mark and Caryn both work at the Solé Salon and Spa and their stations are right next to one another. Mark's daughter Maureen was diagnosed with strep throat and was home from school sick for several days. The following week both Caryn and one of Mark's clients, Jane, are also diagnosed with strep throat after seeing Mark for a haircut.

10. Mark appears to be spreading a(n):

    a. *infectious disease*

    An infectious disease is caused by pathogenic (harmful) organisms that enter the body. An infectious disease may or may not be spread from one person to another person.

11. What should Mark and his salon be doing to prevent the spread of his daughter's illness?

    c. *cleaning and disinfecting the tools, equipment, and surfaces*

    Cleaning and disinfecting procedures are designed to prevent the spread of infection and disease. Cleaning is a mechanical process (of scrubbing) using soap and water or detergent and water to remove all visible dirt, debris, and many disease-causing germs from tools, implements, and equipment. The process of disinfection destroys most, but not necessarily all, harmful organisms on environmental surfaces.

12. Disinfectants used in the salon should be:

    a. *bactericidal, virucidal, and fungicidal*

    Disinfectants used in salons must be bactericidal, capable of destroying bacteria; virucidal, capable of destroying viruses; and fungicidal, capable of destroying fungi. Be sure to mix and use these disinfectants according to the instructions on the labels so they are safe and effective.

13. Mark appears to be spreading bacteria called:

b. *streptococci*

Streptococci are pus-forming bacteria arranged in curved lines resembling a string of beads. They cause infections such as strep throat and blood poisoning.

14. How might Caryn have been exposed to the bacteria that caused her strep throat?

b. *by breathing the same air as Mark*

Streptococci rarely are able to move about on their own, rather the bacteria are transmitted in the air, in dust, or within any substance in which they settle. By being in a confined space, Caryn could easily have contracted the bacteria from Mark by breathing the air he exhaled.

15. Bacteria that are disease-causing are called:

a. *pathogenic*

Pathogenic bacteria are harmful bacteria that can cause disease when they invade plant or animal tissue.

16. Strep throat is:

d. *an infection*

An infection occurs when body tissues are invaded by disease-causing bacteria, such as streptococci.

17. When Caryn looks inside her mouth she can see _____, which indicates that she has an infection.

c. *pus*

Pus is a fluid product of inflammation and white blood cells and the debris of dead cells, tissue elements, and bacteria. Its presence indicates infection.

18. A disease that can spread from Maureen to Mark to Caryn is said to be:

b. *communicable*

A contagious disease, one that can be passed from person to person, is considered to be communicable. As cosmetologists, Mark and Caryn must be very aware that they could potentially expose clients and coworkers to disease and that they must take action to protect the public from the disease.

Three of the five nail clients Thomas has seen today have a strange yellow-green spot just under one of their nails. His first client of the day, Marci, has the spot on her large toe, which Thomas noticed while giving her a pedicure. Gina has a similar spot under a nail enhancement on her left hand, and Bonita has a spot on a fingernail on her right hand. Marci is a waitress and likes to take good care of her feet. She has been a loyal pedicure client of Thomas's for the past five years. Gina, a swimming instructor, is a tried and true nail client, coming into the salon every two weeks for a monomer liquid and polymer powder fill-in. She has worn these nail enhancements for the last three years. Bonita, a schoolteacher, is a natural nail client who has a manicure and pedicure about once a month. When Thomas attempts to wipe away the discolored area he is unable to.

19. What is the yellow-green spot that Thomas has detected likely to be?

c. *fungi*

Fungi are microscopic plant parasites that include molds, mildews, and yeasts. They can produce contagious diseases, such as ringworm.

20. Why can't Thomas remove the yellow-green spots he sees?

a. *because they are a disease*

A disease is not topical—sitting on top of the nail—and therefore cannot simply be wiped away.

21. How could the fungus have been brought into the salon?

b. *Gina may have had moisture trapped under a nail.*

A very common source of nail fungus is moisture that may become trapped and caught under a nail enhancement.

22. How could the fungus have spread from one client to another?

a. *improper disinfection of manicure implements*

If an implement comes into contact with a fungus and then is not cleaned and disinfected properly before being used on someone else, it may cause spread of the fungus.

Each year Lucille and Frank, who are the co-owners of the Serious Skin Care Center, take many precautions to ward off becoming ill during the cold and flu season. Frank makes it a habit to go to the doctor each year and to get a flu shot, because he knows that if he doesn't he will undoubtedly get a cold or flu at some point during the season. Lucille, on the other hand, makes a concentrated effort to take extra note of the vitamins she takes, to get a little extra sleep and relaxation, and to be sure to wash her hands frequently throughout the day, especially after servicing each client.

23. Both Lucille and Frank are attempting to enhance their _____ to disease.

   a. *immunity*

   Immunity is the ability of the body to ward off disease that has gained entrance to the body.

24. Frank's flu shot is considered to be:

   d. *an acquired immunity*

   An acquired immunity is an immunity that the body develops after it overcomes a disease or after a vaccination.

25. Lucille's ability to stave off the flu by taking excellent care of herself is an example of someone with:

   a. *a natural immunity*

   Someone with a natural immunity has partly developed immunity through hygienic living and has also probably inherited an inclination toward immunity.

Jason is the new salon manager for the Good Looks Salon and he is very concerned with the cleanliness of the salon and with preventing the spread of disease. In order to assess how the salon is doing in its efforts to control the spread of harmful disease and to make recommendations to his styling staff, Jason is about to review the salon's cleaning and disinfecting practices with the cleaning crew that has been hired to clean the salon each week. Ginger is the crew's supervisor, and she tells Jason that the salon is regularly cleaned and then disinfected with chemical disinfectants. Ginger also mentions that the cleaning crew follows all of the manufacturer's directions for use of each of these cleaning and disinfecting agents and they follow OSHA guidelines.

26. In order to remove the pathogens and other substances that linger on the surfaces of the salon and on implements, the salon must be willing to:

   a. *decontaminate*

   Decontamination is the removal of pathogens and other substances from surfaces and tools.

27. When Ginger's crew disinfects the salon they are using chemical agents to destroy bacteria and viruses on:

   b. *surfaces and equipment*

   Disinfectants are used only on tools and surfaces and never on human skin because their strong chemicals can damage skin.

28. When Ginger considers the types of products for the crew to use, she must first decide if the product has the correct _____ for getting the job accomplished.

c. *efficacy*

A product's efficacy refers to its effectiveness at achieving the required results.

29. The cleaning crew may use a quat because it is:

d. *effective for disinfecting implements*

Quats, short for quaternary ammonium compounds, are a type of disinfectant usually used to disinfect implements. Implements should be removed from the solution after the specified period, rinsed (if required), dried, and stored in a clean, covered container.

30. Jason can require the salon's stylists to use a _____ for disinfecting salon tools.

a. *phenol disinfectant*

A phenol disinfectant is a powerful tuberculocidal disinfectant with a very high pH. Phenolic disinfectants are a form of formaldehyde, have a very high pH, and can damage the skin and eyes. Phenolic disinfectants can be harmful to the environment if put down the drain. They have been used reliably over the years to disinfect salon tools; however, phenol can damage plastic and rubber and can cause certain metals to rust. Phenolic disinfectants should never be used to disinfect pedicure tubs or equipment. Extra care should be taken to avoid skin contact with phenolic disinfectants. Phenolics are known carcinogens.

31. The cleaning crew's ability to decontaminate is limited mainly to the practice of:

a. *cleaning tools, surfaces, and implements with liquid soap, rinsing them in clean water, and disinfecting them*

Since most salons do not yet use sterilization as a means of decontaminating, the salon must always be sure to clean with liquid soap and water, rinse, and disinfect tools, surfaces, and equipment between use on each client.

32. For multiuse tools and implements the cleaning crew must:

c. *clean and disinfect them after use*

Every multiuse tool and implement must be thoroughly cleaned and disinfected before use on another client. Not doing so puts you and your clients at risk of contracting contagious diseases.

Keith is a busy cutter at Martin's Salon and Spa. In between each client he quickly rinses his combs and brushes with warm water and drops them into a disinfecting solution. Keith allows them to become saturated and then reaches into the jar, pulls the implements out, and wipes them dry with a towel and places them on his roll-about so he can access them easily before the next client is finished being shampooed and is delivered to his station by his assistant.

33. Before immersing his implements into the disinfecting solution, Keith should have:

b. *cleaned them with soap and water*

Before putting soiled implements into a jar of disinfectant, Keith should wash them thoroughly with soap and water and rinse them.

34. To protect himself, Keith should wear _____ when working with disinfecting solution.

d. *gloves*

It is important to wear gloves while disinfecting nonelectrical tools and implements to protect your hands from unintentional contact with the disinfectant and to prevent possible contamination of the implements by your hands.

35. How should Keith mix the disinfecting solution?

c. *according to the manufacturer's guidelines*

All too often professionals do not take the time to read the manufacturer's directions for how to mix and properly use disinfectants. Their unwillingness to do so may cause the mixture to be ineffectual, and therefore they will not truly be disinfecting as they thought they were.

36. How long should Keith's implements be immersed in the disinfecting solution?

c. *as long as the directions recommend*

Again, by not following the manufacturer's directions, people using the disinfectant solution may not achieve the desired results if they remove implements from the solution too quickly. Furthermore, they will not prevent any additional spread of disease by leaving their implements in the solution longer than recommended.

37. After the implements have been removed from the disinfecting solution, Keith should:

b. *rinse, dry, and place them in a clean, covered container*

Storing or placing implements or tools in anything but a clean, dry, disinfected container will only serve to infect them again.

While cutting his client's hair, Mitch accidentally nicks his finger and his cut begins to bleed. He knows that he must follow the Universal Precautions for an exposure incident.

38. The first thing Mitch should do is:

c. *stop the service and notify his client*

Once there is a presence of blood, stop the service immediately and inform your client that you have been cut or that you have nicked her.

39. Mitch asks Jan, one of his colleagues, for help. She immediately retrieves:

b. *the salon's first aid kit*

Every salon should have a fully stocked first aid kit available. The kit should be placed in the same location at all times so that everyone knows where it is and can retrieve it when needed.

40. What should Jan be wearing while she cleans Mitch's cut with an antiseptic wipe and bandages his cut once the bleeding has stopped?

c. *gloves*

Jan should immediately put on a pair of gloves to protect herself from coming into contact with the blood and to protect Mitch from coming into contact with any contaminants Jan may have on her hands.

41. Mitch should now put on gloves and:

c. *clean and disinfect his styling station with a disinfectant designed for cleaning blood and body fluids*

Mitch must clean his styling station and then use the appropriate type of disinfectant to disinfect his station and to prevent the chance that his blood contaminated these surfaces and could potentially contaminate another person.

42. Mitch will need to discard all of his contaminated single-use implements and materials by:

d. *double bagging them and putting a biohazard sticker on the bag before putting it into a container for contaminated waste*

Discard all contaminated single-use objects such as wipes or cotton balls by double-bagging (place the waste in a plastic bag and then in a trash bag). Place a biohazard sticker (red or orange) on the bag, and deposit the bag into a container for contaminated waste.

43. Mitch will need to make sure that all multiuse tools and implements that have come into contact with blood or other body fluids are thoroughly cleaned and completely immersed in a(n)_____ designed for cleaning blood and body fluids or 10 percent bleach solution.

c. *EPA-registered disinfecting solution*

Make sure that all multiuse tools and implements that have come into contact with blood or other body fluids are thoroughly cleaned and completely immersed in an EPA-registered disinfectant solution designed for cleaning blood and body fluids, a 10 percent bleach solution for at least ten minutes, or for the time recommended by the manufacturer.

44. Mitch's multiuse tools and implements must be immersed in the solution for at least _____or for the time recommended by the manufacturer.

b. *10 minutes*

Always follow the manufacturer's directions for mixing and using disinfecting solutions of any kind.

45. Before returning to the client and resuming the service, Mitch should:

a. *wash and dry his hands and rebandage his cut*

Mitch should wash his hands using the proper hand washing procedure, dry his hands thoroughly, rebandage his cut, and, as long as his bleeding has stopped, he may proceed with the service.

Heather has just hired a new pedicurist, Allie, who has finished her training and is eager to start work at her very first salon job. Heather gives Allie a quick tour of the salon and then instructs Allie on where the salon's disinfectants are stored and on how to disinfect the foot spas that are used for pedicure clients. Heather gives Allie instructions on how and when to clean and disinfect the foot baths.

46. Heather instructs Allie to _____ after each client.

b. *scrub all visible residue from the inside walls of the basin*

The foot basin must be scrubbed to remove all visible residue from the inside walls of the basin with a clean, disinfected brush and liquid soap and clean, warm water. Use a clean, disinfected brush with a handle. Brushes must be cleaned and disinfected after each use.

47. Next, Heather explains that Allie will need to refill the basin, making sure that the water level covers the jets and circulate the correct amount of _____ disinfectant, according to the manufacturer's directions.

c. *EPA-registered*

Refill the basin with enough clean, warm water to cover the jets and circulate the correct amount (as indicated in the mixing instructions on the label) of the EPA-registered disinfectant specified by the manufacturer through the basin for ten minutes or for the time recommended by the manufacturer.

48. At the end of each day, Heather tells Allie that she will need to:

d. *remove the screen and clean the debris trapped behind it*

Clean the screen and other removable parts and the areas behind them with a clean, disinfected brush and liquid soap and clean, warm water to remove all visible residue. Replace the properly cleaned screen and other removable parts.

49. At the end of the day, Allie should use an EPA-registered disinfectant and circulate it through the basin for _____ minutes.

c. *ten minutes*

At the end of the day, the basin is filled with an EPA-registered disinfectant and is circulated through the basin for ten minutes, or the time recommended by the manufacturer, then drained and rinsed.

50. Heather tells Allie that at least once a week she will need to fill the foot spa tub with an EPA-registered disinfectant solution, circulate it, and then let the solution sit:

c. *overnight*

This solution should sit in the foot spa tub overnight and then, in the morning, before customers come in for service, the tub should be drained and the system should be flushed with clear, clean water.

CHAPTER 6 General Anatomy and Physiology

Malik has been feeling ill for quite some time when he finally decides to go to a doctor. The doctor performs a number of tests, and diagnoses Malik with a disease that affects his cells' ability to remain healthy and reproduce.

1. Malik's cells contain _____, a colorless, jelly-like substance in which food elements and water are present.
  b. *protoplasm*
  Malik's cells and the cells of all living things are composed of protoplasm, which can be compared to the white of a raw egg.

2. The nucleus of Malik's cells plays a vital role in:
  c. *reproduction*
  The nucleus is dense, active protoplasm found in the center of the cell and it also plays a significant role in metabolism.

3. If Malik's cells are unable to repair themselves, the problem most likely lies in the cells':
  d. *cytoplasm*
  The cytoplasm is all of the protoplasm of a cell except the nucleus and is the watery fluid that contains the food material necessary for growth, reproduction, and self-repair.

4. The two phases of metabolism that Malik's cells undergo are:
  c. *catabolism and anabolism*
  Anabolism is the constructive part of metabolism; it is the act of building up larger molecules from smaller ones. Catabolism is the phase that involves the breaking down of complex compounds within cells into smaller ones.

In her training, Robin is studying the body's tissues and their uses. Since tissues are a collection of similar cells that all perform a particular function, Robin, in her work as an esthetician, knows that she will need to be aware of their effect on her clients, especially during services such as facials and massages.

5. The _____ tissue is responsible for supporting, protecting, and binding together other tissues of the body.
  c. *connective*
  Some examples of connective tissue are bone, cartilage, ligament, and fat or adipose tissue.

6. The tissue that carries food, waste, and hormones through the body is called:
   b. *liquid*
   Liquid tissue such as blood and lymph carry vital elements and by-products through the body.

7. As a skin care specialist, Robin will be very interested in the epithelial tissue since it includes the:
   c. *skin*
   The epithelial tissue is a protective covering on body surfaces and includes skin, mucous membranes, and the lining of the heart and digestive and respiratory organs.

8. When giving a facial massage, Robin will be coming into contact with the _____ system:
   d. *muscular*
   Muscular tissue contracts and moves various parts of the body.

9. When facial clients realize that they feel relaxed and calm as a result of Robin's facial manipulations, it will be because the _____ tissues are carrying those messages from the brain to the rest of the body.
   a. *nerve*
   Nerve tissues not only carry messages to and from the brain, they are also responsible for the coordination and control of all bodily functions.

Richard is losing his hair and realizes that for many reasons, especially esthetic reasons, he wants to do whatever he can to naturally slow the process down. He speaks with his dermatologist, who advises him to massage the top of his head, especially the areas where he sees the most hair loss, to eat a balanced diet, and to stop drinking soft drinks and to replace them with plenty of water. His doctor also suggests that Richard begin taking long walks in the park and that he take time to sit in a peaceful place and breathe in the clean air. Richard also realizes that because his skin is so dry he should use a moisturizer to avoid skin breakage and cracking.

10. When Richard is advised to massage his scalp, the doctor's intention is to increase Richard's blood circulation, which is a function of the:
    c. *heart*
    The heart is responsible for all of the body's blood circulation, and by gently massaging his scalp Richard is increasing the blood flow to that area.

11. Drinking plenty of water will allow Richard's body to eliminate waste products through the work of the:

    a. *kidneys*

    The kidneys are responsible for eliminating excess water and waste from the body. Drinking plenty of water helps the kidneys to have enough fluids to healthfully excrete waste and toxins when needed.

12. Supplying oxygen to the blood is the work of Richard's:

    c. *lungs*

    Oxygen in the bloodstream helps the cells of the body to perform their functions.

13. Using a cream or lotion will moisturize Richard's skin, which is responsible for:

    d. *forming an external protective covering for the body*

    The skin is the organ that completely encloses and encases the body and all of its organs.

Billy volunteers his time and his talent one day a week by going to a nearby nursing home and helping the residents by servicing their hair and beauty needs. Many of the residents at the home have very serious health problems. While Billy knows he should never try to treat the patients, he is aware of the symptoms of their illnesses, and able to notify the nurse on duty to watch out for the patients' well-being. On his schedule today are Mrs. Hammil, Mrs. Boxing, and Mrs. Reyper, all of whom want hair services.

14. While setting her hair, Billy notices that Mrs. Hammil's legs and ankles are swollen, which indicates that her _____ system is not working properly.

    d. *excretory*

    The excretory system which consists of the kidneys, liver, skin, intestines, and lungs purifies the body by elimination of waste matter. Swollen legs indicate that Mrs. Hammil's body may be holding onto fluid instead of releasing it and the waste it contains.

15. Mrs. Boxing has difficulty controlling the position of her head during her service; she is experiencing difficulty with her:

    b. *muscular system*

    The muscular system covers, shapes, and supports the skeletal tissue, and it contracts and moves parts of the body.

16. During her perm Mrs. Reyper sounds like she is having difficulty breathing. This is the work of the:
    d. *respiratory system*
    The respiratory system enables the body to breathe, which supplies oxygen to the body and eliminates carbon dioxide as waste product.

David is a businessman with a very stressful job. He has an appointment with Christy for a haircut and he decides to add on a scalp and head massage before his haircut. David complains of head and neck aches to Christy and tells her that he isn't sleeping as comfortably as he would like to be.

17. In the first part of the massage, Christy will begin at the crown and work her way down to the _____, which is above the nape.
    d. *occipital bone*
    The occipital bone is the hindmost bone of the skull, below the parietal bones. It forms the back of the skull, above the nape.

18. The muscle that Christy will be massaging when she works on David's crown and occipital area is the:
    b. *occipitalis*
    The occipitalis is in the back of the epicranius and is the muscle that draws the scalp backward.

19. The bone that forms David's forehead is called the:
    b. *frontal*
    The frontal bone is the large bone across the front, upper part of the face.

20. The muscle that allows David to raise his eyebrows is the:
    a. *frontalis*
    The frontalis is the anterior portion of the epicranius. It is the muscle of the scalp that raises the eyebrows, draws the scalp forward, and causes wrinkles across the forehead.

21. The bones that are at David's temples are the:
    c. *temporal bones*
    The temporal bones are the bones that form the sides of the head in the ear region.

22. To relieve his neck aches, Christy suggests that David sleep with a soft pillow to support the seven bones of his:
   c. *cervical vertebrae*
   The cervical vertebrae are the seven bones that form the top portion of the vertebral column located in the neck.

23. The muscles that allow David to lower and rotate his head are the:
   d. *sternocleidomastoideus*
   These are the muscles of the lower neck and they rotate the head.

Betty has been told time and time again by her clients that the best part of the manicure is the hand and arm massage. Today she takes extra time with Pam, an administrative assistant who spends a lot of time on her computer; Betty takes special care of Pam's fingers and wrists.

24. When Betty massages Pam's fingers, the muscles responsible for separating the fingers are the:
   c. *abductors*
   Abductors are the muscles that separate the fingers, and massaging them often provides relief from stiffness and fatigue.

25. By massaging Pam's fingers Betty will be concentrating on the bones of the:
   c. *phalanges*
   The phalanges are the bones in the fingers. There are three phalanges in each finger and two in the thumb.

26. Because of her work, Pam is in danger of having pain in her_____, which is the result of repetitive movement.
   b. *carpus*
   The carpus is in the wrist. It is a flexible joint composed of a group of eight small, irregular bones held together by ligaments.

27. When massaging the palm of Pam's hand, Betty would come into contact with the:
   d. *metacarpus*
   The metacarpus in the palm of the hand consists of five bones between the carpus and phalanges.

28. Betty finishes Pam's treatment by massaging her upper arm, also called the:
   b. *humerus*
   The humerus is the uppermost and largest bone of the arm extending from the elbow to the shoulder.

29. The muscle that allows Pam to rotate her palm outward is the:

a. *supinator*

The supinator is the muscle that allows the forearm to rotate back and forth.

Alma is a middle-aged facial client of the Skin Deep Salon and she asks her esthetician, Cindy, what she can do to help her tone and maintain the muscles of her face. Alma points out that she has noticed her skin starting to wrinkle, especially around her mouth, eyes, and nose and says, sarcastically, that she wants to remain looking as young as she can without having cosmetic surgery. Cindy explains that there are several muscles in those areas that could benefit from gentle massage.

30. The muscle in Alma's forehead that is responsible for vertical wrinkles is the:

d. *corrugator*

This muscle is located beneath the frontalis and draws the eyebrow down as well.

31. The muscle between the cheek and upper and lower jaw that compresses the cheeks and gives Alma the appearance of high cheek bones is the:

c. *buccinator*

The buccinator is a thin, flat muscle of the cheek between the upper and lower jaw.

32. The muscle around Alma's eye socket, toned to reduce the tiny wrinkles around her eyes, is the:

a. *orbicularis oculi*

This is a ring muscle of the eye socket that enables a person to close her eyes.

33. The muscle that causes wrinkles across the bridge of Alma's nose is the:

b. *procerus*

This muscle covers the bridge of the nose and lowers the eyebrows.

34. When she made her sarcastic comment about looking young, Alma employed her _____ muscle to lower her lower lip and draw it to one side.

c. *depressor labii inferioris*

This is the muscle surrounding the lower lip.

35. The muscle that would allow Alma to draw her lips in a sexy pout is the:

d. *levator anguli oris*

This muscle raises the angle of the mouth and draws it inward.

Sean is a very successful hairdresser who works a lot to accommodate his clients' needs. He has recently read a number of articles about how important it is for truly successful people to take excellent care of their bodies as well as their minds. Sean spent some time thinking about this and evaluating his life, and he decided to commit to a regular exercise routine, going to the gym three times a week and eating a health-conscious diet. Sean's workouts involve lifting weights and working out on machines designed to build his strength. Sometimes the workout routine leaves Sean out of breath and light-headed. For his protection, the gym requires Sean to frequently stop and check his heart rate, which is often elevated. Sean also sometimes experiences leg cramps in his sleep.

36. The system whose activities are responsible for Sean's thought processes about exercise is the:

c. *central nervous system*

The central nervous system controls all consciousness and mental activities, including all body movements and facial expressions.

37. When Sean realizes that he feels tired as a result of his workout, the realization is the _____ system at work.

b. *peripheral*

The function of this system is to carry messages to and from the central nervous system.

38. When Sean's heart rate becomes elevated, it is the response of the _____ system to the workout.

a. *autonomic*

This system controls the involuntary muscles such as the heart, blood vessels, and glands.

39. The nerves that carry the message from Sean's brain to his muscles, thus allowing him to pick up and move weights during his workout, are called:

c. *motor*

These nerves carry impulses from the brain to the muscles, and the transmitted impulses produce movement.

Stress can sometimes run high at the Stop Here Salon, which employs more than 20 stylists and is located in a busy strip mall. In order to relieve some of the tension from the hectic schedule, the salon manager Jo has decided to introduce a new technique called Expression Therapy during a staff meeting. When stylists are feeling the stress of the day, they are encouraged to go to the break room, close the door, and make funny faces into the mirror, then take a deep breath, laugh at themselves, and return to their styling station. They all agree to give it a try. To start, Marty decides to pull his ears away from his face and bend them downward. Next, Anne puts her index finger on the tip of her nose and lifts it up slightly. Missy follows by extending her lower lip and chin into a huge pout. Laughing, Matt raises his eyebrows, as if he has just been shocked or surprised by something terrible. Finally, when Patsy pushes her lower lip and chin out from her face, the whole group can't stop laughing. They all agree that this technique would be a great stress reliever. Jo flashes a huge smile at the staff and then dismisses the meeting.

40. When Marty pulls his ears away from his face and bends them downward, he is affecting the _____ nerves.

c. *auriculotemporal*

These nerves affect the external ear and skin above the temple up to the top of the skull.

41. When Anne puts her index finger on the tip of her nose and lifts it up slightly, she is affecting the _____ nerve.

a. *nasal*

This nerve affects the point and the lower side of the nose.

42. When Missy extends her lower lip and chin into a pout, she is affecting the _____ nerve.

c. *mental*

This nerve affects the skin of the lower lip and chin.

43. When Matt raises his eyebrows as if he has just been shocked or surprised, he is affecting the _____ nerve.

b. *supraorbital*

This nerve affects the skin of the forehead, scalp, eyebrow, and upper eyelid.

44. When Patsy pushes her lower lip and chin out from her face, she is affecting the _____ nerve.

d. *mandibular*

This nerve affects the muscles of the chin and lower lip.

45. When Jo flashes a huge smile at the staff, she is affecting the _____ nerve.

c. *buccal*

This nerve affects the muscles of the mouth.

After running up and down the stairs from the salon's retail and reception area to the stock room where additional retail products are stored, John is completely out of breath and his heart is pumping hard. He just spent the last hour recording what products were depleted and restocking the salon's shelves.

46. The circulatory system consists of John's _____, arteries, veins, and capillaries.

b. *heart*

The heart is often referred to as the body's pump and is the cone-shaped muscle that keeps the blood moving throughout the body.

47. John's body is employing _____ circulation when it sends blood from the heart throughout the body and back to the heart again.

c. *systemic*

There are two systems that attend to the body's circulation: pulmonary and systemic circulation.

48. John's heart is a(n):

d. *organ*

The heart is a muscular, cone-shaped organ that keeps the blood moving within the circulatory system. It is often referred to as the body's pump.

49. In order to purify it, John's heart will employ _____ circulation to send his blood to his lungs for purification.

a. *pulmonary*

During pulmonary circulation the blood is sent from the heart to the lungs for purification.

50. The thick-walled, flexible muscular tubes that carry oxygenated blood away from John's heart to the capillaries are called:

c. *arteries*

Arteries carry the oxygenated blood away from the heart to the capillaries, and the largest of these is the aorta.

51. John has _____, which are thin-walled blood vessels that are less elastic than arteries.

B. *capillaries*

Capillaries are tiny, thin-walled blood vessels that connect the smaller arteries to venules. Capillaries bring nutrients to the cells and carry away waste materials.

52. John's veins contain _____ which are situated between the chambers of the heart and allow blood to flow in only one direction.

a. *valves*

Valves open and close. They open to allow blood to flow and close to prevent the back-flow of blood.

53. John's _____ are minute, thin-walled blood vessels that connect the smaller arteries to venules.

b. *capillaries*

These bring nutrients to the cells and carry away waste materials.

54. John's red blood cells:

d. *carry oxygen to the body's cells*

The red blood cells, also called red corpuscles, contain hemoglobin, a complex iron protein that gives the blood its bright red color.

55. John's white blood cells:

b. *destroy disease-causing toxins and bacteria*

White blood cells destroy disease-causing toxins and bacteria to keep the body healthy.

56. The plasma in John's blood is responsible for:

a. *carrying food to cells*

The plasma carries food and secretion to the cells and carries away carbon dioxide.

57. Which of the following is NOT a function of John's lymphatic/immune system?

a. *provide waste to cells*

The lymphatic/immune system carries waste and impurities away from the cells and protects the body from disease by developing immunities and destroying disease-causing microorganisms.

Karen has recently begun to feel sudden and overwhelming rushes of heat which she calls hot flashes. They are so severe at times that she has to stop servicing clients and excuse herself to the restroom until they pass. After an episode, Karen is typically covered in perspiration and her clothes are wet. To help her relax after such an episode, Karen practices deep breathing exercises that are designed to help calm her and return her heart rate to a normal and natural rate.

58. The name of the system that affects the growth, development, and health of Karen's entire body is the _____ system:

b. *endocrine*

The endocrine system is made up of a group of specialized glands that affect the general health of the body.

59. Karen's endocrine glands secrete _____ into her bloodstream, which influence(s) the well-being of her entire body.

a. *hormones*

Hormones, such as insulin and estrogen, stimulate functional activity and secretion in other parts of the body.

60. The _____, which is part of Karen's excretory system, is responsible for eliminating waste through perspiration.

c. *skin*

The skin purifies the body by eliminating waste through perspiration.

61. When she practices deep breathing exercises, Karen is employing her:

d. *lungs*

The lungs take in oxygen and then enable the body to exhale carbon dioxide.

62. The muscular wall that helps Karen control her breathing is the:

c. *diaphragm*

The diaphragm is a muscular wall that separates the thorax from the abdominal region of the body and helps to control a person's breathing.

63. When Karen breathes in and oxygen is absorbed into her bloodstream, the process is called:

a. *inhalation*

The first part of the breathing cycle is inhalation.

64. When Karen breathes out and carbon dioxide is expelled from the body, the process is called:

c. *exhalation*

The second part of the breathing cycle is exhalation.

65. Karen's skin, oil and sweat glands, sensory receptors, hair, and nails all belong to which of the following body systems?

b. *integumentary*

The integumentary system serves as a protective covering and helps in regulating the body's temperature; it consists of the skin, accessory organs such as oil and sweat glands, sensory receptors, hair, and nails.

After a long day of servicing clients at the salon, Susan realizes that she hasn't eaten and is feeling very hungry. She decides to drive through a fast food restaurant for a burger on her way home from the salon. She arrives at the order window at 9 p.m. and orders a hamburger, French fries, and a large iced tea. She pays for her food and then sits in her car and eats her dinner.

66. The system responsible for changing Susan's burger into nutrients and waste is the _____ system:

d. *digestive*

The digestive system is responsible for changing food into nutrients and waste.

67. Susan's _____ will be busy at work changing certain kinds of foods into a form that can be used by the body.

c. *digestive enzymes*

Digestive enzymes are responsible for changing certain types of foods into a form that can be used by the body for fuel.

68. If Susan eats her burger at 9:15 p.m., what time will it be when her body completes the entire digestive process?

d. *6:15 a.m.*

The entire digestive process takes approximately 9 hours to complete.

CHAPTER 7

Skin Structure, Growth, and Nutrition

Clare has returned from a week-long vacation in the Bahamas and has made an appointment with Donna, an esthetician, for a facial. While examining her skin, Donna notices that Clare has a tan and that, in certain areas on her face and neck, the skin is taut, pink, dry, and painful to the touch. Clare complains that she is beginning to see wrinkles around her mouth and eyes, that the skin on her nose is a bit oily, and there are dark spots imbedded in the skin.

1. During her examination Donna is observing Clare's:
a. *epidermis*
The epidermis is the outermost layer of the skin, and it provides the body with a thin, protective covering.

2. Clare's tan is a result of the effect of ultraviolet light that increased the amount of _____ in her skin.
c. *melanin*
Melanin protects the sensitive cells below the skin from the destructive effects of the sun.

3. The appearance of skin that is taut, pink, and dry indicates that Clare may have a(n):
c. *sunburn*
Skin that is taut, pink, and dry indicates that it has been overexposed to the damaging ultraviolet rays of the sun and that those rays have caused the skin to burn.

4. What is causing Clare's wrinkles?
b. *loss of collagen and elastin*
Collagen is a fibrous protein that gives the skin form and strength; as the fibers become weakened the skin begins to sag and wrinkle.

5. Which nerves are responsible for the pain Clare feels?
b. *sensory nerve fibers*
Sensory nerve fibers are the ones that react to cold, heat, touch, pressure, and pain, and these receptors send messages to the brain.

6. Which nerves are responsible for Clare's nose being oily?
d. *secretory nerve fibers*
Secretory nerve fibers are distributed to the sweat and oil glands of the skin; they regulate perspiration and the flow of sebum.

7. The dark spots that are imbedded in the skin on Clare's nose are called:
   b. *comedones*
   When sebum hardens and the duct becomes clogged a pore impaction, or comedone, is formed.

8. These dark spots are caused by:
   a. *hardened sebum in a hair follicle*
   These spots appear most frequently on the nose and forehead and create a blockage at the mouth of the follicle.

9. These dark spots are considered to be a disorder of the:
   c. *sebaceous glands*
   The sebaceous glands are connected to the hair follicles and secrete sebum, a fatty or oily secretion that lubricates and preserves the softness of the hair.

Marlee is a hard-working stylist with three young children to care for. She has just returned from her yearly doctor's visit, where she complained of feeling tired all of the time. Marlee told the doctor that she not only feels tired, but that she thinks she looks tired too. Her skin is always dry, no matter what type of moisturizer she uses on it, her jawline is sagging, and when she gets cuts and scratches it takes a long time for her skin to heal. The doctor asks Marlee how much time she spends in the sun. She tells him that since she lives near the beach, she often takes her children there on the weekends to swim and play while she relaxes and catches up on magazine reading. Her doctor also asks her about her regular diet and water intake. Marlee tells him that she is very busy and quite often eats a lot of fast food and doesn't like to have too many liquids during the day because she wants to avoid having to leave her clients frequently to use the restroom. Her doctor recommends eating a more balanced diet, packed with the essential vitamins and nutrients she needs for overall better health, and drinking plenty of water. Marlee agrees to take better care of herself.

10. In order for her to take better care of herself, Marlee will need to create an eating plan that includes the following six nutrients:
    b. *carbohydrates, fats, proteins, vitamins, minerals, and water*
    There are six classes of nutrients that the body needs: carbohydrates, fats, proteins, vitamins, minerals, and water. These essential nutrients are obtained through eating and drinking. The body cannot make nutrients in sufficient amounts to sustain itself properly and therefore every person must design his eating plan to include these categories, in sufficient amounts, to maintain good health.

11. Marlee does a little research and finds out that there are five basic food groups. Those food groups are:

c. *grains, vegetables, fruits, milk, and protein*

The United States Department of Agriculture (USDA) developed a food pyramid to help people determine the amounts of food they need to eat from the five basic food groups. Those food groups are: grains, vegetables, fruits, milk, and protein (meat, poultry, fish, and beans). Eating the recommended amounts of foods from the five basic groups is the best way to support and maintain the health of the body and of the skin

12. Which of the following should Marlee *avoid* when trying to eat a balanced diet?

b. *eating large amounts of salt and sugar, including the sodium and modified sugars that are in prepared food products*

The United States Department of Health and Human Services has established the dietary guidelines to assist people with maintaining a balanced diet, and one recommendation is to eat only moderate amounts of salt and sugar, including the sodium and modified sugars that are in prepared food products. In addition, it is recommended that every person balance his or her diet with the right amount of physical activity and maintain or lower his or her weight.

13. One thing Marlee can do while deciding what items to purchase in the grocery store is:

c. *read the food's product label before she purchases it*

If you are trying to follow a healthy diet, you will want to learn how to read food labels. Food labels can help you select healthy foods. These labels also contain nutrition facts about serving size, number of servings per container, calorie information, and the quantities of nutrients per serving.

14. Marlee promised herself that she would drink more water every day. How can she determine how many ounces of water is appropriate for her to drink?

c. *by dividing her weight by two*

An easy formula that will help you determine the number of ounces of water you should be drinking each day is to divide your body weight by two. The result is the number of ounces of water that you should drink every day. Example: 160 pounds ÷ 2 = 80 ounces of water. Keep in mind that the average water bottle that most people carry with them holds just about 16 ounces (1 pint); therefore, a person who weighs 160 pounds should drink at least 5 bottles of water (80 ounces ÷ 16 ounces = 5 bottles) each day. People who are very active should drink more water.

Drinking pure water is essential to the health of the skin and body because it sustains the health of the cells, assists with the elimination of toxins and waste, helps regulate the body's temperature, and aids in proper digestion. All these functions, when performing properly, help keep the skin healthy, vital, and attractive.

15. If Marlee wishes to enhance her skin's elasticity, she should consider taking:

d. *vitamin A*

Vitamin A supports the overall health of the skin and aids in the health, function, and repair of skin cells. It has been shown to improve the skin's elasticity and thickness.

16. If Marlee wishes to enhance her skin's ability to repair itself, she should consider taking:

c. *vitamin C*

Vitamin C is an important substance needed for the proper repair of the skin and tissues. This vitamin aids in and accelerates the skin's healing processes. Vitamin C also is vitally important in fighting the aging process and promotes the production of collagen in the skin's dermal tissues, keeping the skin healthy and firm.

17. If Marlee wishes to enhance her bone health, she should consider taking:

b. *vitamin D*

Vitamin D enables the body to properly absorb and use calcium, the element needed for proper bone development and maintenance. Vitamin D also promotes rapid healing of the skin.

18. If Marlee wishes to enhance her ability to protect her skin from UV light, she should consider taking:

a. *vitamin E*

Vitamin E helps protect the skin from the harmful effects of the sun's UV light. Some people claim that vitamin E helps to heal damage to the skin's tissues when taken by mouth.

CHAPTER 8

Skin Disorders and Diseases

Gigi is a runner who has just completed a five-mile run. She has just come across the finish line and is drenched in perspiration and breathing heavily. This was a difficult race for Gigi because it was a very hot day. As a result of running through a wooded area, she also has several mosquito bites on her arms and legs, which she has already been scratching. Under her arms, Gigi notices a mass of small red bumps that burn when she moves her arms back and forth. After a few moments, Gigi takes off her running shoes and notices a foul smell as well.

1. Gigi's perspiration is a function of the:

c. *sweat glands*

The sweat glands regulate body temperature and excrete sweat from the skin. Sweat glands are more numerous on the palms, soles, and forehead and in the armpits.

2. The itchy, swollen lesions caused by Gigi's mosquito bites are called:

d. *wheals*

A wheal is an itchy, swollen lesion that lasts only a few hours. It is caused by a blow, insect bite, or skin allergy.

3. To protect herself from overexposure to the sun while running, Gigi should have worn:

c. *sunscreen*

Since overexposure to the sun can be damaging to the skin and can cause premature aging of the skin, it is best to always wear sunscreen and to advise clients to wear sunscreen.

4. As a result of scratching the mosquito bites on her arms, Gigi has developed a(n):

b. *excoriation*

An excoriation is a skin sore or abrasion caused by scratching or scraping.

5. The small red bumps that burn when Gigi moves her arms back and forth are called:

c. *miliaria rubra*

Miliaria rubra is an acute inflammatory disorder of the sweat glands, commonly known as prickly heat.

6. The foul odor Gigi notices after removing her running shoes is called:
   d. *bromhidrosis*
   Bromhidrosis is foul-smelling perspiration usually noticeable in the armpits and on the feet.

Dr. Tinsley is a dermatologist who sees patients with all sorts of skin disorders. Today she has several patients waiting to see her. Brent is a construction worker who works in many types of weather conditions. His hands have a tremendous amount of hard, dried skin accumulated on them which sometimes cracks and becomes painful. Pam has developed a dark-colored red wine spot on her forehead that only started to appear after a long illness she recently overcame. Mrs. Fagan has noticed a number of small, light brown-colored outgrowths of skin on her neck and wants to make sure they are not harmful to her health. Finally, Maryann has a large, dark raised spot on her chest and has recently noticed a hair growing out of it.

7. As a dermatologist, what kinds of conditions is Dr. Tinsley concerned with?
   a. *disorders and diseases of the skin, hair, and nails*
   A dermatologist is a physician who specializes in diseases and disorders of the skin, hair, and nails. Dermatologists attend four years of college, four years of medical school, and then about four years of specialty training in dermatology. Many have additional training in internal medicine because some skin symptoms may be reflective of internal disease. Cosmetologists refer clients with medical issues to dermatologists more than any other type of physician.

8. Brent's hands contain:
   c. *calluses*
   A callus is a keratoma that is caused by continued, repeated pressure or friction on any part of the skin, especially the hands and feet. If the thickening grows inward, it is called a corn.

9. Pam's discolored spot is called a:
   a. *stain*
   A stain is an abnormal brown or wine-colored skin discoloration with a circular and irregular shape.

10. What causes the discolored spot Pam has?
   c. *there is no known cause*
   The cause is unknown but stains can be present at birth, or they can appear during aging, after certain diseases, or after the disappearance of moles, freckles, and liver spots.

11. Mrs. Fagan's outgrowths of skin are called:

b. *skin tags*

A skin tag is a small brown-colored or flesh-colored outgrowth of the skin. Skin tags occur most frequently on the neck of an older person. They can be easily removed by a dermatologist.

12. When do these outgrowths normally appear?

b. *when a person ages*

Skin tags normally appear when a person ages.

13. What is the dark-colored spot on Maryann's chest?

c. *mole*

A mole is a small brownish spot or blemish on the skin, ranging in color from pale tan to brown or bluish black. Some moles are small and flat, resembling freckles; others are raised and darker in color. Large dark hairs often occur in moles. Any change in a mole requires medical attention.

CHAPTER 9 Nail Structure and Growth

Robin's client, Cheryl, is in the salon for a haircolor and cut. She made her appointment for today because tomorrow her daughter, Elizabeth, is getting married, and Cheryl wants the "works" because she wants to look her best. As the haircolor is applied, Cheryl tells Robin that she is considering having a manicure as well and asks her to check the manicurist's schedule to see if an appointment is available while her haircolor processes. Robin consults the schedule and the manicurist and realizes that if she begins the service for the manicurist by removing the nail polish and setting Cheryl's hands to soak in a finger bowl, the manicurist will be able to accommodate Cheryl's last-minute request. Robin obliges her client's request.

1. As Robin removes Cheryl's old nail polish, she finds that her natural nail bed is _____ in color, indicating that Cheryl has healthy nails.

d. *pink*

A healthy nail should be whitish and translucent in appearance, with the pinkish color of the nail bed below showing through.

2. A healthy nail is made up of _____ percent of water.

b. *15 to 25*

A healthy nail may look dry and hard, but it actually has a water content of between 15 and 25 percent. The water content directly affects the nail's flexibility. The lower the water content, the more rigid the nail becomes. Using an oil-based nail conditioner or nail polish to coat the plate can reduce water loss and improve flexibility.

3. Robin notices the white, visible part of the matrix, the part that extends from underneath the living skin of Cheryl's nail. This is called the:

a. *lunula*

The visible part of the matrix that extends from underneath the living skin is called the lunula. The lighter color of the lunula shows the true color of the matrix.

4. Robin also notices that Cheryl's _____ is quite thick. She explains to Cheryl that this is the dead, colorless tissue attached to the nail plate and is incredibly sticky and difficult to remove from the nail plate.
   b. *cuticle*
   The cuticle is the dead, colorless tissue attached to the nail plate. The cuticle comes from the underside of the skin that lies above the natural nail plate. This tissue is incredibly sticky and difficult to remove from the nail plate. Its job is to seal the space between the natural nail plate and living skin above to prevent entry of foreign material and microorganisms, thus helping to prevent injury and infection.

5. Cheryl comments that her nails seem to grow very slowly and asks Robin what the normal growth rate of a nail is. Robin's answer is:
   d. *1/10 inch per month (2.5 mm)*
   The average rate of nail growth in the normal adult is about 1/10 inch (2.5 mm) per month. Nails grow faster in the summer than they do in the winter. Children's nails grow more rapidly, whereas those of elderly persons grow at a slower rate. The nail of the middle finger grows fastest and the thumbnail grows the slowest.

CHAPTER 10 Nail Disorders and Diseases

Ellie has been a nail technician for more than 20 years. In the course of her career, she has had many clients with nail disorders and problems whom she has been able to service and help through regular nail care and maintenance.

1. While recovering from stubbing her finger into a window jam, one of Mrs. Jones's nails developed a dark purplish spot. Ellie recognized the condition as:

a. *bruised nail*

Bruised nails are a condition in which a blood clot forms under the nail plate, causing a dark purplish spot. These discolorations are usually due to small injuries to the nail bed. The dried blood absorbs into the nail bed epithelium tissue on the underside of the nail plate and grows out with it.

2. Ruben gave his daughter a gift certificate for a manicure with Ellie, in the hopes that it would arrest her onychophagy, a condition in which she _____ her nails.

c. *bites*

Nail biting is the result of an acquired nervous habit that prompts the individual to chew the nail or the hardened cuticle around the nail.

3. After losing more than 100 pounds (45 kg), Sabrina noticed that her nails were much thinner, whiter, and more flexible than normal. Ellie explained that this is called _____.

b. *eggshell nails*

Eggshell nails have a noticeably thin, white nail plate and are more flexible than a normal nail. The nail also usually separates from the nail bed and curves around the free edge.

4. Rick has nails that seem to curve into the sides of his fingers. He has:

c. *plicatured nail*

Plicatured nail, also known as folded nail, is a type of highly curved nail plate usually caused by injury to the matrix, but it may be inherited. This condition often leads to ingrown nails.

5. After Sabrina slammed her hand into a table when she fell at home, she noticed a whitish discoloration of her nails. Ellie told her this was called _____ and was caused by injury to the base of the nail.

c. *leukonychia*

Leukonychia are white spots that appear on the nail after injury to the base of the nail bed, but do not necessarily indicate disease of the nail.

Wendy, a loyal monomer liquid and polymer powder nail enhancement wearer, has been going to Cecilia for maintenance procedures for more than three years. Recently she noticed that a dark greenish spot had appeared on her index finger nail. At first she ignored it, but over time it became darker and eventually she noticed that it had a foul odor.

6. The green spot is:

b. *a bacterial infection*

This discoloration is a bacterial infection caused by naturally occurring bacteria on the skin that has grown out of control under a certain set of circumstances and has caused an infection.

7. The green spot is most likely caused by:

b. *using contaminated instruments*

Infections are caused by large numbers of bacteria or fungal organisms on a surface. This is why proper cleansing and preparation of the natural nail plate, as well as cleaning and disinfection of implements, are so important.

Raul, a nail technician, is attending a nail care seminar. One of the classes is conducted by Dr. Reddy, a medical doctor who is discussing the types of nail diseases. Dr. Reddy uses a slide projector with photo examples of each kind of disease he discusses.

8. Dr. Reddy's first slide shows a nail that is separated from and falling off of the nail bed. This condition is called:

c. *onychomadesis*

Onychomadesis is usually caused by a local infection, minor injuries to the nail bed, or severe systemic illness.

9. The next slide depicts a fingernail with a matrix that is inflamed with pus. The nail also is shedding. This is:

a. *onychia*

Onychia can occur from any opening of the skin which will allow bacteria, fungi, or foreign materials to penetrate.

10. Dr. Reddy shows another slide and explains that the nail has grown into the sides of the finger. This is called:

d. *onychocryptosis*

Onychocryptosis can affect either the fingers or toes. In this condition, the nail grows into the sides of the living tissue around the nail.

11. Dr. Reddy's final slide is of a man's foot with what appear to be red patches between the toes. These are:

a. *tinea pedis*

Tinea pedis is the medical term for fungal infections of the feet. These infections can occur on the bottoms of the feet and often appear as a red itchy rash in the spaces between the toes, most often between the fourth and fifth toe. There is sometimes a small degree of scaling of the skin.

CHAPTER 11 Properties of the Hair and Scalp

Mrs. Brand is a very loyal client of the Hearts Salon. She colors and perms her naturally blond hair and makes a weekly visit to the salon for a wet set and comb out. On her most recent visit, Jean, her regular stylist, notices that Mrs. Brand's hair is very dry and rough looking.

1. When Mrs. Brand has her hair colored or permed, the chemical solution affects which layer of the hair shaft?

   b. *cuticle*

   The cuticle is the outermost layer of the hair, and it consists of a single overlapping layer of transparent, scale-like cells that overlap like shingles on a roof.

2. If Mrs. Brand's hair looks and feels dry and rough, it is most likely a result of:

   d. *too much swelling of the cuticle layer of the hair*

   A healthy, compact cuticle layer is the hair's primary defense against damage. When a chemical such as haircolor or perm solution is administered to the hair, it causes the cuticle to swell to complete its action. Over time the swollen cuticle can have the appearance of dry, rough hair.

3. In order for her permanent haircolor solution to actually change the hair's color, which layer of Mrs. Brand's hair must be affected?

   c. *cortex*

   The cortex, the middle layer of the hair, is where all of the hair's melanin pigment is contained. During a permanent haircolor service, the color molecules must penetrate the cortex in order to permanently change the hair's color.

4. The appearance of Mrs. Brand's hair indicates that:

   c. *the cuticle has been opened many times*

   The dry, rough texture to Mrs. Brand's hair indicates that the cuticle has probably been opened repeatedly as a result of haircoloring and other chemical services.

5. Based on the information you have on Mrs. Brand, it is very likely that her hair is missing a:

   d. *medulla*

   The medulla is the innermost layer of the hair, and it is common for people with fine hair or naturally blond hair to entirely lack a medulla.

6. Mrs. Brand's hair is made up of approximately _____ percent protein.

c. *90*

All hair is made up of 90 percent protein, which consists of long chains of amino acids which, in turn, are made up of elements.

7. When Mrs. Brand's hair is permed, the bonds that are broken are called:

d. *disulfide bonds*

A disulfide bond is a chemical side bond that can only be broken by the action of a chemical hair relaxer or permanent wave solution.

8. When Mrs. Brand's hair is wet set, the bonds that are broken are called:

b. *hydrogen bonds*

A hydrogen bond is a weak physical side bond that is easily broken by water or heat, thus allowing for Mrs. Brand's hair to curl when wet set.

9. Mrs. Brand's natural blond hair is a result of the _____ in her hair's cortex.

c. *pheomelanin*

Pheomelanin provides natural hair colors ranging from red and ginger to yellow/blond tones. Natural hair color is the result of ratio of eumelanin to pheomelanin along with the total number and size of pigment granules.

Marlene is a new client for John, so before he begins the cut and color service she has booked, he performs a hair analysis. While it is still dry, John looks at Marlene's hair and notes that she has what appears to be thick, curly, dark brown hair. When he touches her hair, it feels hard and glassy but slick and greasy, and he notices that she has a lot more strands of hair on her head than some of his other clients have. Upon further investigation John realizes that Marlene's hair grows in a circular pattern in the back of her head, at the crown. After her shampoo, John gently pulls Marlene's hair away from the scalp and sees that it readily springs back to its original place. John must now note all of his findings on a client record card before he begins to cut or color Marlene's hair.

10. In determining the texture of Marlene's hair, John notes that it is:

d. *coarse*

Coarse hair has the largest diameter, is stronger than fine hair, and has a strong structure.

11. Based on John's diagnosis, Marlene's hair diameter and structure are characterized as:

 c. *large and coarse*

 Marlene has coarse hair, which indicates that it is large and strong.

12. John must be aware of Marlene's hair texture because it may affect the outcome of:

 b. *the haircolor service*

 Coarse hair usually requires more processing time than medium or fine hair and may also be more resistant to processing. John must know this in order to plan the service properly.

13. Based on what he felt when he touched her head, John would have noted that Marlene's hair density is:

 d. *high*

 A high hair density indicates that a person has many hairs on her head, but this has no real relation to a person's hair texture.

14. Marlene's hair density indicates that she has:

 d. *a lot of hairs per square inch (2.5 cm) on her head*

 Marlene has very dense hair, which indicates that, regardless of her hair texture, she has many hairs on her head.

15. Based on Marlene's hair color, how many hairs is she likely to carry on her head?

 b. *110,000*

 Generally people with brown hair have approximately 110,000 hairs on their head at any given time.

16. Based on John's diagnosis of Marlene's hair, what is her hair's porosity likely to be?

 a. *low*

 Because of her hair's texture and condition, John realizes that Marlene's hair has low porosity, which means that it is considered resistant.

17. Chemical services performed on hair with Marlene's porosity require a(n):

 c. *alkaline solution*

 John will need to use an alkaline solution on Marlene's hair because it will be necessary to sufficiently open the cuticle to allow for uniform saturation and processing.

18. Based on John's observations, Marlene's hair elasticity would be categorized as:

   d. *normal*

   Marlene's hair elasticity is normal because when it is stretched it is able to return to its normal position. Hair with normal elasticity can stretch up to 50 percent of its original length and return without breaking.

19. The growth pattern that is evident on the back of Marlene's hair is called a:

   b. *whorl*

   A whorl is hair that forms a circular pattern and is normally found on a person's crown.

20. John must remember Marlene's growth pattern especially when:

   d. *cutting her hair*

   John will need to be aware of Marlene's growth pattern so that he can make plans to compensate for the pattern when cutting her hair to make sure he doesn't cut the hair too short in order for it to have an even, finished look.

21. What type of hair and scalp condition does Marlene have?

   d. *oily hair and scalp*

   Based on the feel of the hair—slick and greasy—John can determine that Marlene has overactive sebaceous glands which render the scalp and hair oily.

Bonnie has just taken a new position at a salon that specializes in servicing clients with hair loss. On this particular day she is booked with clients who have various forms of hair loss. Bonnie's first client of the day is Albert, a 70-year-old man whose hairline has receded about two inches (5 cm) but who otherwise has a thick head of healthy hair. Six months after having her baby, Anna, another of Bonnie's clients, is experiencing sudden hair loss and is interested in having her hair cut short to make her daily routine easier and to minimize the appearance of the hair loss. Bonnie's final client of the day, a successful 40-year-old businessman named Martin, has just discovered a small round bald area at his nape and asks Bonnie to be sure to leave the hair above it long enough to cover that spot.

22. As she services Albert and learns about his hair loss, Bonnie realizes that his type of hair loss is categorized as:

   a. *androgenic alopecia*

   Androgenic alopecia is hair loss characterized by miniaturization of terminal hair that is converted to vellus hair; in men, it is known as male pattern baldness.

23. The cause of Albert's hair loss is likely to be his:

b. *age*

Based on his age and the condition of his hair and scalp, which appears to be healthy, Bonnie can safely assume Albert's hair loss is simply a result of aging.

24. Anna's hair loss is categorized as:

d. *postpartum alopecia*

Postpartum alopecia is temporary hair loss experienced at the conclusion of a pregnancy.

25. Anna's hair loss is usually:

b. *temporary, with hair growth returning to normal within a year*

Usually a woman who experiences hair loss during pregnancy can expect her hair growth cycle to return to normal within a year after delivery.

26. Martin's type of hair loss is called:

c. *alopecia areata*

Alopecia areata is characterized by the sudden loss of hair in round patches either on the scalp or on other areas of the body.

27. Martin's hair loss is caused by:

c. *an unpredictable autoimmune skin disease*

Alopecia areata is caused by the person's hair follicles being mistakenly attacked by the person's own immune system with white blood cells stopping the hair growth phase.

Judy has a full day of clients booked for various services. Her day begins with Mrs. Hines, who is 65 years old and has mostly gray hair with several areas of hair that are striped—both gray and dark. Joe, another of Judy's clients, wears his hair at a medium length but notes that his hair feels knotted and that he is experiencing lots of hair breakage; he is also finding lots of small white flakes when he brushes or combs his hair. Joe's wife, Sandra, is also in the salon today. She is booked for an upper lip waxing because, she complains, she has dark, coarse hair on her face that almost looks like a man's mustache. When Jan arrives for services today, Judy asks one of the salon's assistants to shampoo her long hair and apply a deep penetrating conditioning treatment for 20 minutes to help her combat her spitting ends. On her day off, Judy will go to her son's third-grade class and speak to the students about hair and scalp care, and she will warn them not to swap hats, especially if someone in the class may have head lice.

28. The technical term for Mrs. Hines's gray hair is:

a. *canities*

Canities is the technical term for gray hair, and it is caused by the loss of the hair's natural melanin pigment.

29. The technical term for Mrs. Hines's striped hair is:

d. *ringed hair or hypertrichosis*

Ringed hair is a variety of canities and is characterized by alternating bands of gray and pigmented hair throughout the length of the strand.

30. The dark hair on Sandra's upper lip is a result of:

b. *hirsuties*

Hirsuties is a condition of abnormal hair growth.

31. The technical term for Jan's split ends is:

d. *trichoptilosis*

Trichoptilosis is usually caused by hair damage and may be treated by deep-conditioning services or by simply trimming off the affected hair.

32. The technical term for Joe's knotted and breaking hair is:

b. *trichorrhexis nodosa*

Trichorrhexis nodosa is characterized by brittleness and the formation of nodular swellings along the hair shaft.

33. The small white flakes Joe finds when brushing or combing his hair are called:

d. *pityriasis*

Pityriasis is the medical term for dandruff, small white scales that appear on the scalp and in the hair.

34. The technical term for head lice is:

c. *pediculosis capitis*

Head lice are animal parasites that infest the hair and scalp and cause itching and infection.

CHAPTER 12 Basics of Chemistry

On his way into the salon for a full day of servicing clients, Jack realizes that he needs to fill his car with gas. He stops at a service station, fills his car's tank, purchases a small bottle of water and some chewing gum, pays for all of these, and then heads to the salon. When he arrives, he finds that the sprinkler has just completed a cycle and the front of the salon is drenched with water. He steps over the puddles and walks into the salon. His first two clients are already there waiting for him—Mr. Ramirez, who will be having his hair cut and colored, and Ms. Crespa, who will be having a steam facial, a perm, and styling. With no time to waste, Jack gets to work.

1. The gasoline that Jack put into his car is considered to be:
b. *organic*
Gas is considered organic because it is manufactured from natural gas and oil, which are the remains of plants and animals that died millions of years ago.

2. Jack's gasoline is considered organic because it contains:
b. *carbon*
Any substance that contains carbon is considered to be organic.

3. Jack's car, made of metal and steel, is considered:
d. *inorganic*
Since Jack's car is made of metal, a nonliving entity, it is considered to be inorganic.

4. The bottle of water that Jack bought is an example of:
b. *matter*
Matter is any substance that takes up space. It can be a liquid, solid, or gas.

5. Jack's pack of chewing gum exists in what form?
d. *solid*
The pack of chewing gum Jack bought is a solid because it occupies space and is tangible.

6. The haircolor that Jack will apply to Mr. Ramirez is considered to be:
a. *an organic substance*
Haircolor is an organic substance because it is made from either a natural or synthetic source of an organic compound.

7. The permanent wave solution that Jack will apply to Ms. Crespa's hair is considered to be:
   a. *an organic substance*
   Permanent wave solution is an organic substance because it is made from either a natural or synthetic source of an organic compound.

8. Ms. Crespa's steam facial is an example of water in what form?
   c. *gas*
   Steam is considered to be a gas because it does not have definite shape or volume.

9. When Jack evaluates Mr. Ramirez's natural hair color level he is determining its:
   c. *physical properties*
   Physical properties are those things that can be determined without a chemical reaction and don't cause a chemical change in the substance.

10. When Jack assesses the change in curl from before Ms. Crespa's perm to after it, he is assessing its:
    a. *chemical properties*
    A chemical property can only be observed through a chemical change in the original substance, such as a permanently curled section of hair.

11. When Mr. Ramirez's hair is cut, the change is considered to be:
    b. *physical*
    It's a physical change because it did not require a chemical reaction to change the substance.

12. When Mr. Ramirez's hair is colored, the change is considered to be:
    a. *chemical*
    The haircolor is considered a chemical change because it did require a chemical reaction to change the substance.

Nancy is booked for a full facial and makeup application and then a conditioning treatment and blowdry at her favorite salon. She arrives at the salon and her esthetician, Sierra, takes her right in and begins to perform the facial. First, Sierra takes a powder from a bag and mixes it with water and applies it to Nancy's face and lets it sit on the skin for three minutes. After removing this mixture, Sierra applies a facial scrub that is both smooth and rough because it contains small, hard particles smattered throughout. Next she applies a cold cream to Nancy's skin, which cools and soothes her face. Throughout the service, Sierra rinses her tools several times in water. When the facial is completed, Sierra shampoos Nancy's hair and applies the deep conditioning treatment. Once the hair is rinsed, dried, and rolled on hot rollers, Sierra removes bottles and tubes of cosmetics and begins the makeup application with foundation. The foundation that she chooses looks like it has separated in the bottle. Sierra shakes it vigorously and then applies it to Nancy's face as a base.

13. The water that Sierra uses to rinse her tools is an example of a:

a. *chemical compound*

Water is a chemical compound because it is composed of atoms from two elements that combine to create a substance that is totally different from the elements with which it was made.

14. The foundation that Sierra used on Nancy's face during the makeup application is an example of a:

b. *physical compound*

The foundation is a physical compound because, although two elements were mixed together to form something else, they still held onto their original properties.

15. When Sierra blended the powder and the water for application to Nancy's skin, she created a:

c. *solution*

The powder and water were a blended solution of two or more solids, liquids, or gaseous substances.

16. The powder that Sierra blended into the water is referred to as a:

c. *solute*

A solute is the matter that is dissolved into a solvent, such as the powder was when blended into the water.

17. The liquid into which Sierra blended the powder is considered to be a:

a. *solvent*

A solvent, such as water, is the substance that dissolves another substance to form a solution with a chemical change in the composition.

18. The fact that the water and powder mixed together without separating implies that they are:

b. *miscible*

Miscible substances are those that can be mixed, in any proportion, without separating.

19. Since the foundation that Sierra used had to be shaken every time it was used because the two ingredients kept separating, it is an example of a(n) _____ substance.

d. *immiscible*

An immiscible substance is one that is not capable of being mixed, such as water and oil.

20. The facial scrub that Sierra applied to Nancy's skin is an example of a _____ because it contains solid particles distributed throughout a liquid form.
  d. *suspension*
  A suspension is a state in which solid particles are distributed through a liquid medium.

21. The hair conditioner that was applied to Nancy's hair is an example of a(n):
  d. *oil-in-water emulsion*
  An oil-in-water emulsion is one in which oil droplets are suspended in a water base, such as in the case of a conditioner.

22. The cold cream that was applied to Nancy's skin is an example of a(n):
  a. *water-in-oil emulsion*
  A water-in-oil emulsion is one in which water droplets are suspended in an oil base, such as in the case of a cold cream.

Mike is creating an order list of products the salon needs to replenish for when Allie, their distributor sales consultant, comes into the salon next week. Every day Mike adds to the list, and he has asked all of his fellow stylists to add on items as they notice them becoming depleted. The list currently contains the following: rubbing alcohol, chemical hair relaxer, three jars of hand and skin cream for the manicure tables, and hair spray.

23. Mike's colleagues like using an alcohol that evaporates quickly for their needs in the salon. This type of alcohol is called:
  c. *volatile*
  A volatile alcohol is useful in the salon to cleanse surfaces, and it does evaporate quickly.

24. Which of the items on Mike's list is a form of ammonia?
  d. *chemical hair relaxer*
  Ammonia is a form of colorless gas that is used to raise the pH level; ammonium hydroxide and ammonium thioglycolate are examples.

25. Which of the items on Mike's list contains glycerin?
  c. *hand cream*
  Glycerin is a sweet, colorless, oily substance formed by the decomposition of oils, fats, or fatty acids.

26. Which of the items on Mike's list contains silicones?
  c. *hand cream*
  A silicone is a special type of oil used in hair conditioners and as a water-resistant lubricant for the skin.

27. Which of the items on Mike's list contains volatile organic compounds (VOCs)?

a. *hair spray*

Volatile organic compounds are two or more elements combined chemically that contain carbon and evaporate quickly.

It's another busy day in Marco's salon. He already has two clients in the reception area waiting their turn for services. The first, Barbra, has an appointment for a shampoo, condition, and updo, and Mandy, his second appointment of the day, is booked for a chemical hair straightening. As Marco reviews his scheduled appointments he sees that he has a 1 p.m. appointment with Andrea for haircolor and a 2:30 p.m. appointment with Renee for a perm. Since he has so many chemical services to perform today, Marco takes a moment to remind himself of the issues surrounding pH and to picture the pH scale in his head.

28. When shampooing Barbra's hair, Marco will use pure water, which has a pH of:

c. *7*

Water has a pH of 7, which means that it is neither acidic nor alkaline.

29. The pH of the water Marco will use is considered to be:

d. *neutral*

Water is considered neutral because it is in the middle of the scale, neither acidic nor alkaline.

30. The pH of Barbra's hair and skin is:

b. *5*

Hair and skin have a pH of 5.

31. The pH of Barbra's hair and skin is considered to be:

a. *acidic*

A pH of 5 indicates that a substance is acidic.

32. Pure (distilled) water is _____ than Barbra's hair and skin:

d. *100 times more alkaline*

Since the pH scale is a logarithmic scale, a change of one number indicates a tenfold change, so a change of two whole numbers indicates a change of 10 times 10, or 100 times.

33. The chemical hair relaxer treatment that Mandy will receive will have a pH that indicates it is:

b. *alkaline*

All alkalis have a pH of above 7.

34. An alkaline pH is useful in straightening Mandy's hair because it will:

d. *soften and swell the hair*

The alkaline pH softens and swells the hair and allows the stylist to easily re-form the hair into a shape that the client desires, in this case to straight.

35. When Marco performs his perm service later in the day for Renee, the perm will have a pH that indicates it is:

a. *acidic*

An acidic pH is one that is below 7.

36. An acidic pH is useful in permanent waving hair because it will _____ Renee's hair:

a. *harden and contract*

To have the hair harden and contract around a perm rod and take on the shape of that rod is the purpose of a permanent wave.

37. After relaxing Mandy's hair, Marco will use a normalizing lotion that will neutralize the relaxer by creating a(n):

c. *acid-alkaline reaction*

An acid-alkaline reaction is one in which equal parts of acid are added to an equal amount of alkaline and they neutralize each other, forming water.

38. When Marco's haircolor client, Andrea, has her service, he will witness a(n):

d. *oxidation-reduction reaction*

An oxidation-reduction reaction is responsible for the chemical changes created by combining an element or compound with oxygen.

39. If, when perming Renee's hair, an element is combined with oxygen, _____ will be produced.

c. *heat*

The heat is produced by the addition of oxygen to an element or compound in the oxidation process.

40. If heat is released during her perm, Renee's hair is experiencing a(n) _____ reaction.

c. *exothermic*

Chemical reactions that are characterized by the release of heat are called exothermic. The heat is produced by an oxidation reaction.

CHAPTER 13 Basics of Electricity

Carlene has just parked her car in the salon's parking lot and realizes that, because it has begun to rain, she will need to run to the salon's door to protect her beautiful new silk blouse from rain droplets. As she gets to the doorway, she realizes that she is the first person to arrive at the salon and will need to unlock the door. Once the door is opened she steps into the salon's lobby and fumbles for the light switch in the dark. Finally, she gets the lights on, closes the door, and gets ready for the day. The first thing Carlene does is plug in her battery-operated curling iron so she can use it on her clients without worrying about it losing its power, and then she plugs her straight irons into the wall outlet. Next she makes sure that her cordless electric clipper is in its charger, and then, finally, she goes into the back room to make a pot of coffee.

1. Carlene's car employs a constant, even-flowing current generated by a battery, which is called:

c. *direct current*

Carlene's car battery creates a constant current that travels in one direction only and produces a chemical reaction; this process is called direct current.

2. The form of energy Carlene was fumbling to activate when she entered the salon is called:

b. *electricity*

Electricity is a form of energy that, when in motion, exhibits magnetic, chemical, or thermal effects.

3. An _____ is what accounts for the lights coming on when Carlene flipped the switch.

c. *electric current*

An electric current is the flow of electricity along a conductor.

4. Supporting the switch that Carlene turned on is a(n) _____, which conducts electricity.

c. *conductor*

A conductor is any substance, material, or medium that can easily transmit electricity.

5. Carlene's silk blouse is a:

b. *nonconductor*

A nonconductor is any substance, material, or medium that cannot easily conduct electricity, such as Carlene's blouse.

6. When Carlene plugs her battery-operated curling iron into the wall outlet she is using an apparatus known as a:
   b. *converter*
   A converter is an apparatus that changes direct current to alternating current.

7. When Carlene plugs her straight irons into the wall outlet, she is using:
   d. *alternating current*
   Alternating current is rapid and interrupted current, flowing first in one direction and then in the opposite direction.

8. Carlene's cordless electric clippers are an example of a:
   a. *rectifier*
   A rectifier is an apparatus that changes alternating current to direct current.

Manuel intends to buy the Special Days Hair Salon, but before the deal is finalized he has a walk-through with an electrical inspector, Andy, to be sure the salon is wired properly and able to handle the special electrical needs that a salon requires. They first inspect the outlets where the styling stations will be and where most of the hair drying and curling will take place. Next, they move to the facial rooms and discuss the special needs when providing esthetic services. Finally, they move into the laundry room to inspect the area and outlets for a washing machine and dryer, and Andy explains the fuse box and circuit breaker.

9. Manuel learns that the normal wall sockets that power hair dryers and curling irons are _____ volts.
   a. *110*
   A volt is a unit that measures the pressure or force that pushes the flow of electrons forward through a conductor. The normal rate for voltage power blowdryers and other electrical apparatuses used in the salon is 110.

10. Outlets that can accommodate the correct amount of power for washing machines and dryers are _____ volts.
   b. *220*
   Since the work of a large appliance such as a washing machine or air conditioner requires more pressure, more force, and more power, these apparatuses require a 220 voltage.

11. Andy explains that, due to its _____ rating, a hair dryer cord must be twice as thick as an appliance with a lower rating in order to avoid overheating and starting a fire.
   b. *amp*
   An amp or ampere is the unit of measurement that measures the strength of an electric current.

12. To create an atmosphere that is relaxing in the facial room, Manuel will use a 40- _____ bulb.
   d. *watt*
   A watt is a measurement of how much electricity is being used in a second.

13. Manuel's 2,000-watt blowdryer will use _____ watts of energy per second.
   d. *2,000*
   Each electrical implement or apparatus is labeled with how many watts it uses so that you can be aware of its electrical needs.

14. If a fuse gets too hot and melts, Manuel will know that:
   d. *an excessive current was prevented from passing through the circuit*
   A fuse melts when a wire becomes too hot and overloads the circuit with too much current from too many appliances or from faulty equipment.

15. If too many appliances are operating on the same circuit and they all suddenly stop working, Manuel will know that the _____ has shut off to protect the salon from a dangerous situation.
   c. *circuit breaker*
   A circuit breaker is a switch that automatically shuts off or interrupts electric current at the first indication of overload.

16. Manuel realizes that his salon has several appliances that have a three-prong plug and that this is evidence of _____.
   b. *grounding*
   Grounding completes an electric circuit and carries the current safely away. It is another important way to promote electrical safety.

Karen is booked for a series of facial treatments with Gale, an experienced esthetician at the Red Tree Spa. Karen has some oil and comedones trapped in the skin on her nose and she has some dry patches on her cheeks and temple area. Karen would like to improve the muscle tone of her face and neck, increase the blood circulation, and relieve her skin's congestion. Gale explains to Karen that she will be using various forms of electrotherapy in her treatments, including galvanic current and faradic current, both of which are perfectly safe and useful in treating Karen's problems when administered carefully by Gale. Karen agrees and they begin the treatment.

17. Gale has prepared an electrode which is a(n) _____ for use in treating Karen.
   a. *applicator*
   An applicator made of carbon glass or metal is used for directing the electric current from the machine to the client's skin.

18. Gale determines that the positive electrode she will use, called the _____, is red.

c. *anode*

The anode is usually red and will have a plus sign on it, indicating that it is a positive electrode.

19. The first modality Gale will use is called _____ current, which is a constant and direct current.

b. *galvanic*

Galvanic current is used as a constant and direct current that produces chemical changes when it passes through the tissues and fluids of the body.

20. If Gale wants to force acidic substances into Karen's skin, she must use:

b. *cataphoresis*

Cataphoresis forces acidic substances into deeper tissues using galvanic current from the positive toward the negative pole.

21. If Gale wants to force liquid into Karen's tissues, she must use:

c. *anaphoresis*

Anaphoresis is the process of forcing liquids into the tissues from the negative toward the positive poles.

22. If Gale wants to introduce water-soluble products into Karen's skin, she must use:

a. *iontophoresis*

Iontophoresis is the process of introducing water-soluble products into the skin with the use of electric current such as through positive and negative poles of a galvanic machine.

23. To increase glandular activity, Gale may use a _____ on Karen.

c. *vibrator*

A vibrator is used in massage to produce a mechanical succession of manipulations.

24. To relieve any redness or inflammation that Karen may be experiencing from mild acne, Gale could use a:

c. *microcurrent*

Microcurrent is an extremely low level of electricity that mirrors the body's natural electrical impulses. Microcurrent can be used for iontophoresis, firming, toning, and soothing skin. It also can help heal inflamed tissue, such as acne.

After a couple of days off, Debbie has spent the day running around in the bright, hot sun completing errands and has just entered the salon she owns with her partner, Larry. Larry comments that she has gotten a bit of a tan and that it makes her look very healthy. He asks Debbie if she is ready for their meeting with Beth, their distributor sales consultant. They are going to discuss adding tanning services to their salon menu by putting tanning bed in a small, unused room off the skin care area of their salon. Both Debbie and Larry have some concerns about the safety of tanning and are prepared to discuss them with Beth, who has just been to a training session and should have the answers they need to make the best decisions. Beth explains that tanning beds are safe, as long as clients follow the manufacturer's instructions and guidelines and that tanning beds provide both UV and infrared light. Beth also suggests that Debbie and Larry consider using specialized light bulbs for treating some scalp and skin conditions.

25. The bright sunlight that Debbie saw while running her errands is called:

d. *visible light*

Visible light is electromagnetic radiation that we can see.

26. Since Debbie has a slight tan, she has been exposed to:

a. *UV rays*

UV rays makes up 5 percent of natural sunlight and are the least penetrating of all sunlight. They produce chemical effects and kill germs.

27. Beth explains that infrared rays:

c. *penetrate the deepest*

Infrared rays make up 60 percent of natural sunlight, have long wavelengths and produce the most heat.

28. Beth explains that _____ light is useful for reducing bacteria on the skin.

c. *blue*

Blue light should only be used on oily, bare skin; it is the least penetrating light and has some germicidal benefits.

29. When Larry asks her about improving collagen and elastin production in the skin, Beth recommends using _____ light.

d. *red*

Red light increases circulation and improves the collagen and elastin production in the skin.

CHAPTER 14 Principles of Hair Design

Andie has just returned from a terrific hair show where she attended several educational classes, and she is excited to use some of the techniques she learned there with her clients. One of the classes she attended was all about the elements of designing a great hairstyle that uniquely fits the client's needs and characteristics. In another class—a haircolor class—ways to use haircolor to enhance the client's face shape and hairstyle were described. A third class explored how wave patterns in the hair can be added or subtracted to further emphasize the shine and beauty of the hair.

1. Andie's excitement over what she learned at the hair show and her desire to try out some of the techniques is considered to be:
a. *inspiration*
Inspiration is the stimulus that motivates action and creativity. Andie was inspired by the styles she saw at the hair show to get home and try out what she learned.

2. When designing a style for hair that forces the eye to look up and down, Andie is creating a hairstyle with:
b. *vertical lines*
Vertical lines in a style make it appear longer and narrower as the eye follows the lines up and down.

3. Cathy, one of Andie's clients, is a single mom with three children who is looking for a very simple hairstyle that requires the least amount of care, so Andie must consider a:
a. *single line hairstyle*
Since the single-line hairstyle is the simplest to care for, it is best worn by someone who wants an easy-to-wear and easy-to-care-for look.

4. To create the illusion of a more slender face for her client Joan, Andie could use haircolor that is a:
c. *dark color*
Dark colors make the face look smaller or thinner and create the illusion of a more slender face. Andie should use a dark color where appropriate to do so.

5. To create a hairstyle that reflects the most light for her client Meredith, Andie should consider a style with a _____ wave pattern.
   d. *straight*
   Curly hair, because of its movement and curl, tends to cut up the ability of the hair to reflect light. Straight hair, on the other hand, does not chop up the light and therefore has a super shiny appearance.

Since she was a teenager, Kim has worn the same hairstyle—long, dark, wavy hair that falls to just above the shoulders. Because she really wants to create a new look for herself, Kim makes an appointment with her stylist, Courtney, for a makeover. When she arrives, Kim talks with Courtney and explains what she sees as her problem areas. Kim complains that her face is too wide, that she has a large forehead, that her eyes are set too closely together, and that she has a wide, flat nose. Kim also feels that her hair is too wavy and that for her to keep it tamed, she has to wear her hair flat against her head, which she is bored with. Kim explains to Courtney that she wants to have a new style to accentuate her best features and minimize her flaws.

6. Based on Kim's description of her face, she has a(n) _____ face shape.
   c. *round*
   A round face type is characterized as being round at the hairline and chin line, with a wide face.

7. To help this face shape to appear longer and thinner, the best hairstyle is one that:
   d. *creates volume at the top and is close at the sides*
   The best style for a round face shape is one that creates volume at the top but is close at the sides, thus creating the appearance of a long, narrow line.

8. To minimize the appearance of Kim's forehead, Courtney should style her hair:
   d. *forward over the sides of the forehead*
   By styling Kim's hair forward over the sides of the forehead, Courtney can hide the wideness of the forehead while still maintaining the illusion of a narrow line down the middle of the face.

9. To combat her close set eyes, Kim's hair should be:
   a. *directed back and away from the temples*
   Directing the hair back and away from the temples will open up the eye area and make the eyes appear farther apart.

10. What type of part is best for a face with a wide, flat nose?
    c. *center part*
    A center part gives the appearance of length.

11. To bring more definition to Kim's jawline, which type of line should be used?
    c. *straight*
    A straight line at the chin draws attention to that area and away from the center of the face.

12. When restyling Kim's hair Courtney will need to make sure her wavy hair is _____ at the temple area and _____ at the top.
    a. *close; high*
    To give the round face a more slender appearance, Courtney will need to make sure the hair is close at the temples to eliminate width and high at the top to give the illusion of an elongated shape.

Donny greets his final client of the day, Jason. Jason is middle-aged and balding. To combat the thinning of his hair on top, Jason combs the hair from one side of his head all the way across his forehead to the other side. He recently decided to stop trying to camouflage his thinning hair and has asked Donny for some advice on a new look. Donny considers the options.

13. Donny asks Jason if he would be comfortable wearing a beard. What style might Donny suggest?
    b. *a short beard, keeping the hair closely trimmed to his face*
    A man who is balding with closely trimmed hair could also look very good in a closely groomed beard and mustache. Keeping this facial hair closely trimmed creates a balance between the amount and volume of hair on his head and on his face.

14. When reviewing Jason's eyebrow length, Don suggests:
    d. *trimming them so they are full, but not too bushy*
    Once again, keeping all of Jason's facial hair neatly trimmed will maintain the overall balance of the face shape with the hair on the face. It gives the appearance of perfect balance and harmony, no matter how much hair is on Jason's head.

CHAPTER 15 Scalp Care, Shampooing, and Conditioning

Nestor is taking a course on scalp massage with a product manufacturer. He knows that his clients certainly enjoy having a scalp massage when they get their hair shampooed, but he has some clients who could benefit from scalp treatments as well. He is unsure of how to know when it is appropriate to suggest one or what kinds of products to use. Nestor has made some notes and he has gone into the class with several questions.

1. The instructor explains that there are two requirements for a healthy scalp. They are:

c. *cleanliness and stimulation*

The two basic requirements for a healthy scalp are cleanliness and stimulation. A clean scalp is a scalp that is less likely to contract disease, and a stimulated scalp is one that will function properly with the proper blood flow and circulation.

2. Scalp treatment products and massage may be given before the shampoo if:

a. *a scalp condition is apparent*

If a scalp condition is apparent once the stylist has done a thorough scalp analysis, it is recommended to perform the scalp treatment, including massage, before the shampoo. Treatment products may contain oils or medications that must sit on the scalp to be effective, so performing the treatment before the shampoo allows the time necessary to perform the treatment.

3. Scalp treatment products and massage may be given during the shampoo if:

c. *the client is in need of relaxation*

If the client has no apparent scalp condition and simply wishes to indulge in a scalp massage, it is performed during the shampoo service. Once the conditioner is applied to the hair, the cosmetologist may perform the scalp massage.

4. Nestor learns that the only difference between a relaxation and treatment massage is:

c. *the products used during the massage*

The scalp manipulations are exactly the same for both a relaxation and treatment massage; the only difference will be in the treatment product used. For a relaxation massage an aromatic conditioner may be used, but for treatment of a scalp condition, a more medicinal type of product will be used in the hopes of improving the symptoms of the scalp condition.

5. The purpose of a general scalp and hair treatment is:
   c. *to maintain the cleanliness and health of normal scalp and hair*
   The purpose of a general scalp treatment is to maintain the scalp and hair in a clean and healthy condition. A hair or scalp treatment should be recommended only after a hair and scalp examination.

6. Nestor also discovers that _____ is crucial to maintaining a healthy hair and scalp.
   a. *hair brushing*
   Correct hair brushing stimulates the blood circulation to the scalp.

7. Hair brushing is important because it:
   d. *all of the above*
   Correct hair brushing helps remove dust, dirt, and hair spray buildup from the hair and gives hair added shine. You should include a thorough hair brushing as part of every shampoo and scalp treatment, regardless of whether your client's hair and scalp are dry or oily.

8. Hair brushing is mandatory before which of the following services?
   c. *none of the above*
   There are two exceptions to hair brushing. Do not brush the hair or irritate the scalp before giving a chemical service and do not brush if the scalp is irritated.

Alexia is a receptionist at the Bubbles Salon and is frequently asked to explain the various shampoos and conditioners and their uses to the salon's clientele. She is surrounded by shelves full of products for retailing, and she answers questions and makes product recommendations all day long.

9. Barton is a 15-year-old client who frequently uses a lot of thick styling glue to get his hair to stand up in long spikes. He notices that his hair sometimes feels gooey even after shampooing. Alexia recommends a(n) _____ shampoo for him.
   d. *clarifying*
   Because of all of the product Barton uses on his hair and its formula of ingredients, he is experiencing a buildup of product, and that's what feels gooey to him. A clarifying shampoo contains an acidic ingredient such as cider vinegar that is helpful in cutting through product buildup that can flatten the hair or make it appear less shiny and healthy.

10. Mrs. Kames is a long-time haircolor client and needs a shampoo that will enable her to keep her color looking fresh between retouch visits. She should try a(n) _____ shampoo.

b. *color-enhancing*

Color-enhancing shampoos both cleanse the hair and add the color base back to the hair, acting like a temporary color. These are very useful to clients who want to keep the original tone of their color looking fresh.

11. Alexia usually suggests that a client with _____ hair purchase a moisturizing shampoo.

b. *permed*

A client whose hair may be dry or damaged due to chemicals used in the salon can greatly benefit from a moisturizing shampoo, which will make hair feel smooth and shiny.

12. For Norman's oily scalp, Alexia suggests a _____ shampoo.

a. *balancing*

A balancing shampoo is made especially for oily hair and scalp and will wash away excess oiliness without drying the scalp excessively.

13. For Joyce, who washes, blowdries, and flat irons her hair every day, Alexia recommends a _____ conditioner.

c. *light leave-in*

For someone who mechanically damages her hair as much as Joyce does with her regimen each day, a leave-in conditioner, one that is applied and not rinsed out, is ideal to moisturize and protect the hair from additional damage.

14. For Janice, who has a full head of bleached hair, Alexia recommends an in-salon conditioning service and a _____ conditioner for at-home use.

b. *treatment*

For hair like Janice's that is extremely damaged and dry, a treatment or repair conditioning treatment is excellent. These conditioners are left on the hair for up to 20 minutes, sometimes employing heat, and generally penetrate the cuticle to restore protein and conditioners to dry hair.

Donna, a new assistant at the Tranquil Escape Salon, has retrieved Ashley's haircolor client from the waiting area and has walked her to a shampoo bowl. Also in the shampoo area is Bob's next haircutting client, who is waiting to be shampooed, and Lakeesha, who is already in the midst of having her hair relaxed. Donna helps to seat her client, folds her collar under and into her blouse, puts a paper neck strip and cape over her, and begins her shampoo.

15. How should Donna have draped Ashley's haircolor client?

d. *using two towels and a cape*

A haircolor service is a chemical service and therefore requires a chemical draping. In a chemical drape, the client is draped with two terry cloth towels, one under the cape and one over the cape. The towels remain as a part of the drape until the service is completed and are regularly checked for dryness and replaced by the stylist.

16. How should Bob's haircutting client be draped for her shampoo and service?

a. *using one cape and a neck strip.*

A shampoo draping is used when a client is in the salon for a shampoo and styling or a shampoo and haircutting service. Two terry towels are used to protect the client, one under the shampoo cape and one over the cape. Once the shampoo service is completed and before the haircutting or hairstyling service begins, the terry towels are removed and replaced with a paper neck strip that is secured with a haircutting or styling cape.

17. How should Lakeesha have been draped for her relaxer service?

d. *with two towels and a cape*

A hair relaxer service is a chemical service and therefore requires a chemical draping. In a chemical drape, the client is draped with two terry cloth towels, one under the cape and one over the cape. The towels remain as a part of the drape until the service is completed and are regularly checked for dryness and replaced by the stylist.

CHAPTER 16 Haircutting

Johnny is a master haircutter at a posh, upscale salon in town. He has spent many years perfecting his cutting skills and getting to know the human head form. Today Johnny is booked solid—he has several clients to service and he is ready to get cutting!

1. Erin, Johnny's first customer, wants to wear an old haircutting favorite—the wedge. Johnny will use her occipital bone as his _____ for the entire cut.

   b. *reference point*

   A reference point is a point in the head that marks where the surface of the head changes and is used by haircutters to establish design lines that are proportionate to the head.

2. To determine if the wedge haircut is suitable for this client, Johnny needs to review the width of her _____.

   a. *parietal ridge*

   The parietal ridge, which is the widest area of the head, starting at the temples and ending at the bottom of the crown, should be considered. If her parietal ridge is already very wide, then this style will emphasize the width there; alternatively, if the client's parietal width is narrow, then this style will create weight to that area and help to balance the head form.

3. When cutting Erin's hair, Johnny is careful to observe the _____ for unusual growth patterns such as cowlicks.

   d. *crown area*

   The crown is the area between the apex and the back of the parietal ridge and is usually the site of cowlicks and whorls.

4. To cut Sandra's long hair along the face and to connect the bangs and the nape, Johnny will use a _____ cutting line.

   d. *diagonal*

   Diagonal lines are used to connect two varying lengths and are cut in a slanting or sloping direction.

5. When Johnny cuts Marianne's hair into a one-length bob, he uses a _____ cutting line.

   c. *horizontal*

   Horizontal lines are parallel to the horizon or the floor. Horizontal lines direct the eye from one side to the other. Horizontal lines build weight. They are used to create one-length and low-elevation haircuts and to add weight.

6. When using the line mentioned above to cut Marianne's hair into a one-length bob, Johnny uses _____ degrees of elevation.
   a. *0*
   Zero degrees of elevation give a straight, blunt, one-length haircut.

7. Marianne's bob will be uniform if Johnny makes sure to continuously use his initial _____ guideline when cutting.
   a. *stationary*
   A stationary guideline does not move. To cut the hair, all of the subsections are brought to the guide and cut at that elevation.

8. Darla has very long, one-length hair that she wants shorter and uniformly layered so, in order to create the layers she seeks, Johnny cuts her hair using a _____ guideline.
   c. *traveling*
   A traveling guideline, also known as movable guideline, moves as the haircut progresses. Traveling guidelines are used when creating a layered or graduated haircut.

9. Mindy has very long hair that she wants to be layered, but she also wants to keep all of the length at her nape. In order to accomplish this Johnny will have to _____ the hair as he cuts the layers.
   b. *overdirect*
   Overdirection occurs by combing the hair away from its natural falling position, thus allowing a cutter to keep certain areas of hair significantly longer than other areas while still achieving a blended-looking haircut.

Pat is looking over his appointment book today and sees that his first three clients are coming in for haircuts. Lucy has very thick, coarse, straight hair; Frank has a good amount of hair that is easy to handle and moderately soft to the touch; and Susan has thin, fine hair that usually lies limp no matter what style Pat cuts into it.

10. Lucy is the first client to sit in Pat's chair and she complains that her hair is always too "fluffy" on top and doesn't look good on her. Pat must first determine her _____ to know whether or not the silhouette of her style is right for her.
   B. *face shape*
   By analyzing the face shape, Pat can begin to make decisions about the best haircut for the client. An important thing to remember is that weight and volume draw attention to a specific area. For example, if a client has a wide face, a hairstyle with fuller sides makes the face appear wider, whereas a narrower style will give length to the face.

11. Lucy asks Pat what he thinks about her having her haircut really short so it can just lay flat against her face. Pat explains that a cut like that will cause her hair to:

b. *stand up away from the scalp*

Thick, coarse hair that is cut too short will not lie flat; rather, because the weight will be taken away from the strand, it will spring up and stick out.

12. Which tool should Pat NOT use when cutting Lucy's hair?

c. *razor*

Since a razor gives a soft finish to hair ends, using a razor on Lucy's thick and coarse hair will serve to lighten the ends even more and further cause her hair to stand up on end.

13. What type of haircut should Pat recommend for Lucy, based on her specific hair texture and face shape?

d. *medium length, layered haircut*

With Lucy's hair texture and coarseness, a medium-length style with layers will give her the freedom to wear her hair in a number of ways, while still allowing her enough hair to compensate for her facial shape and any flaws she may wish to camouflage.

14. Based on Frank's hair type and texture, what kinds of styles would work for him?

d. *both of the above*

Frank is fortunate to have the hair texture and density to be able to wear his hair both extremely short and texturized, without worrying about hair that will stick up or out of place.

15. Frank likes to wear his hair short at the nape and sides and fuller on top with a messy look. To achieve this, Pat will need to use _____ on the top.

d. *thinning shears*

Wearing hair "messy" means that the hair will need to be cut into different lengths to achieve the messy look, where the shorter hairs hold up the longer hairs. This is beautifully achieved with the use of thinning shears.

16. To get a clean line at the nape, Pat will employ a(n):

d. *edger*

An edger is a smaller version of a clipper and is mainly used to clean the nape line on very short cuts.

17. To create the impression of thicker hair, Pat needs to create _____ in Susan's style.

b. *weight*

In order to create the illusion of thicker hair, Pat will need to find a way to create weight. This can be done by cutting the hair at a zero-degree elevation.

18. The best cut for Susan's hair is the:

b. *blunt cut*

A blunt cut, or a zero-elevation cut, builds weight lines on the head form and gives the illusion of thicker hair.

19. The best cutting tool for Pat to use on Susan's hair is a:

b. *haircutting shear*

Since Pat wants to get an exacting, blunt cut for Susan's one-length style, the best tool he can use is a simple haircutting shear.

20. The type of comb that Pat will use for each of his haircuts will be the:

d. *styling comb*

A styling or cutting comb is between 6 and 8 inches (15 to 20 cm) long and is considered an all-purpose comb. It is used for most cutting procedures.

Pam is about to graduate from beauty school and has decided that it is time to buy a new pair of haircutting shears. She has saved her money and has thought about how often she will use her shears and has created a list of questions to ask the salesperson at her local distributor's store. She is on her way to make her big purchase.

21. Pam begins by asking the salesperson to show her several brands of haircutting shears. The one she is most interested in has an ideal Rockwell hardness of:

c. *57*

Generally, a shear with a Rockwell hardness of at least 56 or 57 is ideal. A shear with a Rockwell hardness that is higher than 63 can make the shear too hard and brittle to work with; the shear could even break if dropped.

22. Pam begins to pick a couple of shears she likes. The salesperson explains that _____ shears are thought to be the most durable.

c. *forged*

The forging process creates a more durable shear than the casting process. Forged shears are easier to repair if dropped or bent. With new technology in the manufacturing process, a forged shear is similar in price to a cast shear but is of much higher quality and durability. Forged shears last significantly longer than cast shears.

23. Pam asks the salesperson how she should care for a new pair of shears and is told that in addition to daily cleaning, lubrication, and _____, once per week the blades of the shears should be loosened and cleaned and lubricated.

a. *tension adjustment and balancing*

Adjusting blade tension is an important task to make sure shears are functioning correctly and to ensure that the best results can be achieved. If the tension is too loose, it will allow the shears to fold the hair. If it is too tight, it will cause the shears to bind and cause unnecessary wear and user fatigue.

24. The sales person asks Pam what type of blade edge she is interested in. Pam explains that she wants a _____ for the smoothest cut and sharpest edge possible.

b. *convex edge*

For a cosmetology professional, the best blade is a full convex edge. This type of blade will give you the smoothest cut and is the sharpest edge possible. The convex edge glides through the hair easily and smoothly.

25. After making her purchase, Pam asks the salesperson how often she should have her shears sharpened. The salesperson informs Pam that with proper care, sharpening is only needed every _____.

d. *twelve months*

You should only sharpen your shears as needed. Do not fall into the habit of automatically having them sharpened on a three-to-six month cycle, whenever the sharpening technician comes to the salon. Remember, the better you care for your shears, the longer the edges will last between sharpening. On average, you should be able to go one year or longer between sharpening if you follow the oiling and adjustment directions for your shears. When you do need to have your shears sharpened, it is best to have a factory-certified technician sharpen your shears or to send them to the manufacturer to service them.

Manny attends the ABC Beauty School and is enrolled in a cutting class for curly hair. Today, he and his classmates will cut and style three clients with varying amounts of curly hair. Manny's first client, Jen, has very curly hair that falls down in ringlets. Jen wants her blunt cut trimmedabout an inch (2.5 cm) shorter. Sandy, Manny's next client, has medium length wavy hair and wants her new style to be shorter and spiky. Finally, Renee, his third client, wants to show off her curly hair, so she is looking for a mid-length style to showcase the curl.

26. To give Jen the trim she wants, Manny will need to:

b. *cut it straight across the bottom with no tension at all*

Pulling curly hair taut when cutting will cause it to be much shorter when it dries, so to preserve its length, Manny will want to cut it without tension.

27. To achieve the appearance of having cut Jen's hair 1 inch (2.5 cm), Manny will actually need to cut off about:

b. *¼ inch (.6 cm)*

The rule of thumb for cutting curly hair is that for every ¼ inch (.6 cm) that's cut, the hair will shrink by about 1 inch (2.5 cm).

28. Cutting 1 inch (2.5 cm) of hair will make Jen's finished style appear _____ when it is dry.

c. *shorter*

Cutting Jen's hair a full inch (2.5 cm) will make her hair appear much shorter than she wants it to be.

29. When Manny begins cutting Sandy's hair, he must be aware that her curly hair will need to be elevated _____ to achieve the desired look.

c. *less*

Since Sandy wants her hair to be layered, Manny will need to employ some elevation in his cutting technique; however, it should be less elevation when working with curly hair than with straight hair being cut into the same style.

30. To give Sandy's hair the spiky look she desires, Manny will need to texturize her hair using the _____ technique.

c. *notching*

Notching is a more aggressive version of point cutting and delivers a spiky look to the hair.

31. To give Renee the mid-length style she desires, Manny will need to cut the hair at a _____ -degree angle all around the head.

b. *45*

Using a 45-degree angle will give Renee the mid-length layered look she is after.

32. To remove bulk and add movement to Renee's cut, Manny will use a technique called:

d. *slicing*

Slicing is a great technique for removing bulk and adding movement throughout the lengths of the hair.

CHAPTER 17 Hairstyling

Gayle has been styling hair for the movies for a number of years and has recently been asked to work on a movie whose story takes place in the 1920s and 1930s. She will be responsible for styling the hair for the two lead characters, Esther and Johanna. The director explains to Gayle the look he is after for each of the characters. For Esther, he wants Gayle to create a real flapper look, with many wide but uniformly sized dark waves around the head. The hair should be close to the head when dry, perfectly curled into the wave formations, and set so that no matter how much dancing or movement the character experiences, the hair remains in place. The second character, Johanna, will need to wear her hair in a more flamboyant manner, so it should be light blond in color and the hair should sweep forward at the temples and onto the face. Johanna's hair requires lots of volume but the style should also be very controlled and perfectly coifed so that it stays in place. Gayle begins working on her designs and the supplies she'll need.

1. The list of supplies Gayle will need to have handy for styling the two characters includes:

d. *clips, combs, and rollers*

Creating these two beautifully coifed styles will require an artistic eye and wet-set styling tools such as clips, combs, and rollers.

2. In terms of styling aids, Gayle will need to purchase:

a. *setting lotion, styling lotion, and hair spray*

These are the exact types of wet-goods products that are useful in wet setting hair.

3. To achieve the close-to-the head waves the director wants Esther to wear, Gayle will need to create:

c. *a finger wave*

A finger wave, with its perfectly aligned curl formations that lay flat against the head, is the perfect technique to achieve this look.

4. To ensure that Esther's hair lays appropriately for the style, Gayle should use:

c. *her natural part*

Using her natural part ensures that the hair will lie flat instead of fighting with a part line that forces the hair to lay in a direction that it doesn't want to.

5. The best type of comb for Gayle to use when creating Esther's style is a:
   b. *styling comb*
   A styling comb is perfectly balanced and is the correct comb for Gayle to use when forming Esther's style.

6. When Gayle completes styling Esther's hair, the waves should look like a continuous letter:
   c. *S*
   Finger waves that are done correctly should look like one continuous S shape all over the head, and each ridge should be the exact same size and shape as the one before it.

7. How should Gayle dry Esther's hair prior to combing it out?
   d. *with a hooded dryer*
   To dry Esther's hair Gayle should use a hair net to protect the style from excessive blowing and then put her under a hooded dryer until the style is completely dry.

8. To create Johanna's style, Gayle will use:
   d. *a hooded dryer, rollers, and pin curls*
   To get the kind of volume and hold needed for this role, Gayle will need to use a wet set.

9. To create the most volume she can on the top of Johanna's head, Gayle will place:
   a. *rollers on base*
   By rolling the hair on the roller and placing it directly on top of its base, Gayle ensures that Johanna's curls will have the greatest volume and mobility.

10. In order for Johanna's hair to sweep forward at her temples, Gayle will place pin curls into a _____ shaping.
    c. *C*
    The C shaping will first sweep the hair at the temple area back, off the face and then forward again, onto the face.

11. In order to get a tight, long-lasting curl without too much mobility, Gayle will use:
    a. *no-stem pin curls*
    The no-stem pin curl is placed directly on the base of the curl and delivers a tight, firm, long-lasting curl with little mobility.

12. To achieve a smooth, directed shape, Gayle will need to use a(n) _____ base pin curl at the temple area of Johanna's style.

c. *arc*

Arc-based pin curls are carved out of a base shaping, give good direction, and are used around the hairline.

13. When combing out the finished style, Gayle will certainly need to _____ the hair on the top of Johanna's head to achieve the height required and to ensure the shape lasts as long as needed.

b. *backcomb*

Backcombing or teasing involves combing small sections of hair from the ends to the base, causing shorter hair to mat at the base and form a cushion or base.

Marcia has decided that, after many years with the same styling tools and implements, she needs to purchase new, better quality ones. In preparation for going to her distributor's store to purchase her new equipment, Marcia thinks about her various clients and their hair needs and makes a list of the new tools she will need to purchase. Marcia also decides to look for some new styling lotions as well.

14. The foundation tool for all of Marcia's styling begins with her:

c. *blowdryer*

A blowdryer is an electrical device designed for drying and styling hair in a single service. The blowdryer is considered a basic necessity for today's stylist.

15. Marcia's blowdryer must have a(n) _____ attachment that allows the hair to be dried as if it were being air dried.

c. *diffuser*

A diffuser attachment causes the air to flow more softly, which in turn allows the hair to dry so as to accentuate natural texture and definition.

16. For her clients with mid- to longer-length hair, Marcia will need a:

b. *paddle brush*

The paddle brush has a large, flat base and ball-tipped, staggered nylon pins and is great for use on mid-to-long hair lengths because the pins do not snag or catch the hair.

17. For clients with fine hair or for adding lift at the scalp area, Marcia will need a:

c. *vent brush*

A vent brush has a ventilated design and is useful in speeding up the drying process as well as for adding volume at the scalp area.

18. For clients who need a strong-hold styling preparation, Marcia picks up:

c. *styling gel*

Styling gel is a thick, usually clear, preparation that has a strong hold factor. It is used to create strong hold, or control, in styles.

19. For clients who want to add weight to their hair and achieve a piecy, textured look, Marcia purchases:

d. *styling pomade*

Styling pomade adds considerable weight to the hair by causing hair strands to join together and by causing significant separation in the hair.

20. To add gloss and shine to a finished style, Marcia will need:

c. *silicone shiners*

Silicone shiners are used to add shine and gloss to the hair without adding weight. These products may also create textural definition.

Brandis has an appointment with Shereen for a shampoo and styling. Brandis has medium length, layered hair and likes to wear it straight, close to the head, and curled under around the face and at the neckline. Brandis is an African-American client who does not chemically straighten her hair.

21. In order for Shereen to style Brandis's hair she will need to determine:

d. *how much curl to remove from it*

Shereen will need to know what type of finished look Brandis is trying to achieve, and then she will need to assess the natural curl in her hair to best determine how much curl to remove from it and how to accomplish the style.

22. To remove 100 percent of Brandis's curl, Shereen will need to use a:

c. *hard press*

A hard press involves the application of the thermal pressing comb twice on each side of the hair to adequately remove all of the curl.

24. Before pressing, Shereen should add _____ to Brandis's hair and scalp.

c. *pressing oil*

Adding pressing oil will make the hair softer and prepare and condition it for the pressing treatment, as well as protect the hair and scalp from the heat of the comb.

CHAPTER 18 Braiding and Braid Extensions

Darlene is interested in having his hair extended through braids and has made an appointment with Tameka for the service. She is told by the receptionist that she will need to be in the salon for several hours so she plans accordingly. Darlene arrives at the salon on time and Tameka begins the service with a client consultation, hair and scalp analysis, and then a discussion about the type and length of the braid and extensions Darlene is looking for. Tameka also takes the time to inform Darlene how to wear and care for her braids before beginning the actual service.

1. Tameka informs Darlene that she uses natural hairstyling techniques, which means:
   c. *she will not use any chemicals in providing Darlene's services*
   Braiding salons practice what is commonly known as natural hairstyling, which uses no chemicals or dyes and does not alter the natural curl or coil pattern of the hair. While the origins of natural hairstyling are rooted in African-American heritage, people of all ethnicities appreciate its beauty and versatility. In the twenty-first century, natural hairstyling has brought a diverse approach to hair care.

2. Tameka explains that a complicated braid style can last for up to:
   d. *90 days*
   Since many braids are beautifully complex and can take several hours to complete, they can, if taken care of, last for as long as 90 days before they need to be rebraided or touched up.

3. One of the most important aspects of Tameka's client consultation will be to assess the _____ of Darlene's hair.
   d. *texture*
   Darlene's hair texture—whether it is coarse, medium, or fine; whether it feels oily, dry, or wiry; and whether it is straight, curly, or coiled—will be a very important clue as to the hairstyle that will work best for her and be easiest to maintain.

4. Tameka determines that Darlene would look best in a braid style that is full on top and at the neckline, but close to her head at the temples because she has determined that she has a(n) _____ facial type.
   d. *diamond*
   A diamond face shape is widest at the center of the face and so requires that a hairstyle, in order to balance the face, add fullness to the forehead and jawline areas.

5. In addition to the combs, brushes, and blowdryer Tameka will need for the service, she also sets up her station to include the extension materials, _____.
   c. *drawing board and hackle*
   A drawing board has flat leather pads and fine teeth that sandwich the human hair extensions and allow the needed hair to be extracted without disturbing or loosening the rest of the hair. A hackle is a board with fine nails used to detangle and comb out the hair.

6. Since Darlene intends to wash her hair once a week and let it dry naturally without the use of heat or irons, and since she desires a shiny, reflective finished look, the material Tameka considers using is:
   c. *nylon*
   Since nylon is a synthetic fiber that delivers high shine and can reflect light, and based on how Darlene plans on caring for her hair, it is the perfect choice for her extension material.

7. Tameka decides to use an underhand technique for braiding, which means that:
   c. *the side sections go under the middle section*
   An underhand technique, also known as plaiting, is one in which the left section goes under the middle strand, then the right section goes under the middle strand. This technique is often used for cornrowing because many braiders believe it creates less tangling.

8. Darlene explains that she wants a braid that looks like two strands of hair are wrapped around one another. This style of braid is called a(n):
   b. *rope braid*
   The rope braid is made with two strands that are twisted around each other. This technique can be used on layered or one-length hair.

It's prom time and there are several teen-aged clients waiting for their "special" hair styles in the Braided Up Salon reception area. One client, Maria, has very long, one-length hair and is looking for a braided style to which she can add flowers or a hair accessory. Another client, Stephanie, is hoping to try something different—she wants to wear a chignon with a couple of braids accentuating it. And finally, Marcus is waiting for a braiding style that will provide a neat, clean look and some extra length for prom night.

9. With Maria's long, one-length hair and her desire to add an accessory to the hair, a _____ braid may be the best choice.
   b. *fishtail braid*
   The fishtail braid is a simple, two-strand braid in which hair is picked up from the sides and added to the strands as they are crossed over each other. It is best done on nonlayered hair that is at least shoulder length.

10. Stephanie is planning to wear a very traditional updo to the prom but wants to add a braid design to the finished style. Which of the following techniques might work best for her?
   c. *single braid*
   Single braids, also known as box braids and individual braids, are free-hanging braids, with or without extensions, that can be executed using either an underhand or overhand technique. Single braids can be used with all hair textures and in a variety of ways. For instance, two or three single braids added to a ponytail or chignon can be a lovely evening look.

11. What type of braid will provide Marcus with the clean-cut look he seeks?
   a. *cornrow*
   Cornrows, also known as canerows, are narrow rows of visible braids that lie close to the scalp and are created with a three-strand, on-the-scalp braiding technique. Consistent and even partings are the foundation of beautiful cornrows. Cornrows are worn by men, women, and children, and can be braided on hair of various lengths and textures. The flat, contoured styles can last several weeks when applied without extensions, and up to two months when applied with extensions.

12. In order to get the additional length that Marcus is looking for, his stylist will need to give him:
   c. *a cornrow with extensions*
   Extensions can be applied to cornrows or individual braids to add length to the finished style.

CHAPTER 19 Wigs and Hair Additions

Carlotta has had a number of clients ask her about wigs lately and so she has decided to create a special area within her salon that is dedicated to these items. Clients who are interested in being fitted for a wig or who want to experiment with various wigs will be welcomed to try them out in her salon. Carlotta has several clients who are interested in using the wigs as fashion accessories and others who are experiencing hair loss, so she orders a number of different items from her local distributor.

1. For clients who want the highest quality wigs to cover 100 percent of their hair, Carlotta orders:

c. *human hair wigs*

Human hair wigs are of the best quality and look the most natural because human hair wigs react to wear just as natural hair would.

2. If a client is interested in a product that is ready-to-wear, that comes in fantasy colors, and whose color will not fade, Carlotta should recommend a:

a. *synthetic wig*

Synthetic hair wigs can simulate natural hair wigs, are less expensive, are usually ready to wear and easy to care for, and can come in lots of interesting and attractive colors.

3. For a client who is interested in a wig that has spaces for air to flow through and is less structured, Carlotta should suggest a:

b. *capless wig*

A capless wig is one that is less structured and is open, airy, light, and comfortable to wear.

4. For a client who may have significant hair loss, a ____ wig would be a good suggestion.

c. *cap wig*

Cap wigs are constructed with an elasticized, mesh-fiber base to which the hair is attached and are available in several sizes. The front edge of a cap wig is made of a material that resembles the client's scalp, along with a lace extension and a wire support that is used at the temples for a snug, secure fit, so they are best for people with severe hair loss or who are bald.

5. Carlotta learns that hand-tied wigs are made:
   a. *by inserting individual strands of hair into mesh foundations and knotting them with a needle*
      Hand-tied wigs, also known as hand-knotted wigs, are made by inserting individual strands of hair into mesh foundations and knotting them with a needle. Hand-tying is done particularly around the front hairline and at the top of the head. These wigs have a natural, realistic look and are wonderful for styling.

6. Semi-hand-tied wigs contain:
   c. *both synthetic and human hair*
      Semi-hand-tied wigs are constructed with a combination of synthetic hair and hand-tied human hair. Reasonably priced, they offer a natural appearance and good durability.

7. To measure a client for a wig, Carlotta will need a:
   c. *soft tape measure*
      A soft tape measure is useful for measuring around the contours of the head.

8. To practice working with wigs, Carlotta should work with the wig while it is:
   b. *on a block*
      A block is a head-shaped form, usually made of canvas-covered cork or foam, to which the wig is secured for fitting, cleaning, coloring, and styling.

9. A hairpiece that has openings in the base through which the client's own hair is pulled to blend with the hair of the hairpiece is called a(n):
   c. *integration hairpiece*
      An integration hairpiece is a hairpiece that has openings in the base through which the client's own hair is pulled to blend with the (natural or synthetic) hair of the hairpiece. These hairpieces are very lightweight, natural-looking products that add length and volume to the client's hair. They are also recommended for clients with thinning hair, but not for those with total hair loss, as the scalp is likely to show through.

Judy has had short hair most of her life and has always wanted to try having long hair but has difficulty letting her fine, thin hair grow long. She discusses this with her stylist Larissa, who recommends that she consider having a hair extension service. Larissa explains that hair extensions come in various forms and amounts and are secured to Judy's existing hair to lengthen the overall style and appearance. Judy books an appointment for the extension service.

10. Before attaching any hair extensions, Larissa will need to ascertain from Judy whether or not to:

   b. *add length or fullness, or both*

   Judy will need to decide how much length she wants to add to her existing hair.

11. When attaching an extension, it should be placed:

   d. *about 1 inch (2.5 cm) from the hairline*

   It is a general rule of thumb to stay about an inch (2.5 cm) from the hairline in the front, at the temples, and at the part line when attaching extensions.

12. Since Judy has fine, thin hair, Larissa will need to:

   c. *be careful to hide the base of the hair weft*

   Since fine hair is usually also thinner than coarse hair, it will be important for Larissa to be aware of where she is attaching the weft of hair and to be sure to have enough hair and length above it to cover the weft.

13. Larissa will have several options for attaching the extension to Judy's hair. Which of the following is NOT an option?

   b. *the bob and weave method*

   There is no such professional method called the bob and weave method.

14. The best method Larissa can use for attaching the hair weft to Judy's fine hair is the _____ method

   d. *fusion bonding*

   In the fusion bonding method, the extension hair is bonded to the client's own hair by a heat-activated bonding material. This is best for fine hair because it doesn't leave any bulk to cover up when completed.

CHAPTER 20 Chemical Texture Services

Nick checks his appointment book and sees that he has three perms scheduled for the day. Ava has short, thick, coarse hair and is booked for a tight perm so she can wear her hair curly and let it dry naturally. Maureen has medium-length, colored hair that is extremely dry. She wants to create additional body in her hair so that it is easier to style and will hold the style a bit longer once she has blown it dry and curled it. Reva has very long, straight, one-length virgin hair that she is bored with. Instead of cutting her length, Reva wants to try a long and very curly style. To get prepared, Nick stocks his rollabout and retrieves each client's record card.

1. Ava's hair texture indicates to Nick that her hair may:

c. *require more processing time*

Based on her hair texture, Ava has coarse hair, which usually requires more processing time.

2. Since Maureen's hair is colored, Nick must take special care to notice her hair's:

a. *porosity*

Since Maureen's hair has been colored, she has already opened the cuticle layer of her hair and slightly damaged it, so Nick will need to assess how much damage the hair has undergone in order to assess the porosity level, the hair's ability to absorb liquid, and prepare accordingly.

3. When wrapping Ava's hair, Nick will employ the _____ technique in order to achieve a tighter curl at the ends and a looser curl at the scalp.

c. *croquignole*

Using the croquignole technique means the hair is wrapped from the ends to the scalp in overlapping layers, which produces a larger curl at the scalp and a tighter curl at the ends.

4. In order to achieve a uniform curl throughout the entire hair strand, Nick will wrap Reva's long hair using the _____ technique.

a. *spiral*

In the spiral wrap technique, the hair is wrapped either from the ends to the scalp or from the scalp to the ends evenly, without much overlap, so the result is a more even curl formation.

5. To achieve a tighter curl in the center of each strand and a looser curl on the outer edges, Nick will use _____ rods when wrapping Maureen's hair.

b. *concave*

Concave rods have a smaller circumference in the center of the rod and a wider circumference on the outside edges, which produces a tighter curl on the inside of the curl.

6. To protect the many layers in Maureen's haircut while perming, Nick will employ the _____ wrap.
   b. *double-flat*
   The double-flat wrap employs two end papers, one under the hair and one over the hair, to protect the hair and its layers when wrapped around the rod.

7. To perm Ava's thick, coarse hair, Nick should select a(n) _____ wave.
   a. *exothermic*
   An exothermic wave has an alkaline pH base of 9.0 to 9.6 and employs a heat reaction during the waving process.

8. To perm Maureen's extremely damaged hair, Nick should select a(n) _____ wave.
   b. *true acid*
   A true acid wave with a pH of 4.5 to 7.0 is best used for extremely damaged hair or extremely porous hair and is perfect for hair such as Maureen's.

9. To perm Reva's virgin hair, Nick should select a(n) _____ wave:
   a. *alkaline/cold*
   A cold or alkaline wave, with a pH of 9.0 to 9.6, is perfect for hair that is coarse, thick, and resistant, such as Reva's hair.

Mrs. Carr, who was in the salon two weeks ago for a perm service, has come back into the salon today to tell her stylist Jill that the perm "fried" her hair; she also complains that her hair is curly at the scalp and about halfway down the strand but the bottom half of the strand is straight, dry, and frizzy. Jill finds Mrs. Carr's record card and reviews the perm she selected and the procedure.

10. Based on Mrs. Carr's description of her hair, her hair is:
   c. *overprocessed*
   Overprocessed hair usually has a weak curl or results in straight hair.

11. The perm solution that Jill chose was most likely too:
   c. *strong*
   Overprocessed hair means that the waving lotion was either too strong or was left on the hair too long.

12. Mrs. Carr's hair doesn't have enough strength left to:
   c. *hold the desired curl*
   Mrs. Carr's hair doesn't have the strength to hold the curl because too many disulfide bonds were broken during the perming process.

13. Mrs. Carr's hair cannot hold its curl because too many _____ bonds were broken during the perm processing.
   b. *disulfide*
   When hair is overprocessed, it means that too strong a solution was used on the hair and that many disulfide bonds were broken, rendering the hair unable to hold its new shape. A properly processed permanent wave should break and rebuild approximately 50 percent of the hair's disulfide bonds.

14. Jill realizes that because the perm solution she used was too strong, the damage to Mrs. Carr's hair occurred in the _____ minutes of the service.
   c. *first five to ten*
   If a client's hair has been overprocessed, it probably happened within the first five to ten minutes of the service, and a weaker permanent waving solution should have been used. You should take care to check the curl formation every few minutes, but you can check more often if you are concerned about the hair's condition.

15. Mrs. Carr asks Jill for another perm. Jill explains that another perm at this time will:
   c. *make the hair even straighter*
   Contrary to what many people believe, overprocessed hair does not necessarily mean hair that is overly curly. If too many disulfide bonds are broken, the hair will be too weak to hold a firm curl. Overprocessed hair usually has a weak curl or may even be completely straight. Since the hair at the scalp is usually stronger than the hair at the ends, overprocessed hair is usually curlier at the scalp and straighter at the ends. If the hair is overprocessed, further processing, which will only break more disulfide bonds, will make it straighter.

Melinda has two clients arrive at the salon for appointments. Both Charlotte and Brenda have extremely curly hair that they want to have relaxed. Charlotte wants to wear her hair perfectly straight in a chin-length blunt style. Brenda wants her hair to be layered, and she wants the curl reduced but not completely taken out so that she can wear her hair wavy. After reviewing their record cards, Melinda realizes that Charlotte had some scalp irritation as a result of her last haircolor appointment. Melinda prepares for the services.

16. To completely straighten Charlotte's hair, Melinda will use a:
   b. *chemical hair relaxer*
   Using a chemical hair relaxer is the only way to permanently remove all of the curl from Charlotte's hair, in order to achieve her desired look.

17. To remove some of the curl from Brenda's hair, Melinda will use a:

c. *soft curl permanent*

Since Brenda only wants to have more control over the amount of curl she wears instead of eliminating it completely, Melinda will use a soft curl permanent to re-form the curl.

18. What can Melinda do to minimize the potential reaction Charlotte's scalp may have to the service?

d. *use a protective base*

Since Melinda knows that Charlotte has a sensitive scalp, she should opt to use a protective base to protect her scalp before the application of the straightener.

19. A relaxer containing which of the following active ingredients is most appropriate for Melinda to use on Charlotte's hair, given her sensitive scalp?

d. *guanidine hydroxide*

Guanidine hydroxide has a pH of 13 to 13.5, causes less skin irritation than other hydroxide relaxers, and is a good choice for someone such as Charlotte.

20. What strength relaxer is best used on Charlotte?

a. *mild*

Since Charlotte's hair has already been colored, a mild formula is the best choice for a straightening product.

21. Brenda's soft-curl perm will:

c. *reformulate the amount of curl she has*

A soft-curl perm does not remove curl; it simply changes the type and amount of curl so that it can be more easily worked with.

22. How many services are required for Melinda to complete the soft curl perm procedure on Brenda's hair?

b. *2*

A soft-curl perm requires two services. The first is a relaxing service with a thio relaxer, and the second is the wrapping of the relaxed hair on tools to re-form the curl.

23. Which of the following is involved in Melinda performing the soft-curl perm on Brenda's hair?

b. *relaxing the hair and then re-curling it*

This process doesn't really straighten the hair, what it actually does is make the client's existing curl softer and looser.

CHAPTER 21 Haircoloring

Danny is a master colorist at the Suprema Salon. He has a long list of color clients who see him each day. Today, he notices that he has three color correction services planned. The first is Mary, who wears light blond highlights and is a swimmer. After swimming in a chlorinated pool every day for the past three months, her hair has a greenish tinge which is unsightly and needs to be corrected. Danny's next client, Amber, colored her own hair at home but was unhappy when her hair turned a brassy orange color. Amber wants to return to her natural color, a deep brown without so much red in it. And, finally, Zeena, who recently had her hair lightened from root to ends, wants Danny to change her color because she feels it is too "lemony looking."

1. To counteract the greenish tinge to Mary's haircolor, Danny will need to select a shade that has a _____ base color.

c. *red*

To counteract a greenish tinge to her hair, Danny will need to determine which color is opposite the color he wants to cover on the color wheel and use a new shade with that base color to change the greenish hair to a more natural shade.

2. To prevent Mary's highlighted hair from becoming too dark during the correction procedure, Danny must be careful not to select a shade with too much _____ in it.

a. *blue*

The addition of blue to a color darkens the overall shade.

3. The color Danny will use to correct Mary's hair color is a(n) _____ color.

a. *primary*

A primary color is a pure or fundamental color that cannot be achieved through a mixture of other colors.

4. To return Amber's haircolor to the desired shade, Danny will need to use a _____ tone.

d. *cool*

Since Amber complains that her hair is too brassy, or orange (i.e., a warm tone), Danny will need to use a cool shade to counter the red tones.

5. Typical colors in the tone range Danny will use on Amber's hair have a(n) _____ base.

d. *blue*

Any cool color will have some degree of blue in its base tone.

6. The color Danny will use to correct Amber's brassy tone is a(n) _____ color.
   b. *complementary*
   Complementary colors are a primary and a secondary color positioned opposite each other on the color wheel.

7. Once achieved, Amber's deep brown haircolor will be a level:
   d. *3*
   Level is a unit of measurement used to identify the lightness or darkness of a color. If Danny achieves the dark brown shade Amber desires, he will have achieved a level 3 haircolor for her.

8. If Zeena wanted her lightened hair to have a cooler, more platinum look instead of the lemony color it is now, Danny would need to select a shade that has a _____ base.
   d. *violet*
   To counteract the lemon-yellow color, Danny would need to choose a blue-based color for Zeena. Violet is a blue-based color and is opposite yellow on the color wheel, making it the right choice for a platinum blond look.

9. If Zeena wanted her lightened hair to have a strawberry blond color instead of the lemony color it is now, Danny would need to select a shade that has a _____ base.
   c. *red*
   A strawberry blond shade is a mixture of yellow and red, so since the hair is already very yellow, Danny would need to use a red-based shade on Zeena to achieve the strawberry color.

10. A strawberry blond shade would indicate that Zeena preferred a _____ tone in her hair.
    a. *warm*
    Any color with a red or yellow base is a warm color.

11. Once Zeena's lightened hair has achieved a platinum shade, her haircolor will be a level:
    a. *10*
    A level 10 is the lightest shade and since Zeena wishes to be a platinum blond, she is asking for the lightest shade.

Another colorist at the Suprema Salon, Sarah, also has a busy day ahead. She has her first client, Gina, booked for a color service. Gina has about 25 percent gray hair and wants something close to her natural medium brown color to blend and cover her gray. Maya is another of Sarah's clients; she is a natural redhead who wants to have a few chunky blond highlights around her face. And Katie, who loves to wear her hair short and funky and who has been lightening her hair, is booked for a full head bleach retouch on a two-inch (5 cm) regrowth area.

12. Since Gina has about 25 percent gray hair, what is the overall situation Sarah will encounter when coloring Gina's hair?

    c. *Gina has more pigmented hair than gray hair.*

    Sarah's assessment of Gina's hair is that she has 25 percent gray hair, which means that the remaining 75 percent of Gina's hair is pigmented.

13. To effectively blend Gina's gray hair, Sarah should use a:

    c. *demipermanent color*

    Demipermanent haircolor is a deposit-only haircolor, which means that it does not lighten the hair during the coloring process. It deposits color and coats the hair shaft with dark color, which is an excellent way of coating and therefore blending gray hair with pigmented hair.

14. The type of color product Sarah uses on Gina should:

    c. *deposit color*

    Since the only required outcome with this service is to deposit color onto the unpigmented hair, the only thing the color needs to do is cover the gray.

15. When formulating Gina's color, to assure proper coverage, Sarah should:

    d. *select a shade two levels lighter than the desired shade*

    Since demipermanent color simply "dumps" color onto the hair shaft, it is important that the shade not become too dark to naturally blend with the pigmented hair. It is usually recommended that a lighter shade is used.

16. To achieve the chunky highlights that Maya desires, Sarah will need to use a(n):

    d. *off-the-scalp bleach*

    Since chunky highlights appear in various areas on the head and not at the scalp, an off-the-scalp bleach is appropriate for use.

17. Since Maya's natural hair color is a bright shade of red-orange, her hair will go through _____ degrees of decolorization to achieve the yellow base shade she desires for her highlights.

    c. 5

    The darker the natural color the hair is when decolorizing, the more stages of lightening the hair will go through. Since Maya's hair is already in the red-orange shade, she will have to go through five more stages of decolorization to achieve the blond highlights she requested.

18. Since Maya has so much red pigment in her hair naturally, Sarah may opt to use a _____ technique to achieve a pleasing finished tone to the highlighted hair.

c. *double-process coloring*

A double-process technique, which involves first bleaching the hair and then toning it with a haircolor shade, will help Sarah to get rid of the unflattering red-orange tones that are naturally present in Maya's hair.

19. To lighten Katie's regrowth area Sarah will use a(n):

a. *on-the-scalp bleach*

Since the regrowth area is at the scalp, Sarah will need to use an on-the-scalp bleach to lighten Katie's regrowth.

20. To boost the lifting power of the cream bleach, Sarah will use a(n):

b. *activator*

An activator is an oxidizer added to hydrogen peroxide to increase its chemical action, in this case, its lifting power.

21. Before applying the toner to Katie's hair Sarah may choose to use a(n) _____ to protect and condition the previously bleached hair.

d. *conditioner filler*

A conditioner filler is used to recondition hair prior to the haircolor application. Color can be applied right over the conditioner filler and in this way both products are working together to color and condition the hair.

22. After her hair is lightened to the desired level, Sarah should formulate and tone Katie's hair using a _____ -volume developer to simply add color and lessen the amount of damage done to the hair.

a. *10*

Since the hair will have already been lightened, a low-volume developer is all that is needed for toning the prelightened hair.

23. Which of Sarah's clients require a patch test before she begins their services?

d. *all of them*

Since all of Sarah's clients received color services using an aniline derivative tint, they all require a patch test.

CHAPTER 22 Hair Removal

Joanie is a fashion-conscious businesswoman who deals with the public all day long. She is very careful to present a professional and attractive appearance. Joanie has always had a problem with superfluous facial and body hair. Once a week she shapes her eyebrows at home with a pair of tweezers, and every other week she books an appointment for removal of unsightly facial hair on her upper lip, chin, and neck. Joanie has noticed that sometimes her face is irritated by waxing. Joanie usually shaves the hair on legs and underarms every other day but her skin often feels bumpy from shaving. Joanie wants to investigate some other options for hair removal that may make her personal grooming routine easier and less bothersome. She discusses her options with Amy, her esthetician.

1. Before determining the appropriate methods of hair removal, a positive answer to which of the following questions would indicate to Amy that she should not be providing hair removal services for Joanie?

c. *Do you currently use Retin-A?*

The use of Retin-A or similar products is a contraindication for hair removal, which means that it should not be considered for the client.

2. When Joanie shapes her own eyebrows with a pair of tweezers, she is using a method called:

d. *temporary hair removal*

Tweezing is a form of temporary hair removal because the hair that is removed will grow back.

3. If Joanie wanted to learn more about permanent hair removal methods, Amy would suggest:

d. *electrolysis, photoepilation, and laser hair removal*

Electrolysis is removal of hair by the use of an electric current; photoepilation is the removal of hair by means of using an intense light to destroy hair follicles; and laser hair removal uses a laser beam pulsed on the skin to impair the hair follicles.

4. A quick and easy method of temporary hair removal Amy could suggest to Joanie for removing the hair on her legs that would leave the skin smooth, but requires a patch test is:

a. *a depilatory*

A depilatory is a caustic substance which is applied to areas of the body and dissolves superfluous hair at the skin level.

5. A milder but equally effective way of removing Joanie's facial hair could be to:

d. *sugar*

Sugaring is an epilation treatment that employs a thick, sugar-based paste and is especially appropriate for people who have sensitive skin.

6. To minimize the irritation to Joanie's underarms, Amy suggests the use of:

d. *cold wax*

A cold wax is not heated before it is applied and therefore is milder, making it ideal for use on sensitive areas.

CHAPTER 23 Facials

Rebecca, an esthetician, is asked by a high school counselor to visit a class of graduating students to discuss skin care with them. She arrives with product samples and begins to explain about the skin, its function, and how best to care for it. When she opens the floor to questions, she receives many questions from three students—Jane, Anne, and Andrea—about types and uses of skin care products available on the market and how best to use them. Rebecca is happy to answer the questions and reduce confusion.

1. Anne asks Rebecca about the difference between a foaming cleanser and cleansing milk. Rebecca tells her that:

d. *a foaming cleanser is useful for people with oily skin, a cleansing milk is best for dry skin*

A foaming cleanser is best used for a person with oily skin while a cleansing milk is best used on a client with very dry or mature skin.

2. Jane explains that she has some acne, and asks what she should use to cleanse her face. Rebecca suggests a:

b. *foaming cleanser*

Using a foaming cleanser can cut excess amounts of oil on oily or combination skins.

3. For Andrea's sensitive but oily skin, Rebecca recommends using a(n) _____ after cleansing.

c. *toner*

Toners and astringents are usually stronger products, often with higher alcohol content, and are used to treat oilier skin types.

4. Jane complains that her skin appears bumpy and lumpy. Rebecca recommends that she use a(n) _____ two to three times a week.

d. *exfoliant*

An exfoliant is an ingredient that, when added to a facial preparation, aids in the peeling and shedding of the horny outer layer of the skin.

5. Andrea tells Rebecca that her esthetician suggested an enzyme peel but that she wasn't sure what it was. Rebecca responded by explaining that it is a(n):

d. *exfoliating procedure using keratolytic enzymes*

An enzyme peel is a chemical exfoliation whereby dead skin cells or the intercellular "glue" that holds them together is dissolved by a chemical agent.

6. Jane asks Rebecca if there is anything she can use on her skin daily to reduce dryness. Rebecca suggests:
   c. *moisturizer*
      A moisturizer is a product formulated to add moisture to the skin.

7. Alyssa begins by using a technique that involves a light, continuous stroking movement called:
   b. *effleurage*
      Effleurage involves a light, continuous stroking movement applied with the fingers or the palms in a slow, rhythmic manner; no pressure is used.

Trisha has booked a facial at her favorite salon and can't wait for the soothing massage to begin. She arrives, changes into a facial gown, and waits patiently for her esthetician, Alyssa, to arrive. The lights are dim and there is a soft music playing in the background. Before entering the room Alyssa reviews Trisha's client record card and notices that the last time she was in Trisha commented that she wanted to tone her muscles and improve her circulation and general health. Alyssa enters the room and discusses these notes with her client. Once they have agreed on a course of action, Alyssa begins the service.

8. To offer deep stimulation to Trisha's muscles, Alyssa employs:
   a. *pétrissage*
      Pétrissage is a kneading movement performed by lifting, squeezing, and pressing the tissue with a light, firm pressure.

9. To increase Trisha's circulation and glandular activity, Alyssa uses a(n) _____ technique.
   c. *friction*
      Friction is a deep rubbing movement in which pressure is applied to the skin with the fingers or palms while moving it over an underlying structure.

10. Alyssa uses _____ on Trisha's neck to tone her muscles.
    c. *tapotement*
       Tapotement consists of short, quick tapping, slapping, and hacking movements.

11. Alyssa is always careful to massage from the:
    c. *insertion to the origin*
       Muscles that are massaged in the incorrect direction could result in the loss of resiliency and sagging of the skin and muscles.

George sells electric facial machines that help enhance the effectiveness of facial treatments. He has a meeting with Joyce to review her needs for additional equipment and special appliances. When George arrives, Joyce is ready and waiting for him with a list of questions.

12. Joyce asks if there is any electrotherapy treatment that will help to liquefy sebum stuck in the hair follicles on the face of a client. George explains that the application of _____ will do just that.

a. *galvanic current*

Galvanic current is the most commonly used current and can produce significant chemical changes to the skin.

13. To stimulate blood flow and help products to penetrate, Joyce is interested in using:

d. *high-frequency current*

High-frequency current, discovered by Nikolas Tesla, can be used to stimulate blood flow and help products penetrate. It works by warming tissues, which allows better absorption of moisturizers and other treatment products

14. Joyce asks George to explain how the use of microdermabrasion can help her clients. George explains that microdermabrasion is a _____ and leaves the skin looking_____.

d. *mechanical exfoliant, younger*

Microdermabrasion is a type of mechanical exfoliation that involves shooting aluminum oxide or other crystals at the skin with a hand-held device that exfoliates dead cells. Microdermabrasion uses a closed vacuum to shoot crystals onto the skin, bumping off cell buildup that is then vacuumed up by suction. Microdermabrasion is a popular treatment because it produces fast, visible results. It is used primarily to treat surface wrinkles and aging skin. Performance of safe and effective microdermabrasion treatments requires extensive training.

CHAPTER 24 Facial Makeup

Amanda has booked a makeup appointment with Sandra for the morning of her wedding. She has discussed with Sandra the color of her wedding gown—off-white—and her belief that she looks best in orange or coral tones. Sandra notes that Amanda has deep auburn-colored hair, light pale skin, and large green eyes. The morning of her wedding, Amanda arrives at the salon with a freshly cleansed, toned, and moisturized face but she has a blemish on her forehead and some dark circles under her eyes. Sandra starts the application.

1. From the information that Sandra has received about Amanda's color preferences and from analyzing her skin, she determines that her skin tone is:
   d. *warm*
   A warm skin tone is evident if the client has yellow undertones in her skin and looks best in gold, red, or orange shades.

2. Before any other product goes on Amanda's face, and to even out her skin tone and create a base for the makeup application, Sandra applies:
   b. *foundation*
   Foundation is a tinted cosmetic that is used as base or as a protective film before makeup or powder is applied.

3. To cover Amanda's blemish and reduce the discoloration around her eyes, Sandra should apply a concealer whose color is:
   b. *the same as the skin tone*
   A concealer that is matched to the skin color is best used to blend skin blemishes and discolorations.

4. To set the foundation and concealer and to give the face a matte finish, Sandra pats on a:
   c. *face powder*
   A face powder is a fine cosmetic powder used to add a dull or matte finish to the face.

5. To keep Amanda's makeup matte-looking, Sandra adds _____ cheek color.
   c. *powder*
   Dry cheek color imparts a matte finish and is applied with a brush or cotton puff.

6. To harmonize with Amanda's coloring, she should wear a _____ color on her cheeks.
   c. *coral*
   A coral shade will harmonize Amanda's red hair and her warm skin tone.

7. To keep Amanda's lip color from feathering, Sandra applies:
   d. *lip liner*
   Lip liner is a colored pencil used to outline the lips prior to the application of lipstick.

8. Sandra fills in Amanda's lips with:
   a. *lip color*
   Lip color is applied to enhance the natural color and shape of the lip or to redefine the lip. Lip color is available in a myriad of shades and glosses.

9. The best lip color to apply to Amanda is:
   a. *warm-toned*
   A warm-toned color will have orange and red undertones and is best for use with a makeup palette of similar tones.

10. To make Amanda's green eyes a focal point, Sandra should select a _____ color:
   c. *plum*
   Since red is the color opposite green on the color wheel, a red-toned color will be best to accentuate green eyes.

11. Sandra highlights Amanda's eyes with a color that is:
   a. *lighter than the skin tone*
   Highlighting is a technique used to draw attention to a certain area; in this case, a color lighter than the natural skin tone will draw attention to the eyes.

12. To make Amanda's eyes appear larger and more open, Sandra should apply:
   d. *mascara on top and bottom lashes*
   Curling the upper lashes and applying mascara to both the top and bottom lashes will make the eyes appear larger and more open.

Linda is a makeup artist who works for a very high-end cosmetics line that is sold exclusively through salons and spas. Today, a distributor is hosting an educational conference where Linda will be the guest educator. The topic of today's class will be corrective makeup techniques and Linda will be demonstrating these techniques using the cosmetics line she represents. Instead of hiring models, the conference participants will analyze and perform the corrective techniques on one another. Kelly, one of the class participants, is first. She has a wide forehead and cheek area but a rather narrow jawline, with small eyes, and she also has a very long, thin neck. Carmen, another participant, has a very full, round face, with a wide and somewhat flat nose, protruding eyes, and a rather thick chin and neck area. Rita has a very low forehead and a thin upper lip.

13. What face shape does Kelly have?

d. *inverted triangle*

Kelly has a face shape that is wider at the forehead and narrower at the chin; this is called an inverted triangle.

14. To make Kelly's face appear more oval, Linda will need to:

b. *minimize the width of the forehead and increase the width of the jawline*

To achieve the most desirable look for her client, Linda will want to reduce the appearance of the forehead while making the jaw appear wider.

15. To make Kelly's small eyes appear larger, Linda will:

d. *extend shadow above, beyond, and below the eyes*

To make small eyes appear bigger, Linda will extend the eye shadow around the eyes, making them look larger than they actually are.

16. To create more fullness to Kelly's neck and jawline area, Linda decides to apply a _____ to the area.

c. *light foundation*

Since light colors attract attention and since Linda wants to make the neck area appear larger, she will use a light-color foundation in this area.

17. To make Carmen's round face appear slimmer, Linda will need to:

d. *slenderize and lengthen the face*

Linda will use a darker foundation around the outside perimeter of Carmen's face to make her face seem slimmer and more oval-shaped.

18. To correct Carmen's wide, flat nose Linda will:

c. *apply a dark foundation on either side of the nostrils*

By applying a dark foundation on either side of the nostrils, Linda will reduce the appearance of the nose width.

19. To minimize Carmen's protruding eyes, Carmen should:

b. *blend a deep shade of shadow over the upper lid and to the eyebrow*

A medium to deep eye shadow shade should be used over the prominent part of the upper lid, carrying it lightly toward the eyebrow.

20. To slenderize Carmen's neck and jawline area, Linda will apply a _____ to the area.

a. *dark foundation*

A dark-colored foundation will make a wide neck and jaw area appear slimmer.

21. To give the appearance of a more balanced face, Rita can offset her low forehead with eyebrows that have:

c. *a low arch*

A low arch gives more height to a very low forehead, giving a balanced look to the face overall.

22. How can Linda correct Rita's thin upper lip?

c. *by using a lip pencil to make the curves of the upper lip proportionate to the nostrils*

To increase the size and appearance of her thin upper lip, Linda can use a lip pencil to draw in the peaks of the upper lip, using the nostrils as a guide, and then by filling in the lip with a medium- to light-colored lipstick.

CHAPTER 25 Manicuring

Josie is a new nail technician at the Helpful Hands Nail Salon. On her first day, she sets up her manicure station with all of her tools and implements and gets ready for her first client, Wanda. Wanda arrives and requests a natural nail manicure and gives Josie a bottle of bright-red nail polish she has selected from those provided by the salon.

1. Before beginning the manicure, Josie and Wanda should:

a. *wash their hands*

Before any and every service performed in a salon, a cosmetologist must wash her hands. If performing nail services, clients must also wash their hands before sitting down for a service.

2. Once at the table, the first thing that Josie does is:

c. *remove the old nail polish*

Before she does anything else, Josie must remove Wanda's old nail polish so that she can clearly see the nails and fingers.

3. To shape Wanda's nails, Josie will use a(n):

d. *nail file*

A nail file is a disposable manicuring implement with two abrasive sides used for shaping and smoothing the nail.

4. Wanda explains that she would like her nails shorter, so Josie uses a(n) _____ to shorten them to the desired length.

d. *nail clipper*

A nail clipper is a reusable metal instrument used to shorten very long nails.

5. Josie recommends that Wanda consider using a _____ daily to correct and prevent brittle nails and dry cuticles.

c. *penetrating nail oil*

Penetrating nail oils are designed to absorb into the nail plate (or surrounding skin) and increase flexibility. These oils will also help seal in valuable moisture.

6. Once the manicure is completed and before the polish is applied, Josie begins the hand and arm:

   c. *massage*

   A massage is one of the client's highest priorities during the manicure, and often it is the most memorable part of the manicure. Massage manipulations should be executed with rhythmic, long, and smooth movements, and one hand should always be on the client's arm or hand during the procedure.

7. The manipulation in which Josie's hands glide over Wanda's hand and arm is called:

   a. *effleurage*

   Effleurage is a succession of strokes in which the hands glide over an area of the body with varying degrees of pressure or contact.

8. The manipulation that involves lifting, squeezing, and pressing the tissue is called:

   b. *pétrissage*

   Pétrissage or kneading is lifting, squeezing, and pressing the tissue.

9. _____is a rapid tapping or striking motion of the hands against the skin.

   d. *Tapoment*

   Tapotement is a rapid tapping or striking motion of the hands against the skin.

10. Vibration is a continuous _____movement applied by the hand without leaving contact with the skin.

    a. *trembling or shaking*

    Vibration is a continuous trembling or shaking movement applied by the hand without leaving contact with the skin.

11. _____incorporates various strokes that manipulate or press one layer of tissue over another.

    d. *Friction*

    Friction incorporates various strokes that manipulate or press one layer of tissue over another. The pressure and manipulation of the tissues should be done lightly, with an end goal of inducing relaxation, not treatment.

12. Before applying the base coat and polish, Josie applies a _____ to strengthen the nails and prevent them from splitting or peeling.

d. *nail hardener*

Nail hardeners or strengtheners are designed to prevent nails from splitting or peeling and are applied to the nail before the base coat.

13. How should Josie remove excess nail polish from around Wanda's nails?

b. *with a cotton-tipped wooden pusher dipped in polish remover*

Josie will carefully wipe a cotton-tipped wooden pusher dipped in polish remover over the areas where the excess polish is and clean up her polish lines.

Mariel lives in a cold climate and during the winter months, when the temperatures fall below freezing, her hands frequently become dry and even chapped. She also experiences stiffness in her hands and only a warm hand bath seems to help alleviate her symptoms. While in the Nails Forever Salon, Mariel tells her nail technician James about her situation and he says he may be able to recommend a service that can help.

14. What type of service could James be thinking of?

b. *a paraffin wax treatment*

A paraffin wax treatment is considered to be a luxurious add-on service and can be safely performed on most clients.

15. What is the benefit of this type of treatment for Mariel?

c. *It will trap moisture in the skin.*

Paraffin wax treatments are designed to trap moisture in the skin while the heat causes skin pores to open. Besides opening the pores, heat from the warm paraffin increases blood circulation.

16. James and Mariel decide to do the treatment before her manicure that day because it will:

a. *pre-soften rough or callused skin*

Performing the paraffin wax treatment before beginning a manicure is advantageous because it allows the client to have her nails polished immediately at the end of the manicure service, and it is an effective way to pre-soften rough or callused skin.

17. Before beginning the service, James asks Mariel to:

c. *wash her hands*

Remember, in order to perform any kind of service, especially a nail service, the hands of both the cosmetologist and the client must be properly washed.

18. Since she has never had this treatment before, James performs a:

d. *patch test*

A patch test for heat tolerance should be performed on all clients the first time they have the service. A patch test will also reveal any allergies or sensitivities to the wax before beginning the service. To perform the patch test, place a small patch of wax on the client's skin to see if the temperature can be tolerated.

19. James checks the temperature of the wax, which is a perfect ____ degrees.

d. *125 to 130 (52 to 55 C)*

Special heating units melt solid wax into a gel-like liquid and maintain it at a temperature generally between 125 and 130 degrees Fahrenheit (52 to 55 C). When using this treatment, only use the equipment that is designed specifically for this use. Never try to heat the wax in anything other than the proper equipment. This can be very dangerous and may result in painful skin burns or a fire.

20. Before applying the wax, James checks Mariel's hands for:

a. *open sores, wounds, or abrasions*

James must check the hands carefully for open wounds, diseases, or disorders. It is not appropriate to apply heat to clients with abnormal skin conditions. If it is safe to perform the procedure, ensure the client's hands are clean and continue with the service.

21. Once he has determined that he can proceed, James applies _____ to Mariel's hands.

c. *moisturizing lotion*

By applying moisturizing lotion or penetrating oil to the client's hands and gently massaging it into the skin, additional moisture is present when the heat from the wax is applied, aiding in the retention of moisture and the softening of the hands.

22. James prepares Mariel's hand for dipping into the paraffin by placing the palm facing down with the wrist slightly bent and the fingers:

b. *straight and slightly apart*

By keeping the wrist slightly bent and the fingers straight and slightly apart, once the hand is dipped into the wax, every part of the hand can be bathed in the wax, thus encouraging the benefits of the treatment.

23. James dips Mariel's hand into the wax up to the wrist _____ times.

b. *three to five*

By dipping the hand into the wax and allowing the wax to solidify for a couple of seconds before dipping it into the bath again, you can ensure that the hand is properly coated.

24. Once each hand is dipped into the wax, James places Mariel's hands into:

d. *plastic mitts*

Once the hands are completely dipped, wrap the hands in plastic wrap or insert them into plastic mitts designed to protect the wax from peeling off. Then put them into terry cloth or warming (electric) mitts. Have the client relax for approximately five to ten minutes.

25. Once the treatment is over, James peels the wax from Mariel's hands and _____.

c. *disposes of it*

Used wax should never be stored, reused, or re-melted. It should only be disposed of.

CHAPTER 26 Pedicuring

Carla is a retail store manager who spends over 40 hours a week on her feet. For her birthday, her husband Leonard has booked an appointment for her to have a pedicure with Joya, a pedicurist at their local salon. When she arrives for the appointment, Carla explains to Joya that she is eager to have his feet massaged. Joya begins the service.

1. The first step of the service involves Joya instructing Carla to:
   c. *place her feet into the bath*
   Every pedicure service begins with the client soaking her feet in the pedicure foot bath. The bath may vary in design from the basic stainless steel basin to an automatic whirlpool that warms and massages the client's feet. The soak bath is filled with comfortably warm water and a product to soak the client's feet. The bath must be large enough to completely immerse both of the client's feet comfortably.

2. Carla's feet should be left soaking for about _____ minutes.
   b. *five*
   Allow the feet to soak for about five minutes to clean and soften them before beginning the pedicure.

3. Once the first foot is removed from the foot bath and dried, Joya must:
   a. *remove any toenail polish*
   Old nail polish must be removed from the toes so that the pedicurist can properly examine the condition of the toenail and complete the pedicure service.

4. In the next step of the pedicure, Joya should clip the toenails _____ across the top and even with the end of the toes.
   b. *straight*
   Clipping the toenails straight across the toe helps to discourage any instances of the toenail growing into the side of the nail, causing an ingrown toenail. Also, be careful to make the nail smooth across without any hooks that could cause a tear in the skin or infection.

5. Joya will use her nail rasp to:
   d. *file and smooth the edges of the nail plate*
   Carefully use the foot rasp, if needed. The rasp is narrow and will only file the nail in one direction. It can be used to remove, smooth, and round off any sharp points on the free edges that might eventually cause infection. Do not probe with the rasp or point the tip toward the hyponychium. Gently draw it along the side free edge that you have just trimmed. Small, short strokes with the file will accomplish the task.

6. Joya uses a professional strength _____to soften and smooth thickened tissue on Carla's heels and over other pressure points.

   a. *callus softener*

   Professional strength callus softeners are products designed to soften and smooth thickened tissue (calluses). They are applied directly to the client's heels and over pressure-point calluses. They are left on for a short period of time, according to the manufacturer's directions. After the product softens the callus, the callus is more easily reduced and smoothed with files or paddles.

7. Joya will use a foot _____ to reduce Carla's thickened calluses.

   a. *file*

   After the callus softener softens the callus, the callus is more easily reduced and smoothed with files or paddles. Be careful not to smooth the calluses down too much, as this can cause pain to the client.

8. To gently remove cuticle tissue from the nail plate, Joya will use a:

   d. *cuticle remover and a cotton-tipped wooden pusher*

   After the foot is removed from the towel wrap, use a cuticle remover and a wooden pusher to gently remove any loose, dead tissue, but be careful to stay away from the eponychium and take care not to break the seal between the nail plate and eponychium.

9. To complete the pedicure Joya will use a _____, a small, scoop-shaped implement used for more efficient removal of debris from the nail folds, eponychium, and hyponychium.

   d. *curette*

   Next, if necessary, the curette is used on the first foot to gently push the soft tissue folds away from the walls of the lateral nail plate. This allows you to visually inspect the nail plate and the surrounding tissue. If there is extra buildup of debris between the nail plate and surrounding tissue, it should be gently removed with the curette. To use this implement, place the rounded side of the spoon toward the sidewall of living skin. A gentle scooping motion is then used along the nail plate to remove any loose debris. Take care not to overdo it. Do not use this implement to dig into the soft tissues along the nail fold as injury may occur.

10. Joya begins the foot and leg massage by applying _____ and rotating the foot at the _____.

 c. *moisturizing lotion, ankle*

 Apply lotion, cream, or oil to the first foot for skin conditioning and massage. Use a firm touch to avoid tickling your client's feet. Rest the client's heel on a footrest or stool and suggest that your client relax. Grasp the leg gently just above the ankle and use your other hand to hold the foot just beneath the toes; rotate the entire foot in a circular motion.

11. The only place on the foot and/or leg where a friction movement should be performed is on the_____of Carla's foot.

 c. *instep*

 The only place a friction movement is performed in pedicure services is on the bottom of the foot, called the instep. Place one hand on top of the foot, cupping it, and make a fist with your other hand. The hand on top of the foot will press the foot toward you while your other hand twists into the instep of the foot. This helps stimulate blood flow and provides relaxation. Repeat three to five times.

12. To begin the leg massage, Joya will grasp Carla's leg from behind the ankle and perform _____movements up the leg, to just below the knee.

 d. *effleurage*

 Place the foot on the footrest or stabilize it on your lap. Then, gently grasp the client's leg from behind the ankle with one hand. Perform effleurage movements from the ankle to below the knee on the front of the leg with the other hand. Move up the leg and then lightly return to the original location.

13. Joya will perform these manipulations _____ times on the front, sides, and back of Carla's legs.

 b. *five to seven*

 Perform five to seven repetitions of these manipulations, then move to the sides of the leg and perform an additional five to seven repetitions.

CHAPTER 27 Nail Tips and Wraps

Roberta has been a nail technician for many years and has a thriving clientele. Roberta's clients, like many nail clients, love long nails and so aren't shy about wearing nail extensions and enhancements. Today she will be seeing a long-time client, Kaila, who is scheduled for tips and wraps.

1. After Kaila has washed and dried her hands thoroughly and is seated at Roberta's manicure table, she is asked:

c. *how much extra length she would like added*

It's important for Roberta to know how long Kaila would like her nails to be, so she can determine what length the tips should be that are affixed to Kaila's nails. The lenth of nail extensions is also dependent upon the client's lifestyle and work. This is a perfect time to discuss these issues and concerns.

2. To add extra length to Kaila's natural nails, Roberta will use nail tips, which are made of:

b. *plastic*

Nail tips are plastic, pre-molded nails shaped from a tough polymer made from acrylonitrile butadiene styrene.

3. Roberta will use ____ to put the tips on to Kaila's natural nails.

c. *nail tip adhesive*

The bonding agent used to secure the nail tip to the natural nail is called nail tip adhesive. Adhesives can be purchased in either tubes or brush-on containers and are available in several different forms, depending on the thicknesses of the adhesive.

4. After the nail extensions have been applied, a(n) _____ must be applied over the natural nail and nail tip for added strength.

c. *overlay*

An overlay is a layer of any kind of nail enhancement product such as fabric (silk), fiberglass material, or even paper that is applied over the natural nail and nail tip for added strength.

5. In order to determine the best type of wrap for Kaila, Roberta will need to ask her which of the following questions?

c. *How rough are you on your hands and nails?*

Each type of nail wrap has specific conditions that make it more suitable for one type of client over another. By asking Kaila how she uses her hands, Roberta will be able to recommend a suitable procedure for her needs.

6. Kaila explains that she is a landscape artist and she works outdoors planting and gardening all day long. Based on this, Roberta recommends that she wear _____ wraps for their durability.
   c. *linen*
   Linen provides a durable wrap and is much thicker than silk or fiberglass; it requires a colored polish to cover the material once applied.

7. Roberta recommends this type of wrap material because it is the:
   c. *strongest*
   Given what Kaila does for a living and that her work will be tough on her nail extensions, Roberta chooses the strongest of all of the linen wraps, fiberglass.

8. Roberta begins to pull out the products she needs to perform this service for Kaila. The products she gathers include:
   b. *wrap resin*
   A nail wrap resin is used to coat and secure fabric wraps to the natural nail and nail tip. Wrap resins are made from cyanoacrylate, a specialized monomer liquid and polymer powder monomer that has excellent adhesion to the natural nail plate and polymerizes in seconds.

9. Before applying tips or wraps onto Kaila's nails Roberta must wipe the natural nail with ____ to remove any moisture from the nail's surface.
   d. *nail dehydrator*
   A nail dehydrator is a very important aspect of the nail enhancement service. Nail dehydrator is a substance used to remove surface moisture and tiny amounts of oil left on the natural nail plate and a variety of nail tips for the nail tip application.

10. As she prepares to apply the fabric to Kaila's nails, Roberta ____ the fabric to fit her nail size and shape.
    b. *cuts*
    Pre-cutting the fabric before applying it to the client's nail makes managing the fabric easier and makes for a speedier and more manageable application.

11. Before applying the fabric to Kaila's nails, Roberta applies a layer of wrap resin to _____ and then begins applying the fabric wrap.
    d. *all of her nails*
    Apply a layer of wrap resin over the entire surface of the nail and tip on all ten nails. Remember to keep the nail adhesive off the skin. Besides potentially damaging your client's skin, this

could cause the wrap to lift or separate from the nail plate. Begin with the pinky finger of the left hand and apply the wrap resin to all ten fingers. Once completed, return to the first finger and apply the fabric wrap.

12. Roberta uses a small piece of thick plastic to:

b. *smooth the fabric onto the nail*

Using a small piece of plastic to smooth the fabric onto the nail is easier than trying to use an implement or other fabric that will become stuck to the resin.

13. After the second coat of wrap resin is applied to all of the nails, Roberta sprays _____ onto Kaila's nails to speed their drying time.

c. *wrap resin accelerator*

A wrap resin accelerator, also known as an activator, acts as the dryer that speeds up the hardening process of the wrap resin or adhesive overlay. Activators come in several different forms: brush-on bottle, pump spray-on, and aerosol. Activator will dissipate in about two minutes after application.

14. Roberta will apply wrap resin and wrap resin accelerator ___ more time(s) before the nails are completed.

a. *one*

Every time wrap resin is applied to the nail, a wrap resin accelerator will also be applied to the nail to aid in drying it. Since most wrap systems require that wrap resin be applied twice to build the proper amount of product and strength to the nail enhancement, so too, the accelerator is applied twice.

15. Kaila asks Roberta about maintaining her new nails. Roberta explains that every two weeks she will need to have her nails maintained, and the maintenance will follow this schedule:

b. *wrap resin only applied two weeks after a fresh wrap is applied, with additional fabric needing to be applied every four weeks*

Proper maintenance of linen-wrapped nails ensures that the nails stay healthy and look good.

CHAPTER 28

Monomer Liquid and Polymer Powder Nail Enhancements

Martine specializes in monomer liquid and polymer powder nail enhancements and has done so for years. She is about to begin servicing Jamie, a new client to her salon.

1. If Jamie wishes to have her nails extended past the length of her natural nails, Martine has two options. She can use _____ or _____.
   c. *nail tips, nail forms*
   Both nail tips and nail forms used with monomer liquid and polymer powder will extend the length of Jamie's natural nails.

2. Jamie wears sculptured nails, so when Martine does Jamie's nails, she uses:
   a. *a monomer liquid and polymer powder*
   Another name for monomer liquid and polymer powder nail enhancements is sculptured nails.

3. To aid in the adhesion and to prepare the nail surface for attachment with the monomer liquid and polymer powder material, Martine will use _____ on Jamie's nails.
   d. *primer*
   Primer (methacrylic acid) is used to enhance the adhesion of enhancements to the natural nail.

4. When Martine combines the monomer liquid and polymer powder on her application brush, a(n) ____ forms.
   d. *bead*
   A natural hair and pointed, round, or oval application brush is the best brush to use for applying these products. The brush is immersed in the monomer liquid. The natural-hair bristles absorb and hold the monomer liquid like a reservoir. The tip of the brush is then touched to the surface of the dry polymer powder, and as the monomer liquid absorbs the polymer powder, a small bead of product forms. This small bead is then carefully placed on the nail surface and molded into shape with the brush and smoothed into place.

5. Martine knows that if she uses twice as much monomer liquid as she does polymer powder the bead is considered:
   d. *wet*
   The amount of monomer liquid and polymer powder used to create a bead is called the mix ratio. A bead mix ratio can be best described as dry, medium, or wet. If twice as much liquid as powder is used to create the bead, it is called a wet bead.

6. Curing is the process by which the monomer liquid and the polymer powder:
   b. *harden*
   Although there appears to be a lot of liquid used in this nail enhancement service, the beads of product do quickly harden by curing (hardening).

7. Martine knows that she must play close attention to the ____ of the nail, because this is where the strength of the nail enhancement lies.
   b. *apex*
   The apex, also known as the arch, is the area of the nail that has all of the strength. Having strength in the apex allows the base of the nail, sidewalls, and tip to be thin yet leaves the nail strong enough to resist frequent chipping or breaking. The apex is usually oval shaped and is located in the center of the nail. The high point is visible no matter where you view the nail.

8. Once applied, monomer liquid and polymer powder overlays should be _____ every two weeks and the shape of the nail should be _____ each time monomer liquid and polymer powder is used.
   a. *maintained, rebalanced*
   Regular maintenance helps prevent nail enhancements from lifting or cracking. If the nail enhancements are not regularly maintained, they have a greater tendency to lift, crack, or break which increases the risk of the client developing an infection or having other problems.

CHAPTER 29 UV Gels

Jen is preparing for a full day of nail clients. Her first client is Falon, who has booked a full set of UV gel nails. Jen has already applied tips to Falon's nails and is ready to begin the application of the gel.

1. In addition to the materials in her basic manicuring setup, Jen will need a _____ to complete the service for Falon.
   b. *UV gel light-unit*
   UV gel light-units are designed to produce the correct amount of UV light needed to properly cure UV gel nail enhancement products.

2. Jen will first apply a _____ to improve adhesion of the UV gel to the natural nail plate.
   b. *bonding gel*
   UV bonding gels are used to increase adhesion to the natural nail plate, similar to a monomer liquid and polymer powder primer. UV bonding gels will vary in consistency and chemical components. The increased adhesion decreases the tendency for enhancements to separate from the natural nail.

3. When applying this UV gel, Jen should firmly brush UV gel onto the _____ nail.
   c. *natural*
   Bonding gels are applied to the natural nail in order to prepare them to receive and adhere to the building gels. Since the natural nail may contain natural oils that make adhesion difficult, the application of this bonding gel could be the difference between overlays that separate from the natural nail and those that do not.

4. To create the right arch in Falon's nail, Jen will apply a _____.
   d. *building gel*
   UV building gels include any thick-viscosity resin that allows the cosmetologist to build an arch and curve to the fingernail.

5. After the building gel is applied, Jen may choose to apply a _____, which will create a smooth finish on the nail and requires less filing.
   c. *self-leveling gel*
   UV self-leveling gels are thinner in consistency than building gels, allowing them to settle and level during application. These gels are used to enhance thickness of the overlay while providing a smoother surface. Cosmetologists who are experienced in UV gel application often choose to apply a UV building gel first, and then apply a self-leveling UV gel to reduce filing and contouring.

6. Curing the gel means:
   d. *allowing it to harden*
      UV gel products cure or adhere when the client's hand is properly positioned in the UV lamp for the required cure time as defined by the manufacturer. Always cure each layer of the UV gel for the time required by the manufacturer's instructions. Curing for too little time can result in service breakdown, skin irritation, and/or sensitivity. Improper positioning of the hands inside the lamp can also cause improper curing.

7. The inhibition layer left on the nail after the UV gel has cured is:
   a. *tacky*
      UV gels cure with a tacky surface called an inhibition layer. This layer can be removed by filing with a medium abrasive (180- to 240-grit) or with alcohol, acetone, or other suitable remover on a plastic-backed cotton pad to avoid skin contact.

8. This layer must be:
   d. *cleaned from the nail*
      An inhibition layer is a tacky surface left on the nail after a UV gel has cured. When removing the inhibition layer from the UV gel, avoid cleaning the nail in a manner that would put the gel onto the surface of the skin. Using your nail wipe, start at the top of the fingernail nearest the cuticle and wipe away from the cuticle to the free edge of the fingernail.

9. Jen must remove the inhibition layer from Falon's nails:
   b. *before polishing the nails*
      The inhibition layer must be removed just before the final nail filing and smoothing.

CHAPTER 30 Seeking Employment

Samuel has just received notice from his state board of cosmetology that he is scheduled to take his licensing exam in two weeks. He is happy but also nervous about taking the exam. He wants very badly to pass the test on his first try, but test-taking always makes him nervous. Samuel pulls out his textbook and study materials and begins to schedule his study and preparation time.

1. Samuel should begin studying:

   d. *several weeks before the exam*

   By giving himself several weeks to study for the important state board exam, Samuel has plenty of time to review all of his subjects and to concentrate on topics that are not quite so clear for him instead of cramming a few days before the exam.

2. In order to get ready for his written exam, Samuel should:

   d. *review past quizzes, tests, and homework assignments*

   Using his past homework assignments, tests, and quizzes is an excellent way for Samuel to prepare for the exam. These materials are sure to cover the most important pieces of data and remind him of vital information he may have overlooked.

3. The evening before the exam Samuel should plan to:

   d. *get a full night's sleep*

   The best thing Samuel can do the night before the exam is to get enough rest and sleep to ensure that he feels great in the morning and is calm, well-prepared, and thinking clearly for the exam.

4. Once he is given the exam, Samuel should:

   c. *read through the exam and all of the directions before beginning the test*

   It is always best to read through all of the information on a test before plunging into answering the questions, although answering all the questions first, without reading through the test, may have been Samuel's first reaction. Reading through the test first gives the test-taker an overview of the test and of what can be expected.

5. If Samuel is stuck on a question, he can _____ and then determine which are possible correct answers.
   b. *eliminate answers he knows are incorrect*
   Since all of the state board written exams are multiple-choice format, Samuel should go through the all of the possible answers and eliminate the ones that he knows are incorrect. This will leave him with one or two that are the most appropriate and he can assess the best possible answer.

Amira has graduated from beauty school and received passing grades on her exams. She wants to find a good salon job and begins looking in various local newspapers for job openings. She makes a list of salons that have openings and then schedules several appointments with salons that have run help-wanted ads in the newspapers. She dresses well in a beautiful outfit with matching shoes and handbag, has her hair and makeup done expertly, and washes her car so that she presents a great-looking appearance to her prospective salon manager.

6. When she arrives at the first salon, the salon manager asks Amira for her credentials. Amira should hand the manager a:
   b. *resume*
   A resume is a written summary of your education and work experience, and it is expected that a person applying for a job would have one.

7. What kinds of information will the salon manager need to ascertain about Amira before determining if she right for the open position?
   b. *her job history*
   The manager will want to know what type of jobs Amira has held, what were her responsibilities, and for how long she remained in each position.

8. Another tool Amira should consider creating to take with her on interviews is a(n):
   c. *employment portfolio showing before and after photos of past clients*
   Creating a portfolio of styles will help a salon manager determine the caliber of Amira's work and to determine what additional training or practice Amira may need once she is hired.

9. In order to validate her claim that she has been a responsible employee while working for others, Amira should provide:
   c. *letters of reference from past employers*
   Letters of reference, in the words of others who have managed Amira, will tell a potential new manager exactly how Amira will perform and what a new employer can expect.

10. If Amira has the opportunity to ask questions of the interviewer, which of the following would NOT be appropriate?

d. *Will someone be fired when I am hired?*

It is not Amira's business to ask if someone else will be fired if she is hired. There are many reasons why a new position may have opened up at this salon. She may ask how there came to be an open position, however.

11 One question that Amira's interviewer is legally prohibited from asking her is:

b. *Do you have any disabilities?*

The Americans with Disabilities Act prohibits general inquiries about health problems, disabilities, and medical conditions. It is important to recognize that not all potential employers will understand that they may be asking improper or illegal questions. If you are asked such questions, you might politely respond that you believe the question is irrelevant to the position you are seeking, and that you would like to focus on your qualities and skills that are suited to the job and the mission of the establishment.

12. After having met and spent some time with the salon manager, Amira should send:

d. *a thank you note for the interview*

It is considered both polite and professional to thank an interviewer for the time and energy she or he spent interviewing you for a position with a firm or salon.

13. If she is offered the position, Amira will have to decide _____ before taking the job.

c. *if the salon has the kind of image, culture, and values that she has*

It is always important for a new employee like Amira to really understand the salon's image, culture, and values and to feel that her beliefs match those of the salon and the staff. Otherwise, Amira could be setting herself up for failure.

CHAPTER 31 On the Job

Today is Marshall's first day at the Jolie Salon, and he is excited. He will meet the entire staff this morning at the weekly staff meeting and then he'll meet with Sara, the salon manager, to go over the rules and regulations of the salon and to discuss the details of his financial remuneration. Marshall also has a few questions he wants to ask Sara and a couple of issues he would like her to clarify.

1. Sara tells Marshall that the salon operates very much like a(n) _____ in that all of the employees are aware of their own duties but are also ready and must be willing to aid their coworkers in whatever needs to be accomplished.

b. *team*

A team environment is an excellent salon environment. In a team situation, every person has value and knows how that work affects the overall salon. Each person also knows that the team leader or salon manager is available for help or assistance, if they are needed.

2. Sara explains that payday is on Friday and that Marshall will make a _____, which is a percentage of his service dollars and an hourly wage.

d. *salary plus commission*

A salary plus commission is an excellent way for a new stylist to get paid when beginning at a new salon, because you are guaranteed a salary and also are rewarded with a commission on your service and retail dollars.

3. Sara explains that after his first 90 days of employment Marshall will have a(n) _____, which will be an opportunity for her to assess his progress and performance and for Marshall to discuss his thoughts and ideas about the salon.

b. *employee evaluation*

An employee evaluation is an excellent way to determine and define expectations both for the employee and the salon.

4. Marshall asks Sara if she can help him to determine what his paychecks might be for the first three months of employment so that he can make a _____ to track his expenses, such as loan repayments and his rent.

c. *personal budget*

A personal budget is an invaluable tool for all salon stylists to have, whether they are new to the business or a 20-year veteran. A personal budget will enable Marshall to know where he sits financially every month and will help him make responsible financial decisions.

5. Sara assigns Marshall to Joyce, a senior stylist who will be responsible for answering his questions, giving him guidance, and helping him when he has difficulty. Joyce will be his:
   d. *mentor*
   Having a senior stylist as a mentor is a tremendous asset for Marshall because Joyce will be someone who can help him, answer his questions, and give him individual guidance and attention whenever he needs assistance. Joyce's only intention will be Marshall's complete and successful transition into this new salon life.

Chantal has just learned that her salon will be retailing a product line that she has used in the past and has wanted to sell to her clients for some time. She is excited because many of the salon's clients can really benefit from the products and the new services their use will introduce to the salon. Chantal's first client is Noreen, who has had her hair colored and chemically straightened and who uses a hot iron to flatten and style her hair about once a week. As a result of the intense chemicals and heat, Noreen's hair is very brittle, dried, and damaged and Chantal feels that any additional pulling or styling may cause Noreen's hair to break.

6. When Noreen comes in for her haircut and styling appointment, Chantal should:
   d. *review Noreen's record card and discuss the condition of her hair*
   For a client such as Noreen, even weekly shampooing and styling can add undue burden on her fragile hair. Chantal is right to review Noreen's record card and her hair condition every time Noreen comes into the salon so that she can make appropriate recommendations.

7. While discussing her hair Noreen mentions that she is having difficulty with her hair being so dry and looking dull. Chantal will want to use this as an opportunity to:
   a. *describe the new line of retail products to Noreen and how they can benefit her*
   By listening to Noreen, Chantal gets lots of clues as to what the client needs and what she can provide in terms of solutions, whether they are additional services or products, or both.

8. Since Noreen's hair is very dry and damaged, Chantal suggests adding a deep-conditioning treatment to today's service. This is called:
   b. *ticket upgrading*
   A ticket upgrade is the practice of recommending and selling additional services to your clients that may be performed by you or someone else in the salon.

9. Once Noreen has had her service and sees the benefit of the treatment, Chantal can use a _____ approach to recommending additional retail products for at-home use, because Noreen already feels their benefit.
   c. *soft-sell*
   A soft-sell approach is one in which Chantal can easily suggest that Noreen purchase the product or service, because Noreen has either already requested it or has benefited from it.

Cassie is worried. She has a great clientele who are very loyal to her, but she knows that if she moves to a bigger salon and rents more space that her expenses will go up and she wonders what she can do to increase her income. She decides to take some time and write out her plan for how to increase her income to cover her expenses by increasing her client base. Cassie gets to work.

10. To obtain important demographic information on her clients, Cassie will need to refer to her:
   b. *client intake form*
   The client intake form, if filled in properly, should contain the demographic information Cassie needs, such as the clients' addresses, their birth dates, and how often they frequent the salon.

11. Cassie notes that she can use her business cards to:
   b. *promote a referral program with current clients*
   Using a business card is the most logical and easiest of all the referral programs a stylist can use. Cassie will simply give her business cards to current clients, ask them to write their names on the cards, and pass them along to their friends. When the cards are presented to Cassie by the referred clients, she can reward the people whose names are on the cards with a discount on their next service.

12. As a reward for her loyal clients and to promote the purchase of additional services and products, Cassie can prepare a _____ and include it in a thank you or birthday card mailing.
   c. *discount coupon*
   Offering a small 10, 15, or 20 percent discount on regular services or products is a great incentive and a good way to thank loyal clients.

13. To make herself visible to new groups of potential clients, Cassie could:
   c. *make herself available to speak at local organizations*
   By offering her time to speak to local organizations and groups, Cassie not only becomes visible to these groups, she also positions herself as an authority in the area of beauty and grooming. This encourages people to take part in her service offerings.

14. Cassie could make use of her relationships with other local merchants by:
   b. *agreeing to cross-promote with merchants who are willing to do so*
   Cross-promoting with other businesses who want to do so, such as florists, bakeries, and dry cleaners, is an excellent way to advertise services to the clients of businesses that do not compete with your business.

15. Cassie realizes that one of the simplest ways to keep her business steady is to:
   b. *book clients for their next appointment before they leave the salon*
   Booking current clients for their next appointment before they leave the salon is one way for Cassie to ensure that she has a steady base of clients and income. Even if a certain percentage of clients cancel the appointment later or before they are due to come in to the salon, another percentage are guaranteed to keep their appointment.

CHAPTER 32 The Salon Business

Don has been a stylist for more than six years and has built a loyal clientele at his current salon. He has thought about opening his own salon for several months and has decided to explore the various options open to him. He calls his friends, Emily, Scott, and Matt, who work at different salons in the area, and they agree to get together to discuss options and share ideas with Don.

1. Emily tells Don that she is a_____, which means that she pays rent to a salon owner for the space she works in and that she supplies all of her own materials and products. She has complete control over her work schedule and appointments.

c. *booth renter*

Booth renting is a very popular way of becoming your own boss, especially for someone who wants flexibility but not the responsibility of managing others.

2. Scott is a _____ of the Scott Salon. He is responsible for determining all the policies of the salon and hiring and paying all of the employees. He also assumes all of the responsibilities of expenses and the profits of the salon.

d. *sole proprietor*

A sole proprietorship is a situation in which one person, the owner of the business, has all of the responsibilities and reaps all of the rewards.

3. Matt explains that he is a _____ with his wife, Anne. They share all of the duties of owning the business and all of the rewards as well. Since Matt is a cosmetologist, he manages the salon while his wife, who is an accountant, manages the finances and operations of the salon.

a. *partner*

In a partnership, two or more people own the business together. Usually, these individuals bring different, yet complementary, skills to the partnership.

4. Scott advises Don to be aware of the area he will be working in. He explains that _____, _____, _____, and _____ are important factors in determining where to open a new salon and whether or not it will be successful.

b. *demographics, visibility, parking, and competition*

It will be important for Don to know who his clients are, where they will and won't go for the type of services he will offer, and how best to position his salon over the other salons that will compete for the same type of clients.

5. Don's friends advise him to develop a _____, which will help him to clarify his vision and determine which type of opportunity is best for him.
   b. *business plan*
   A business plan is a document that forces the entrepreneur to thoroughly think through all of the aspects of a business and make decisions up front so that she or he has a clear vision of the business.

After careful consideration, Don has decided to open his own salon, a sole proprietorship. He writes an extensive business plan, outlining his vision for his business, and creates a budget to determine what his expenses will be to open and run the salon. Don takes his business plan and budget to his local bank and meets with John Burke, a small business loan officer, to see about getting a loan to open his new salon.

6. John asks Don how much _____ he is seeking to run the salon for the first two years.
   c. *capital*
   Capital refers to the amount of financial support, or money, that will be needed to run the business for at least the first two years of operation.

7. John asks Don what percentage of the overall salon revenue he expects to spend on rent for the space and for advertising.
   c. *approximately 16 percent*
   Typically, space rental for a business such as a salon should be about 13 percent of the gross income and advertising should comprise about 3 percent of the gross income, for a total of 16 percent.

8. To make informed decisions about the salon's financial success, Don explains to John that he will keep _____ and _____ records to control expenses and waste.
   d. *purchase and service*
   The purchase of inventory and supplies should be closely monitored. Purchase records help you maintain a perpetual inventory, which prevents overstocking or a shortage of needed supplies, and they alert you to any incidents of theft. Service records help you to look at the use of the inventory you have purchased, identify trends in service, and look for areas of opportunity and growth.

9. Don mentions that _____ supplies such as hair spray and styling products will be on hand to sell to salon clients so that they can maintain their styles at home and that these sales will increase the salon's profitability.

   d. *retail*

   Retail supplies are those products that are on hand for the sole purpose of reselling them to salon clients.

10. John asks to see a copy of the projected _____ so that he can assess whether the salon will have the correct flow and be conducive to the many services and demands of the clients who will patronize it.

   c. *salon layout*

   A salon layout is a drawing or a plan that assesses the flow of traffic and people through the space and allows the new owner to determine whether the space is used efficiently and wisely.

11. Don knows that when he interviews prospective employees for his salon, the following three items are very important:

   d. *level of technical skill, overall attitude, communication skills*

   Don knows that he must look for employees with the appropriate level of skill, educational background, and attitude about education; people who have a mostly positive approach to life and a good overall attitude; and people with good communication skills who can understand the questions being asked of them and whose response to those questions is understandable.